The Troubles
of Journalism

A Critical Look at What's
Right and Wrong With the Press

LEA's COMMUNICATION SERIES
Jennings Bryant/Dolf Zillmann, General Editors

Selected titles in Journalism (Maxwell McCombs, Advisory Editor) include:

Black • Mixed News: The Public/Civic/Communitarian Journalism Debate

Crespi • The Public Opinion Process: How the People Speak

Hachten • The Troubles of Journalism: A Critical Look at What's Right and Wrong with the Press

McCombs/Shaw/Weaver • Communication and Democracy: Exploring the Intellectual Frontiers in Agenda-Setting Theory

Merritt • Public Journalism and Public Life: Why Telling the News is Not Enough, Second Edition

Wanta • The Public and the National Agenda: How People Learn About Important Issues

For a complete list of other titles in LEA's Communication Series, please contact Lawrence Erlbaum Associates, Publishers.

The Troubles
of Journalism

A Critical Look at What's
Right and Wrong With the Press

WILLIAM A. HACHTEN

The University of Wisconsin–Madison

 LAWRENCE ERLBAUM ASSOCIATES, PUBLISHERS

1998   Mahwah, New Jersey   London

Lawrence Erlbaum Associates, Inc., Publishers
10 Industrial Avenue
Mahwah, New Jersey 07430

Cover design by Kathryn Houghtaling Lacey

Library of Congress Cataloging-in-Publication Data

Hachten, William A.
  The troubles of journalism : a critical look at what's right and wrong
with the press / William A. Hachten.
    p. cm.
  Includes bibliographical references and indexes.
  ISBN 0-8058-2649-1 (cl. : alk. paper). -- ISBN 0-8058-2650-5 (pbk.
  alk. paper)
    1. Journalism--United States--History. I. Title.
  PN4855.H24 1988   97-32578
  071'.3--dc21   CIP

Books published by Lawrence Erlbaum Associates are printed on acid-free paper,
and their bindings are chosen for strength and durability.

Printed in the United States of America

10 9 8 7 6 5 4 3 2

In Memory of
Harold "Bud" Nelson (1917–1996)

Contents

Preface

*The human understanding is like a false mirror, which,
receiving rays irregularly, distorts and discolors the nature
of things by mingling its own nature with it.*
                                        —Francis Bacon (1620)

During the early 1930s when I was a youngster in Huntington Park, California, I could hear the cry of newspaper boys walking through the neighborhood, hawking *The Los Angeles Herald Express* or *The Los Angeles Times* calling out "EXTRA! EXTRA!" to announce some breaking news story, such as FDR's first election that required a special edition—an *extra!*—to get the news out faster.

Soon, news announcements made on the radio supplemented and in time replaced the newspaper extra. During World War II, we listened to the radio for breaking news, but with wartime constraints, the time element of major battles and other war-time events was often vague. Newspapers were still important, but so were newsreels, which in the dark of movie theaters provided moving pictures of distant events—Hitler haranguing Nazi crowds in Germany and the abdication of King Edward VIII for example. The immediacy of the newspaper extra was not there.

During the 1936 presidential campaign my family huddled around the radio, listening to ex-President Herbert Hoover addressing the Republican Convention. We were all Republicans and hoped that the GOP would nominate Hoover to take on FDR again. Forlorn hope. My uncle was an International News Service reporter in Washington, DC, and an admirer of Hoover. I later rejected my uncle's politics but not his work. He was my role model for a career in newspapering.

When I studied journalism at Stanford in 1947, the curriculum required students to learn to set type by hand using the California Job Case. Some weekly papers, despite the widespread use of Linotype machines, were still doing it the old way.

During my newspaper days from 1948 through 1956, daily papers were being put together much as they had been for the previous 75 years—local news stories were written on typewriters (preferably Underwood or Royal Standards) while "wire" or telegraph news stories came clattering in on Associated Press (AP) or United Press teletypes. News stories, after being funneled through the city and news desks ended up on the copy desk for close editing and headlines and then were set in type by Linotype operators. Then galleys of body type and headlines were made up on page forms; stereotype mats and lead castings were made and transferred to a rotary press that printed out the newspapers.

At the time, there was a sense of romance and excitement about working on newspapers. A career in newspapering appealed to idealistic young people who wanted to change or improve the world, or at least have fun and interesting jobs, despite the fact that salaries were meager and the hours were long. (When he retired, the late John Chancellor of NBC News commented that when he began as a young reporter on *The Chicago Sun-Times* in 1948, he was having so much fun that he would have worked for nothing.) Then, few worried about the future because there was a certain amount of social prestige and cachet in being a journalist. Then (and now), journalists were always interesting and stimulating people to be around.

World War II produced its journalistic heros, Ernie Pyle, Edward R. Murrow, Hal Boyle, Eric Sevareid, and others. Still in its salad days, listeners admired and relied on radio news. One of its early giants, Eric Sevareid, said later he was in the broadcast end of the news business, not the news end of the broadcasting business as he would later be. As shown later, that was an important difference.

Much has changed since I had my first newspaper job in 1948 at the Santa Paula (CA) *Daily Chronicle* (circulation 3,000 but now defunct). (I later worked as a reporter for *The Long Beach Press-Telegram* and as a copy editor for *The Los Angeles Examiner*, and *The Minneapolis Star*.) As a newspaper man and later journalism educator, I have been dazzled by the changes, for better or worse, that have occurred over the last 50 years.

Some of those changes were technological—new cold-type production methods and computer terminals revolutionized the newsroom and the backshop. Computerized high-speed data transfers assisted by communication satellites greatly accelerated the speed and volume of news and photos. The old-time newspaper city room with its clattering typewriters and its floor strewn with copy paper and galley proofs began to look more and more like an insurance company office—rugs on the floor, reporters and editors quietly peering into computer terminals, and perhaps Muzak playing in the background.

Changes in daily newspaper journalism, however, have been overshadowed in the past 50 years by the impact of television. In many diverse ways, television has remade, glamorized, and expanded the reach and impact of daily journalism. But at the same time, the small, flickering screen has also distorted, trivialized, and, in many ways, corrupted the news business.

Many of the changes in American journalism—economic, social, cultural, and technological—seem mostly related to what television has done *for* and *to* journalism and to society. We have seen how television continues to modify and transform the Olympic Games (away from sport to entertainment) as well as our national political conventions, which no longer choose candidates but merely crown them. The earlier ethic of the near-anonymous newsperson has given way to celebrity journalists appearing on television news and talk shows and commanding large lecture fees.

This volume looks at and evaluates some of the changes in journalism, both positive and negative, and suggests what they may have meant for the nation and the world at large. American journalism—its methods and its standards—has markedly influenced the way millions of others overseas receive news and view their world.

I gladly acknowledge a strong bias: I believe that serious, public affairs journalism is an important resource of American life that should be nurtured and shielded from the various influences that diminish and trivialize the news. This is an inquiry into the causes of the malaise that seem to grip the news business day.

THE PRESS AS A DISTORTED MIRROR?

The mirror is often a metaphor (as well as a name) for the daily newspaper; two of the largest, the defunct *New York Daily Mirror* and the flourishing *Daily Mirror* of London, were sensationalist tabloids. Today there is a sense that the bright, shiny mirror of American journalism has developed some serious cracks, becoming at times a distorted mirror. One astute journalist, Kenneth Walsh (1996) wrote: "The media are no longer seen as society's truth-sayers. In holding up a mirror to America, journalists too often have filtered out the good and embellished the bad, resulting in a distorted image" (p. 281).

I suggest that sometimes our admirable press, as a "false mirror," like Francis Bacon's human understanding, "distorts and discolors the nature of things" by bringing at times its own preconceptions and biases to bear in reporting the news.

ACKNOWLEDGMENTS

This book is based on a 50-year involvement with newspapers and journalism education. My colleagues, teachers, and students, particularly during my 30 years at the University of Wisconsin–Madison, have helped to educate me about the press. Aware that I will omit some, let me name several of the most influential people. Among my teachers, I am indebted to Chilton Bush, Ralph Casey, Edward Gerald, Ray Nixon, Mitch Charnley, Bob Jones, and Harold Chase. Among friends and colleagues, I learned a good deal from Ralph Nafziger, Harold "Bud" Nelson, Wilmott Ragsdale, John McNelly, Graham Hovey, Alex Edelstein, Jim Baughman, Charles Higbie, Jim Fosdick, Steve Chaffee, Jack McLeod, Scott Cutlip, Anthony Giffard, Raymond Louw, and Bill Blankenburg. Students, who later became colleagues and friends, include Dave Nimmer, Don Pember, Al Hester, Dwight Teeter, John Stevens, Bob Stevenson, Don Dodson, Don Shaw, Earl Hutchison, Frank Kaplan, and David Gordon. I owe much to all of them.

Finally, as with everything I have written for publication for many years, this book has benefitted from the careful editing and insightful suggestions by my wife, Harva Sprager Hachten. I thank John McNelly and Jim Fosdick for their comments on this volume. I alone am responsible for the judgments and errors in this book.

William A. Hachten

Introduction

*Most journalism is not about facts but about the
interpretation of what seem to be facts.*
            —Walter Lippmann (1922)

As the end of the 20th century nears, it hardly needs repeating that journalism and mass communication play a central role in modern society. Over time, our newspapers, magazines, radio, television, cable, video cassettes, and movies have been demanding more and more of our attention and leisure time. The media markedly affect our politics, our sports, our recreation, our education, and in general and profoundly, our culture, our perception, and our understanding of the world around us.

Although the news media may lack coercive power (a newspaper cannot draft you and send you off to a foreign war or put you in jail), their influence and pervasiveness are beyond doubt. Yet there are wide disagreements and conflicting views about just how, for better or worse, we are influenced by media in general and by journalism in particular.

The media, in their diverse, ubiquitous manifestations, are everywhere. As Pember (1992) wrote:

> Perhaps no nation in the history of mankind has enjoyed a communication system equal to the one that currently exists in the United States. It must be regarded as one of the technological marvels of the modern world. It is a multi-faceted system of interpersonal and mass communication elements, and some parts of the network touch virtually everyone in the nation. (p. v)

Further, much of the greater world is influenced as well by U.S. mass communications and their cultural by-products and relies heavily on English-language journalism to report global events.

THE IMPORTANCE OF NEWS

The essential and useful information we require for our personal lives and livelihoods comes from the press. Our economy, our government, and our society would have great difficulty functioning without the continuing

1

flow of news and information—the lifeblood of our body politic. An open, democratic society without independent news media is impossible to imagine.

Many Americans have a strong need for, and attachment to, news and use a variety of news sources at least several times a week; about half of the people in the U.S. say they get most of their news from television. A January 1997 Roper poll found that 70% of the public believe that news is either very or somewhat useful to them in making practical decisions. Half of the respondents said they consume news at least 1 hour a day; for many it is 2 hours or more. Two thirds said it would matter some or a lot if they could not get news for a week.

Journalism or what is often called the *news business*—the gathering, the processing, and delivery of important and interesting information and developments by newspapers, magazines or broadcast media—is inextricably entangled in the giant, whirling entity often referred to as *the media*.

Journalism, of course, is concerned with news, which is somewhat different from information because of its public nature. Michael Schudson believes that news is a form of culture that he terms "public knowledge," which he defines as "this modern, omnipresent brand of shared knowing" (Schudson, 1995, p. 3). Many millions of Americans pay close attention on a daily basis to the news.

James Fallows argued that the real purpose of journalism (and news) is to satisfy both the general desire for current information and its meaning. "People want to know the details but they also want to see what the details add up to. Journalism exists to answer questions like, 'What is really going on?' and 'Why is this happening?'" (Fallows, 1996, p. 134).

By definition, news reports should be accurate and objective in order to be believed or to be credible. *Objectivity* means that a news story should be free of a reporter's feelings or opinions and should be based on verifiable facts. *Verification* of a news story means that the story should be convincing so that there can be no argument about its truth or accuracy.

In explaining the meaning or importance of any event, a journalist always runs the risk of being considered biased or partial, hence, the need to be fair and evenhanded. Objectivity and fairness may be difficult, if not impossible, goals to achieve, but it is essential that the journalist try.

News provides perspective by telling people what is important and significant and what is not. Page location and size of headlines can indicate this; any story placed on the right-hand column of page one of a metropolitan newspaper is considered important, usually what an editor considers that day's major story. Most of the time, the first item on a television newscast is considered of prime interest.

Fallows (1996) pointed out that

> During times of scandal our media abandon the pretense of maintaining perspective, and in times without scandal, it hopes for a scandal to come. The financial press does the same thing waiting for the next big takeover deal. The foreign affairs press does so waiting for the next big international disaster. All of them are too busy looking for what is "urgent" to do the daily chore of telling us what is important and why. (p. 134)

This illustrates a long-standing contradiction and dilemma for daily journalism. News should also provide placement in time by not only reporting what is happening, but explaining to us the background or the history of a particular story. When genocidal warfare breaks out suddenly in Zaire or Rwanda, the press should tell us the background and detail of similar tragic instances in that land and elsewhere. News should also point out the similarities and differences in events because many events are important because they fit a certain pattern and as such have added significance. When an airliner, such as the ill-fated TWA Flight 800, explodes in midair, people want to know about similar catastrophes of recent years.

News is not usually a discrete, singular event, although television news often gives that impression. News is a process with a recent past, present, and future, hence, the importance of giving background and context to a story as well as providing follow-up stories. It has also been said that news is a liquid, not a solid.

Much news is interesting and diverting but is important mainly because for many people it is *useful*. A crisis in the Middle East can mean that gasoline will be more expensive at the pump. Other examples: Next Tuesday is election day and polls are open from 8 a.m. to 8 p.m. Here are the candidates. . . . Here is the weather forecast for today. Business sections of newspapers are replete with useful information about changes in the markets and the shifting prices of investments and commodities. Sports pages provide scores. Scores and scores of scores.

In more abstract terms, Harold Lasswell (1971) wrote that the communication process (including serious journalism) in society performs three broad functions: (a) surveillance of the environment, disclosing threats and opportunities affecting the value positions of the community and of the component parts within it (b) correlation of the components of society in making a response to the environment and (c) transmission of the social inheritance to the next generation. According to Lasswell, in democratic societies, rational choices depend on enlightenment, which in turn depends on communication; and especially on the equivalence of attention among the leaders, the experts, and the rank and file. A workable goal of democratic society is equivalent enlightenment among expert, leader, and laymen. If, for example, the president, leading scientists, and the public disagree over the potential threat of global warming, then the society has a problem.

News, as useful public knowledge, is a lot of things as distinct from rumor, titillation, diversion, gossip, and particularly scandal, although any of these elements may contain kernels of news and unfortunately often become involved in news stories. News has a long and fascinating history; one man's news is another man's titillation, entertainment, propaganda, or diversion.

Nonetheless, news in whatever form seems quite essential for any society. Gossip, or just idle talk or rumors about the private affairs of others, are not with purpose and seem to be a human requirement; inquiring minds really do want to know. A sociologist defined news as organized gossip.

What kinds of news do people want to read about? A Pew Research Center for the People and the Press (1996) survey found that crime, the local community, and health were the news subjects that most interest the American public. Culture and the arts, news about famous people, and business and financial news were the least interesting of 14 subjects tested. Other topics of interest were: sports (4th place); local government (5th place); science and technology (6th place); religion (7th place); political news (8th place); international news (9th place); and entertainment (10th place).

Of course, there are marked differences between, say, listeners to National Public Radio (NPR) and C-SPAN and those who watch MTV and tabloid, tell-all television shows. The former were less interested in crime news whereas the latter followed news about crime very closely.

STORIES OF HIGH INTEREST

Other surveys conducted over 5 years by the Pew Research Center for the People and the Press (1997) found that relatively few serious news stories attract the attention of adult Americans, except those that deal with national calamities or the use of American military force. Only one in four Americans (25%) followed the average story closely. Of 480 stories reported over 5 years, the survey found that most attention went to natural or man-made disasters, such as the Challenger spacecraft explosion, and stories about wars and terrorism involving American citizens. Most notably, only 5% of Americans paid very close attention in late 1991 to news about the outbreak of civil war in Yugoslavia.

The public also has a taste for trivia. In early 1990, for example, when only 21% of Americans were following the fall of Communist regimes in Eastern Europe, 74% of Americans had "heard a lot recently" about the Teenage Mutant Ninja Turtles, 78% knew about the recall of Perrier water, and 76% named George Bush's least favorite vegetable—broccoli. People get their information from many sources.

In a broad sense, the term *media* encompasses most of commercial entertainment—movies, popular music, television, radio, books, and video programming as well as print journalism and broadcast news. But more often media are separated into the entertainment media and the news media and that is a distinction I follow in later chapters. *News media*, or simply the press, are used to designate newspapers, journals, news magazines, and those aspects of electronic organizations primarily involved with news and information of public interest and concern. But I quickly add that the intermixing and overlapping of news and entertainment and/or sensationalism is a central concern about today's journalism. Along with this is a trend for opinions to replace facts, particularly in political reporting.

Increasingly, the media, and sadly some serious journalism and some of its best-known practitioners, have become ensnared in the various orbiting worlds of advertising, publicity, public relations, promotion, and that pervasive commercial activity, marketing. In modern America, apparently, no organization is too proud or pure to refrain from trying to market or sell its ideas, its by-products, its people.

The serious news media, which are mainly, but not exclusively, concerned with public affairs news, can at times pursue the same stories and share the news values of trivial or entertainment-oriented media. Even worse, the serious news media can emulate the trash journalism as typified by the supermarket tabloids and various television magazine shows such as *Hard Copy* and *Entertainment Tonight*.

Today, even the best and most responsible of news media are often a mix of hard news, self-help and lifestyle stories, news about celebrities, and some scandal and crime news. The editor's goal is to maintain a balance between the important and the fascinating but yet trivial. That essential balance is easier to achieve on newspapers than in broadcasting because print media have much larger news holes than the network television news's usual 21 minutes to tell everything. (A news hole is the space left over after advertising, comics, features, etc., have been allocated.)

After all, from its beginnings the press has sought to entertain its readers. Even today, a great many people will be interested in or diverted by a good story. (The press is still not too far removed from Hearst's definition of real news: a story whose headline causes a reader to first stagger back in disbelief and then to rush to buy the paper and read all the shocking details.)

Further, due to pressures for profit-making or economic survival, some news media and their journalists are facing an identity crisis—they are becoming increasingly involved in the entertainment business. *Infotainment* is a pejorative term used with derision to describe the mixing of news and titillation that is so widespread today. (Historians may say the press has always sought to profit by seeking the greatest possible audience with content as low or enticing as necessary.)

NEWSPEOPLE'S NAMES MAKE NEWS

A fairly recent trend is that some journalists, from network anchors to television talkshow regulars, have become highly paid celebrities whose names appear in gossip columns and who command large speaking fees. They are famous because they appear regularly on television and may appear in *People* magazine. Some people, with no aparent accomplishments, are famous because they are famous.

Many in journalism are distressed by this trend. Celebrity journalism, it is argued, has undermined press standards and fueled public animosity toward the press.

The identity, if not the soul, of American journalism, appears to be threatened. At times, it seems that the news media have made Faustian bargains with the devil in order to increase their circulations, audience sizes, corporate profits, and, in the case of individual journalists, to maximize their personal wealth. For a few, journalism is a very lucrative career. The best newspapers and magazines, as well as broadcast outlets, have always been in business to make money and indeed must prosper in order to survive in the marketplace. But critics detect a recent willingness to unduly compromise journalistic standards to increase monetary gain. In the past, there were always some news organizations for whom public service was a higher calling than merely making money. Today, that seems to be the case less often.

DISAPPEARING FIRE WALL

Public communication today appears to be marked by a kind of Manichaean struggle—a battle between good and evil propensities of journalists and their masters. There is a sense that public affairs journalism has become seriously tainted.

Veteran newsmen say there used to be a "fire wall" located at responsible news organizations—such as *The New York Times, The*

Washington Post, Time, Newsweek, and CBS News, and a few other media —between serious news reporting and mere sensationalism and entertainment. Some feel that wall has almost disappeared or at least has too frequently been breached in the competitive scramble for audiences, circulations, and profits.

Certain kinds of lurid stories come along that seem to cause some of the most reputable news organizations to forget the fire wall and compete with the "bottom feeders" (i.e., supermarket tabloids) for juicy tidbits about the travails of some celebrity or public figure well-known to television viewers. Examples come along too regularly—the Bobbitt case, the Amy Fisher trial, the Menendez brothers trial, theTonya Harding/Nancy Kerrigan episode, and the JonBenet Ramsey case, among others. Perhaps, the prime example of journalistic waywardness was the way the press reported the prolonged murder trial of O.J. Simpson, the story that had everything—a brutal double murder, a well-known athletic celebrity, spousal abuse, celebrity lawyers, racial overtones, and a prolonged, televised trial. During election campaigns, scurrilous and often unfounded rumors make their way into the news cycle of even the most responsible media.

These trends toward the trivialization of content and decline of serious news reporting are seen as somehow related to the consolidation of newspapers, magazines, television and radio stations into bigger and more pervasive media conglomerates with great economic power and influence both here and overseas. Well-regarded news organizations such as *Time* magazine, the three networks, Cable News Network (CNN), and a long string of once-prestigious daily newspapers such as *The Louisville Courier Journal,* and *The Des Moines Register,* have been swallowed up by media mergers into giant conglomerates. In these multibillion-dollar operations, news organizations devoted to serious journalism represent only a small fraction of a media giant dedicated to maximizing profits from highly profitable entertainment divisions. How have such organizational changes affected the quality and integrity of serious journalism?

For these and other reasons to be discussed later, the American public has become increasingly annoyed and dissatisfied with the news media. Public opinion polls of various kinds show widespread scorn and dislike of much popular culture, the media, and of journalists in general. High-profile journalists such as Diane Sawyer, Sam Donaldson, Cokie Roberts, Barbara Walters, and Dan Rather, among others, have been singled out at times for failing to meet the standards of public affairs journalism.

Public dismay or unhappiness with the media is often confused—and confusing. When the media are under attack, which medium or media personalities are being criticized—your local daily newspaper, Tom Brokaw on NBC News, Russ Limbaugh on talk radio, shouting anchors on Crossfire or smart-aleck comments in *Newsweek*? Equally unclear is what aspects of the media are undergoing scrutiny—violence or sex in the the entertainment media or the lies and distortions of the news media? That is part of the problem. Critical readers and viewers usually treat the media as a monolith, forgetting that media is a plural noun (although the usage is changing) that refers to a complex and multifaceted institution composed of many diverse elements.

Widespread distrust and suspicion of the press exists across the political spectrum from the far left to the far right and even among many political moderates. A few critics such as Fallows believe the press' cynical distortions of political reporting are undermining American democracy.

The public itself, however, is not blameless. The usual comeback of criticized media has long been, "we're just giving the public what it wants." In a sense that is true, and a major failing of Americans today is that too few people are adequately concerned and informed about the serious issues and problems facing the nation. People under 30 years of age read less in general and are not reading many daily newspapers; recently a dramatic drop in watching news on network television occurred among this group.

Many young people get their political news, especially during presidential campaigns, not from serious media, but from entertainment sources such as Music Television (MTV), late-night television comedians such as Jay Leno and David Letterman, and from talk radio's call-in shows. There is an obvious need to create and expand a more attentive and critical audience for serious news.

The crisis in journalism may be related to the reality that we are becoming an increasingly polarized society—a small, affluent, and well-educated upper class that attends to news and public information and the swelling bottom 85% of our population (especially those under 30) that read less and pay less and less attention to public information, opting instead for pop culture and entertainment. The news media themselves reflect these schisms.

I agree with Stephen Hess that the United States is a one-nation-with two-media societies especially in the case of foreign news. Hess (1996) wrote:

> Our society is awash in specialized information, available to those who have the time, interest, money, and education to take advantage of it. The other society encompasses the vast majority of Americans, who devote limited attention to subjects far removed from their necessary concerns. They are content to turn to the top stories of television networks' evening news programs and their community's daily newspaper for their information. (p. 5)

This distinction is central in understanding the strength and weaknesses of American journalism.

THREE MODES OF DAILY JOURNALISM

This analysis may be helped if we consider that the press often seems to operate under three different modes in covering the day-to-day news. Mode one is a routine, normal news day when no one major story dominates the news. The better newspapers will cover a variety of stories, perhaps highlighting a few features or "soft news" stories.Television will do likewise, stressing stories of self-help, medical news, personal advice, or human interest.

Mode two is when a story of major significance breaks: the mysterious explosion of an airliner, results of a presidential election, assassination of a major world leader. Both print and broadcasting will throw all their resources into covering these stories. Evening television may devote an entire program to the story—excluding most or all of the other news. This mode shows U.S. journalism at its best.

Mode three is when a major scandal or sensational story of high interest such as the Simpson case, JonBenet Ramsey murder, or similar stories, takes over the news spotlight. Television news will respond to stories appearing first in tabloids and pick up the story even while decrying such journalism. Often, the coverage of the coverage becomes a compelling story. This mode shows the national media at their worst.

It is worth noting that the current unhappiness with news media and journalists comes during a period of technological change in news communication and entertainment media and their economic underpinnings as well as in a period of rapid societal change. Media—movies, television, pop music, videos, cassettes, CD-ROMs, computer-generated exchanges such as the Internet—are the main conveyor belts of our vast popular culture, mostly generated in America, that have been sweeping the world, for better or worse.

As noted, American journalism in all of its forms is a small but important part of that cultural flow. The old distinction between foreign and domestic news has all but disappeared as well.

Change brought on by electronic media, especially the Internet, as well as computer-assisted information transfers, threatens the viability of traditional ways of reporting the news yet offers promising new ways of disseminating information.

The focus in this book is on serious news coverage, primarily American journalism, and how news is gathered, edited, and disseminated here and abroad. Although faced with such recent disturbing trends as tabloidization, mixing of facts and opinion, trivialization, and media consolidation and commercialization to increase profitability, American journalism is still arguably the most informative and most free anywhere and is an influential and significant source of news for news organizations of other nations.

A great advantage of the free and independent journalism Americans have enjoyed is its ability to correct its own excesses through the process of self-criticism. American journalism has had a long tradition of self-examination throughout the 20th century—from Will Irwin to A. J. Liebling to various journalism reviews and a current crops of astute critics, several of whom are quoted here. Some newspapers have ombudsmen who act as representatives of the public in responding to complaints about media performance.

Many within the field of journalism are deeply concerned about its shortcomings and want to see them corrected. So if it will recognize its faults (some say U.S. journalism is in denial), U.S. journalism can potentially correct and improve itself. Recently, a good deal of self-criticism has been going on within U.S. journalism, a reassuring sign. The power of embarrassment and shame to convince journalistic peers to mend their ways should not be underestimated. There are some indications that media criticism is bringing results.

This volume examines recent trends and current problems that beset American journalism in its schizophrenic, love–hate relationship with the burgeoning entertainment industry—typified by such names as Rupert Murdoch, Time-Warner (and now) Turner, Disney–ABC, the Gannett and Knight-Ridder newspaper chains, NBC, CBS—and with a wary and often hostile public. People often do not like the media, but they still pay attention to the media.

Chapter 1, Best News Media in the World?, examines the American news system as it operates today. It is usually considered the best, most comprehensive, and reliable in the world. Chapter 1 also looks at its key players and major organizations—the so-called national media.

In our rapidly changing world of interdependent economic systems and political uncertainties, American news media have become major players in global news exchanges and mass culture diffusion. In chapter 2, Global Impact of American Media, I analyze the expanded international role of American journalism and note how changes in media structures are impacting on major news events, which in turn influence diplomacy and the relations between nations.

American journalism has enjoyed unusual freedom from government interference and has broad constitutional protections when criticizing public officials. Chapter 3, Freedom of the Press: Theory and Values, shows how the First Amendment and political theory undergird the news media, protecting rights of expression enjoyed by all of us.

A brief historical overview in chapter 4, Recent History of the Press, provides some perspective on current press difficulties. Monopoly, sensationalism, tabloidization, irresponsibility, and public unhappiness with the press have all been around for quite a while. No one designed our news system. It has expanded rapidly and is still evolving.

Bigness, fewness, and like-mindedness are the concerns of chapter 5, which examines how profit opportunities at home and abroad, as well as innovative media technologies, are driving our mass media into bigger and more concentrated conglomerates. Recent megamergers have markedly changed the structure and possibly compromised the integrity of mass communication. Media conglomerates are getting bigger and more powerful in part because there are fewer of them. Further, the number of truly independent news organizations is fast diminishing.

The pervading perceptions of decline in electronic journalism — diminishing audiences, lower status for downsized news staffs, compromised news standards and infotainment trends, all driven by profit squeezes—are analyzed in chapter 6, News on the Air: A Sense of Decline. An examination of the similar malaise of the newspaper business is the focus of chapter 7, The Fading Daily Newspaper? Comparable concerns about downsizing to increase profits, declines in readership and, for big city papers, in retail advertising, are analyzed.

Chapter 8, Why the Public Hates (Some) Journalists, examines widespread dismay with political journalism and with celebrity journalists seen on television talk shows and lecture tours. Some believe that the political culture has been debased by the cynicism and negativism of the political press.

The next three chapters involve international or global perspectives of U.S. journalism. Chapter 9, Changes in Foreign News Coverage, looks at significant changes and problems in reporting foreign news and the changing role of the foreign correspondent. Chapter 10, In the Dark About Africa, examines why the American press does not seem able to report adequately those stricken new nations almost 40 years after political independence. Chapter 11, The Press and the Military, reports on the often-abrasive relations between the press and the U.S. military in the news coverage of military incursions abroad from Panama, Grenada, Persian Gulf War, Somalia, and Haiti to Bosnia.

Chapter 12, Educating Journalists, focuses on how to better prepare young journalists within the context of journalism education in universities.

Will the Internet and the information highway become major players in the journalism of future? If so, why and how soon? Chapter 13, News on the Internet, speculates about some of the short-term changes to be expected in the collection, collation, and distribution of news via cyberspace.

The final chapter, chapter 14, Conclusions: Journalism at a Time of Change, looks at several ways to improve press performance.

1

Best News Media in the World?

There is much to criticize about the press, but not before recognizing a ringing truth: the best of the American press is an extraordinary daily example of industry , honesty, conscience, and courage, driven by a desire to inform and interest readers.

—Ben Bradlee (1996)

A major news event can occur unexpectedly somewhere in the world at any moment—the explosion of a jet airliner in midair, a terrorist bombing of an American military facility, the assassination of a world leader, an outbreak of war in the Middle East, a major oil spill in an ecologically sensitive region.

On hearing about a major news event, millions of Americans then turn to their television sets or radio to learn more—to CNN perhaps, or to an all-news radio station for the first details from the Associated Press (AP) or Reuters or from broadcast reporters. The evening network news shows will give a more full picture and one of the networks—ABC on Ted Koppel's *Nightline* or maybe NBC or CBS—may put together a special report later in the evening.

The next morning more complete stories with additional details will appear in more than 1,500 daily newspapers and hundreds of radio and television stations will recap the story with more developments. If the story is big enough, if it "has legs," *The New York Times* may devote three or four inside pages to more details, related stories, and news photos. Other major dailies may do the same.

Within a week, the news magazines, *Time, Newsweek,* and *U.S. News and World Report,* will publish their own versions, complete with cover stories, more background, and commentary.

If the event is important enough, aware Americans will know the basic essentials—"Terrorists bomb U.S. military housing in Saudi Arabia,"—within 24 hours, and the "news junkies" and interested specialists among us will know a great deal more.

Such near-extensive communication of so much news and information, driven by high-speed computer systems, communication satellite networks, and various databases, is commonplace today. Many Americans will pay little attention and will not be much impressed, but to some of us, such an impressive journalistic performance will be dazzling.

For when it is good, American journalism is very good indeed—as any careful examination of the annual Pulitzer Prizes, DuPont-Columbia Awards, National Magazine Awards, and Peabody Awards should remind us. Probably no newspaper covers the day's news as well and as thoroughly as does *The New York Times*. Rivals that may outperform the *Times* at times (and they often do) would be other major U.S. papers such as *The Washington Post, The Los Angeles Times, The Wall Street Journal,* or *The Philadelphia Inquirer,* winner of numerous Pulitzer Prizes for excellence in reporting.

There are good newspapers of course in other open, democratic societies, many of which serve their readers well. Newspapers are edited for the interests and concerns of their own readers in their own cultures, so comparisons of papers across national boundaries are often interesting but probably pointless.

NATIONAL MEDIA SET AGENDA

These daily papers plus *Time, Newsweek, U.S.News and World Report,* and the television networks—ABC, NBC, CBS, and CNN—plus NPR are often referred to as the national media, and to a large extent they set the news agenda for other media across America.

What the national media decide is major or important news in New York City and Washington, DC, will be important news, or at least noted, in Pocatello and Peoria, because electronic news, as well as AP news, reaches almost every community.

This nationalizing of the American press took place over several decades. News magazines and nationwide radio news were well-established before World War II. A national television news system took on real importance after the 30-minute format took over in 1963. The highly successful *60 Minutes* appeared in 1968 and *Nightline* in 1979 becoming important supplements to the evening news and followed by lesser broadcast newsmagazines. C-SPAN also started in 1979 and CNN in 1980.

In 1970, educational and noncommercial radio licensees formed NPR and out of it came two superior daily national news programs "All Things Considered" and "Morning Report."

Due to facsimile and satellite publication, several major newspapers, *The Wall Street Journal, The New York Times,* and *U.S.A. Today,* are now available to many millions through home delivery, by same day mail, or on newsstands almost everywhere in the nation. In the 1990s an American interested in significant news has almost the same access to these national media as anyone in New York City or Washington, DC.

In this sense, "national" has two meanings. These media are available across the country and they provide news and information of national, not of local or parochial, interest.

This agenda-setting function of the national media flies in the face of the reality that most news is local, as the perusal of page one of any small daily newspaper or local television news show will attest. People are most interested in what happens close to home, whatever seems to most directly affect their lives. A small airplane crash at a nearby airport is a bigger story than a jet going down with 250 aboard in Europe.

But for important news from distant places, the national media decide what is significant or at least highly interesting, and regional and local media generally take heed. The national media also collect and edit foreign news.

The dissemination of that news is assisted greatly by the AP, the cooperative news service owned by U.S. press and broadcast outlets, which is instantly available to almost every daily paper and most broadcasters. Reuters and the news syndicates of the *The New York Times, The Washington Post,* and *The Los Angeles Times* supplement the AP's round the clock coverage. News video on television and cable networks is often syndicated or cooperatively shared with local broadcasters in much the same way. United Press International (UPI) is no longer able to compete with AP and Reuters.

Televised news has evolved as an elaborate process of gathering and disseminating news and video from domestic and foreign organizations. For many millions, the television and perhaps the car radio may be their only source of news. A major reason for the steady decline of afternoon papers in big cities was that the papers' midday deadlines enabled the evening television news shows to offer major stories breaking too late to be reported by those papers.

Although declining in audiences and profits, the three networks news shows, identified with ABC's Peter Jennings, NBC's Tom Brokaw, and CBS' Dan Rather, usually maintain professional standards. Until 1996, Jennings' report was considered the best; ABC's news resources, especially in foreign news, were superior, and Jennings was seemingly less tempted than CBS or NBC to present more entertainment-oriented and trivial features at the expense of hard news. More recently, however, ABC seems to have slipped, CBS is making a comeback in serious news coverage, and NBC News attracted the most viewers during 1997.

Broadcast media and print media each have different strengths in reporting major news stories. For epochal events from the opening night of the Gulf War to the election returns of a presidential content, network television can command the nation's attention for hours on end. Network news, including CNN, easily switches locales to bring information and comment from a variety of sources; at times, widely scattered reporters or experts can be brought together electronically to engage in group discussions—all of which we take for granted. Through video and spoken reports, television viewers get the headlines and the first available facts.

Those who watched network news the day that the Israeli premier, Yitsak Rabin, was assassinated, learned not only the news of how and why he died, but also, despite some repetitions, a good deal about the current crisis and background of Israeli and Arab politics.

Newspapers and news magazines, however, have the space and the time to provide more details, background, and analysis than broadcasting. Moreover, print media are much better on follow-up stories to inform the public about what really happened during, say, the Gulf War or President Clinton's struggle with Congress over health care.

NEW CATEGORIES OF NEWS

This volume is critical of some current journalistic practices, so it is important to realize that in many ways the news media today are better than they have ever been.

Forty years ago, most newspapers considered the news was covered adequately if they reported some government affairs and politics; a smattering of foreign news, local crime and disaster stories; some business news; and sports. In addition, light and human-interest features to divert and entertain were usually included.

In recent years, this same subject mix is still being covered but in much more detail and depth. For journalism is very much a part of the information explosion and news media now have far larger amounts of news available. More importantly, the definitions of what is news have been greatly expanded to include news and developments about science, medical research, reviews of movies, the arts and popular culture, the entertainment business, a wide range of social problems, education, legal affairs, information technology and the computer revolution, personal health, nutrition, and many facets of the business and financial world.

Much of this expanded reporting is done by specialists with professional training in their fields. (These expanded news categories should not be confused with the gossip, trivia, and celebrity-oriented sensationalism that so many deplore in some of today's media.)

This broader newspaper and broadcast coverage is supplemented by a plethora of specialized magazines, journals, and books that deal with such topics in a more leisurely and detailed manner.

Any person living in America who is determined to be well-informed and be on top of the news can do so by owning a television set with cable, subscribing to a national newspaper such as the *The New York Times* or *The Wall Street Journal*, listening to NPR, selectively watching CNN and C-SPAN, and subscribing to several magazines such as *Time, Harper's, The New Republic, The New Yorker, Atlantic, Foreign Affairs,* or *The Economist,* plus getting a good state or regional daily newspaper.

Our hypothetical news junkies can get access to a lot more news if they also own a computer with a modem to scan the news and information available from online services such as America Online, CompuServe, or Prodigy, or the interactive editions of about 700 newspapers on the World Wide Web (WWW; see chap. 13).

At this time of media-bashing, it is well to remember that a lot of good reporting still gets done by newspapers. Phillips (1996) commented:

> Anyone with an hour for a Nexis computer search can come up with 50 courageous exposes of special interests buying congressional favors, lobbies run amok, the plight of the Middle Class and such like in *The New York Times, The Washington Post, The Wall Street Journal, The Chicago Tribune, The Philadelphia Inquirer, The Los Angeles Times,* and *The Boston Globe.* The ghost of Lincoln Steffens is not gone from the nation's newsrooms. (p. 8)

Press critic Ben Bagdikian commented that newspapers are much better today than they were 40 years ago and report a great deal more news than before. But, he added, newspapers now need to be better than before because much more and varied information is required to cope with today's complex and changing world; further, many Americans today are better educated and desire, indeed require, more sophisticated and specialized news for their lives and their jobs.

As always, what some people consider to be very important news does not get reported. Most news is mainly of local or parochial interest and does not make it beyond city or state borders. Sometimes, major stories, such as the savings and loan scandals of the 1980s, will be reported in some national media but fail to make an impression on other media and hence, do not attract the attention of the public in general.

Further, despite the availability of so much news each day, the same space and time constraints still persist. ABC, CBS, and NBC have only 21 minutes each evening for their major newscasts. Sometimes a major breaking story, such as the TWA Flight 800 disaster, will take the entire 21 minutes; no other news gets reported on that broadcast. Radio's news on the hour usually takes 5 minutes or less. Many daily newspapers have small news holes for the day's news after all the retail advertisements, features, comics, advice columns, classifieds, stock market reports, and sports have been included. Most people probably devote less than 1 hour a day to news from various media.

Journalism, as that proverbial "watchman on the hill" keeps its eyes open and sees more because news gatherers can penetrate almost all corners of the world, but not always. Between 1928 and 1938 an estimated 10–20 million people were killed or starved to death in the Soviet Union as a result of Stalin's brutal and disastrous policies, but little news about this horror reached American readers. Similarly, in the early 1960s little was reported about the 20–30 million Chinese who perished during Mao's Great Leap Forward. Today, it is less likely that an autocratic regime could hide calamities of such proportions from the world's view.

To better understand what is ahead, we need to provide a concise overview of the American press as it exists today.

THE "MIGHTY WURLITZER" OF U.S. JOURNALISM

The two main arms of U.S. journalism today, print media and electronic media, are divided into three main approaches:

1. The "new news"of daily journalism as exemplified by the daily newspaper, evening television news, or radio "news-on-the-hour" with the latest from AP;
2. weekly or periodical journalism as typified by *Time* as well as the better television discussion shows like *Meet the Press* or *Washington Week in Review*, and
3. commentary or opinion journalism in various periodicals; *The New Republic, Nation, Foreign Affairs, Atlantic Monthly*, and others as well as books, are examples.

The expectations for objectivity, balance, and fairness are much higher, naturally, for daily journalism, which reports the first version of events, than for the more leisurely weekly and opinion publications or the talk shows of weekend television. Daily journalism also has room for editorial comment and interpretation, but the expectation is that comment should be clearly identified and separated from hard or just-appearing news.

The Print Media

Daily Newspapers. Although viewed by some as a twilight industry, the daily newspaper is still the most effective means of supplying large amounts of serious late-breaking news to the American public. A total of 1,516 dailies were published in 1997—roughly 40% in the morning and 60% in the afternoon—with a total circulation of about 63 million. Almost all metropolitan papers come out in the morning to better compete with television.

Circulations vary widely. Fifteen dailies have a circulation of more than 500,000, whereas more than 1,129 dailies have a circulation under 25,000 and are primarily concerned with serving small cities and communities.

The backbone and intellectual leadership of daily journalism comes from the 40–45 dailies each with circulations of more than 250,000 and includes all those considered the best plus a number of mediocre or fading dailies.

Largest and presumably the most influential dailies include:

The Wall Street Journal (circulation about 1.8 million) is primarily a business publication but is noted for its excellent news coverage and fine writing on nonbusiness topics. Owner is the Dow Jones Co. which has 14 other papers.

USA Today (circulation about 1.5 million) is also distributed nationally and is owned by the Gannett Co. which has 93 dailies and a total daily circulation of more than 5.8 million. *USA Today* has had mixed reviews but is considered to be improving and is carrying more hard news.

The New York Times has a circulation about 1.1 million, of which about 200,000 comes from its national edition. Although undergoing marked changes in recent years, the *Times* is still considered by many as the nation's most influential newspaper.

As mentioned, the large circulations of *The Wall Street Journal, USA Today,* and *The New York Times* are due in part to their national distribution, facsimile newspaper pages are sent via satellite to regional printing plants around the nation.

The Los Angeles Times (about 1.1 million) is one of the notable success stories in U.S. journalism, changing in the past 40 years from a parochial, partisan paper into the finest newspaper west of the eastern seaboard. The Times Mirror Co. owns 10 other papers with a total daily circulation of 2,624,426.

The Washington Post (circulation 800,000) is highly regarded and wields great influence in the political vortex of the nation's capital. The Washington Post Co. also owns *Newsweek* as well as broadcast and cable properties. The *Post* competes head-to-head with the *Times* on major stories in Washington, DC.

The New York Times, The Washington Post, The Los Angeles Times, and *The Wall Street Journal* all maintain significant numbers of their own reporters in key capitals overseas. In truth, concern about the global economy and political instability of the world beyond our shores and the willingness to report foreign news, is one of the hallmarks of a great news medium. Much of this outstanding reporting finds its way to other dailies through syndication. *USA Today* and other Gannett papers, despite the profitability of the group, are notable for their lack of overseas coverage.

Another major newspaper group is Knight-Ridder Inc. with 29 papers enjoying a circulation of 4,136,770. Highly regarded among its properties are *The Miami Herald, The Charlotte Observer, The Detroit Free Press,* and *The Philadelphia Inquirer,* each an outstanding daily with great influence in its cities and nearby suburbs. For $1.65 billion, Knight-Ridder acquired two big additions, *The Kansas City Star,* circulation 291,000, and *The Forth Worth Star-Telegram,* circulation 240,000, from the Disney Co. in April 1997.

Finally, Newhouse Newspapers includes 26 dailies with circulation of 2,960,360, including *The Portland Oregonian.* Newhouse also owns *The New Yorker,* Conde Nast magazines, and the giant Random House book publishing house.

Weekly Newspapers. At the other end of the circulation scales are the 7,400 to 7,500 weekly newspapers that average about 7,500 subscribers each. Total circulation of these publications, so important in so many small communities, is about 55 million, more than double the mid-1960s total. Although often small and unimposing, these papers are close to their readers and usually serve their communities well. Local news dominates these papers (Strentz & Keel, 1995).

Magazines. Certainly the most diverse and perhaps the most changeable yet resilient of the mass media have been magazines, of which there are about 4,000 published, up from 2,500 in the mid-1980s. Carmody (1995) reported that 832 new magazines started in 1994; 67 of these were about sports and 44 were related to sex. Each year about 80% of newly launched magazines fail.

Comparatively few magazines are mainly concerned with journalism and news but overall magazines contribute tremendous amounts of diverse information and entertainment available to the public. As seen later, U.S. magazines are increasingly popular overseas.

Leading news magazines and their approximate circulations are: *Time* (4.1 million); *Newsweek* (3.2 million), and *U.S. News and World Report* (2.3 million). Business magazines such as *Money* (2.2 million), *Business Week* (900,000), and *Fortune* and *Forbes* (each about 770,000), contribute to news flow as do, of course, *Atlantic, Harper's*, and *The New Yorker*.

Though modest in circulations, opinion journals such as the *New Republic, Nation*, and *National Review* have a disproportionate influence on politicians, opinion makers and intellectuals, particularly in Washington, DC and New York City.

Books. Over 50,000 new book titles are published annually in the United States and a significant number contribute directly to the swirling cauldron of journalism. Ever since Theodore H. White wrote *The Making of the President, 1960* after John Kennedy defeated Richard Nixon, journalists have been writing numerous books on national politics and public affairs. Bob Woodward of Watergate fame released his latest, *The Choice*, well before the 1996 presidential conventions and *Newsweek* broke the news of the book by excerpting parts of it. Three well-publicized books in 1996—*My American Journey* by Colin Powell, *It Takes A Village* by Hillary Rodham Clinton, and *Unlimited Partners* by Bob and Elizabeth Dole—all contributed to political news and indeed were part of journalism. However, the two political best sellers of 1996—*Primary Colors* by Anonymous (Joe Klein) and *Rush Limbaugh is a Big Fat Idiot* by Al Franken—were essentially satire and entertainment, not political journalism.

Three of the books most critical of American journalism in 1996 were written by journalists; *Breaking the News: How the Media Undermine American Democracy* by James Fallows; *Hot Air: All Talk, All the Time* by Howard Kurtz; and *Feeding the Beast* by Kenneth T. Walsh. I include quotations from all three later.

Electronic Media

Radio. Radio is ubiquitous and has been for most of the 20th century. Receiving sets are everywhere—in almost every car, scattered around the house, and carried by young people and joggers. There are 500 million sets in America. The nation is served by more than 8,454 radio stations of which 3,764 are AM stations and 4,690 are FM stations. About 70% of the audience listens to FM. Many big city radio stations today are quite profitable.

Hard hit by the advent of television, radio was slow in finding a new niche. It no longer seeks its previous mass audience and offers instead narrow formats in various kinds of music and news, plus a smattering of network programming, especially in news. Radio's survival has offered additional proof that older media are supplemented by new media, not replaced by them.

Radio's journalistic contributions appear to consist mainly of brief newscasts stressing local and regional news, as well as headlines and brief reports on national and foreign events. As mentioned, two shining exceptions are NPR's "Morning Report" and "All Things Considered" heard all over the nation on public stations. These programs make excellent contributions to reporting and analysis of public affairs. Public radio has disproved the conventional wisdom that government support of broadcasting compromises journalistic quality and independence.

Television. A good deal is written about television news and its ups and downs. To set the scene briefly, here are a few basic facts: More than 1,290 commercial licenses have been granted by the Federal Communications Commission (FCC). Of these, about half are VHF, with a far-reaching signal, and half are UHF stations, more numerous and limited in reach.

Viewers have access to about 350 noncommercial or public television stations. More than 400 commercial stations are independents, not affiliated with the four major networks—CBS, ABC, NBC, and Fox. Television markets vary widely from New York City with about 7 million television households, all the way to Alpena, Michigan, with just 15,600 households with television sets (Strentz & Keel, 1995).

Ninety eight percent of homes have television sets and research suggests that sets are on 7 hours a day in a typical home. About 80% of homes have a video cassette recorder (VCR) and 60% receive cable. Both VCR and cable percentages are steadily increasing as are satellite receivers. In 1997, there were 1,594 total cable systems across the nation.

Most Americans are aware of television's importance as a news medium. If at any time there are rumbles of a disaster or other ominous event, people turn on their television sets or, if away from home, their radios.

Public television stations have made their own significant contributions to broadcast journalism primarily in recent years through the *MacNeil-Lehrer News Hour* (now the *News Hour with Jim Lehrer*) and various documentary news programs such as *Frontline, Nova, The American Experience,* and so on. With the exception of CBS' *60 Minutes,* news documentaries or news magazines on commercial networks rarely reach the journalistic quality of those on PBS.

Another important contributor to broadcast news is C-SPAN, the nonprofit cable channel created to report on the legislative process in the U.S. Congress. In addition it provides television coverage, without comment or interpretation, of a wide variety of meetings, conferences, or seminars, all of which have some involvement with public affairs. C-SPAN has a small but devoted group of listeners who care about public affairs.

As mentioned, we are largely concerned with the so-called national media, all of which have the capability of reaching most of the nation—either directly on indirectly. There are other important regional news media in Chicago, Boston, Philadelphia, Detroit, Los Angeles, San Francisco, Seattle, Phoenix, Houston, Dallas, Denver, Atlanta, and other urban areas but the national media have an agenda-setting capability and influence extending beyond their locales.

These national media have overlapping audiences and to a great extent reach the movers and shakers of the American establishment—leaders in government, politics, social affairs, business, and academia, especially along the eastern seaboard from Boston to Atlanta and in the midwest.

As shown later, these trends raise concerns about just where the news media are headed. For one thing, it means that the great majority of Americans are not being reached by serious journalism. Whether the U.S. news media are the best in the world or not may be a pointless argument. The more important question is whether they are as good as they should be or could be? Nonetheless, as seen in chapter 2, the impact of American journalism on the world has been significant.

CHAPTER
2

Global Impact
of American Media

*Mankind has become one, but not steadfastly one as
communities or nations used to be, nor united through years
of mutual experience. . . . nor yet through a common native
language, but surpassing all barriers, through international
broadcasting and printing.*

—Alexandr Solzhenitsyn

Most Americans who keep up with the news are unaware of the influence
and reach of American journalism beyond the borders of their nation.
During the past 50 years, the U.S. news media, in doing their basic job of
reporting the news for local audiences, have participated in and helped
shape a world that is economically more interdependent while being, since
the end of the Cold War, more politically fractured and threatening.

In addition to American-generated news in print and broadcasting, our
movies, pop music, television programs, and lifestyles have penetrated the
minds and cultures of European and non-Western people with tremendous
impact. With results both positive and negative, transnational communication
is undeniably evolving toward a single, integrated global communication
system that espouses free, independent journalism as well as favors market
economies and Western popular culture. As seen later, the current wave of
major media mergers can be viewed in part as corporate strategies to better
compete for overseas markets and profits in both entertainment and news.

The enhanced ability of Western journalism (Britain and other
industrial democracies contribute as well) to report quickly and fully on
global crises and trends enables leaders of nation states, the United Nations,
and business and nongovernment organizations to respond to such
challenges. News media can and do alert nations to a kaleidoscope of such
dangers as environmental disasters, changing facets of terrorism, human

rights clashes, economic trends, and incipient political crises whether in Bosnia, Zaire, Chechnya, or Algeria.

It has been said with some but not much exaggeration that an American's right to know is the world's right to know. Any news story that gets into the American news media can and often does flow rapidly around the world and can appear in local media anywhere if it gets by the various gatekeepers that select and reject the news of the day.

Since the end of the Cold War and the demise of Communist news systems in the Soviet Union and other Eastern bloc nations, the American approach to international news, based on independent and wide-roving journalists free to report (at least in theory) whatever they want and wherever they wish, has gained influence.

English is the dominant language of global news just as it is of computers and the Internet. Global news gathering is now more cooperative and less confrontational (or competitive) than it was in the Cold War days, and more countries are now open to foreign journalists.

Autocratic regimes still exist, of course, and many often restrict their own journalists, as well as foreign reporters, trying to control the news, but they have not been as successful as they once were. Despite press controls in such currently authoritarian states as Indonesia, Nigeria, China, Cuba, and Algeria, the news does get out sooner or later.

GLOBAL NEWS SYSTEM

This global news system, although largely American, is greatly enhanced by such British media as the great BBC World Service (mainly shortwave radio) and BBC World television (a recent competitor to CNN International), Reuters news agency, *The Financial Times*, *The Economist*, and the long tradition of foreign coverage in several elite newspapers such as *The Guardian, Times of London, Sunday Times, The Independent,* and *Daily Telegraph.* Reuters Television, (successor to Visnews) and World Television News (WTN), two Anglo-American enterprises, daily gather and distribute video news packages to television stations all over the world.

Among U.S. daily newspapers, most of the foreign reporting, some of high quality, comes from just seven groups—*The New York Times, The Washington Post, The Los Angeles Times, The Wall Street Journal, The Chicago Tribune, The Christian Science Monitor,* and *The Baltimore Sun*—which all maintain overseas news bureaus. These papers, whose total daily circulation is about 11 million, represent only about 20% of newspaper circulation of all U.S. dailies. Companies controlling 80%of daily newspaper circulation have been making little effort to produce sustained international coverage; the list includes such prominent newspaper owners names as Gannett, Newhouse, Thomson, Hearst, McClatchy, and Pulliam. *USA Today* distributed overseas has been called a newspaper with a "foreign editor but not foreign correspondents" (Hess, 1966, pp. 3–4).).

Most dailies rely on the AP's widespread correspondents for news from abroad. AP is probably the single most important agency that collects and distributes news globally. By the agency's count, more than 1 billion people have daily access to AP news. To collect foreign news abroad, AP maintains bureaus in 67 countries staffed by 617 full-time foreign correspondents. Like Reuters, its closest competitor, AP uses an extensive network of leased satellites circuits, submarine cables, and radio transmissions to supply newspapers and broadcasters with up-to-the-minute news around the world 24 hours a day. AP broadcast services are used by 6,000 radio and television stations. Three key centers—New York, London, and Tokyo—channel the millions of words and pictures daily to both U.S. and foreign subscribers.

The New York Times, The Washington Post, and *The Los Angeles Times* syndicate their foreign news stories thereby extending the impact of U.S. journalism overseas. The New York Times News Service, including Cox newspapers and *The Boston Globe,* sends more than 50,000 words daily to 550 clients, of which more than 130 are newspapers abroad. Its close competitor is the Los Angeles Times/Washington Post News Service, which transmits about 60,000 words daily to 50 nations or about 600 newspapers, half of which are outside the United States.

Hess (1994) reported other U.S. news services with bureaus abroad include the greatly shriveled UPI, Cox Newspapers, Knight-Ridder Financial News, Hearst Newspapers, and Scripps-Howard. Broadcasters (and the number of bureaus) are ABC (5), ABC Radio (9), CBS (4), CBS Radio (4), CNN (19), Mutual Radio/NBC (1), NBC (11), and NPR (3).

Time, Newsweek, and *U.S. News and World Report* have long maintained substantial bureaus overseas in major news capitals.

Since 1980, CNN has added a new dimension to global television journalism—the ability to broadcast news around the clock via satellite, aided by cable, to millions of television sets abroad. Broadcast news from ABC, NBC, and CBS is also found on foreign cable and satellite systems.

U.S. global journalism is augmented by two important U.S.-owned daily newspapers. *The International Herald Tribune* (IHT), published in Paris, is a joint venture of the New York Times and Washington Post companies and carries stories and features from both papers in addition to reports generated by a staff of 40. *IHT,* a marvel of newspaper distribution, sells about 200,000 copies 6 days a week in 164 countries (in Europe alone sales number about 135,000) and is printed by plants in London, the Hague, Marseilles, Rome, Zurich, Singapore, Hong Kong, and Miami. Although still an American paper in outlook and content, it has acquired an important non-American readership. Nearly half its readers are an elite group of European internationalists—businessmen, diplomats, and journalists fluent in English. *IHT* is the first newspaper in history to publish the same edition simultaneously for distribution to all continents.

The Asian Wall Street Journal covers a 16-country, 6,000 square-mile business beat from Manila to Karachi. Averaging about 12 pages an issue, roughly one third the size of the domestic edition, the paper tries for the same mix of authoritative business and political news, a risky effort for a region with so little press freedom. *The Wall Street Journal* also has a European edition, written and edited in Brussels and printed in the Netherlands. The Asian Journal has nearly 33,000 circulation, and the European Journal about 47,000.

American magazines are influential abroad as well. Two internationalized versions of *Time* and *Newsweek*—in English—are widely read globally. Among non-news U.S. magazines, Hearst publishes *Cosmopolitan, Esquire, Good Housekeeping,* and *Popular Mechanics* in 14 languages in 80 nations. The Russian language edition of *Cosmopolitan* carried 110 pages of ads and sold 225,000 copies in 1995. A long-time overseas success is *Reader's Digest,* which in 1995 had 47 international editions in 18 languages, circulating 13 million copies a month overseas. Many millions reading the Digest overseas are unaware that it is an American magazine.

Also important in spreading U.S. and world news abroad is the U.S. Information Agency's Voice of America (VOA), which broadcasts via shortwave radio in 48 languages and has an audience in the tens of millions. A BBC study found that 200 million people daily tune in to shortwave radio on about 600 million shortwave receivers around the globe—half in Asia and Africa. In the last 20 years, the total number of nations that broadcast internationally has risen to more than 100 and the number of hours broadcast has risen to about 30,000 hours annually, almost double that of the 1960s.

MAJOR EFFECTS OF GLOBAL NEWS

The increasing capability to broadcast and publish news globally has changed our world as well as our perceptions of our world. Some effects have been global or geopolitical in nature, others are more media-related, and some are felt mainly by individuals. (Several of the following topics are expanded later in this book.)

Triumph of Western Journalism. Since the fall of the Communist "second world," the Western concept of journalism has become the dominant model around the world and is widely emulated. Non-Western nations have adopted not only the gadgets and equipment of the U.S. press and broadcasting but also its practices, norms, ethical standards, and ideology. Journalists abroad increasingly seek editorial autonomy and freedom from government interference. These journalists aspire to the professional values of fairness, objectivity, and responsibility as well as the so-called *checking effect,* that is, the role of the press as a watchdog and critic of government and authority. They want to report the news as they see it, not as their government wants it seen.

Electronic Execution of Communism. Today many experts agree that news and popular culture from the West contributed to the demise of the USSR and Communist regimes in Eastern Europe. Western media, including Voice of America, BBC World Service, and Radio Free Europe, provided news not otherwise available and delivered the forbidden fruit of Western movies, videocassettes, rock music, lifestyles, as well as promises for a better life—democracy, market economies, and a higher standard of living. Western mass communication, by going over, under, and around the Iron Curtain, played a significant role in raising expectations and breaking the Communists' monopoly on news and pop culture.

Some observers believe the breakup of the Communist system began with the successes of the Solidarity trade union in Poland. There the Communists' monopoly on information was broken in two ways: the rise of alternative newspapers challenging the government and supporting Solidarity goals, and second, a triangular flow of news among the alternative newspapers inside Poland, foreign reporters, and international broadcasters. It worked this way: foreign journalists reported news of Solidarity to their Western media; this news was beamed back to Poland via international shortwave radio, particularly BBC, Deutsche Welle, and Radio Free Europe; these stories were then picked up by listeners and by the alternative papers inside Poland.

Western media suggested that political change was possible, that times were changing, and that the world was watching. Potential demonstrators in other nations saw that the unthinkable was indeed possible. Thus events in East Berlin, Budapest, Prague, and Bucharest reinforced each other.

Mass Culture Accepted. In recent decades, Western mass media have also conditioned much of the world to use the media for entertainment and leisure. (Political indoctrination by the media has been rejected, at least currently, by peoples everywhere, including even China, the last great

Communist nation.) Ever-growing audiences appear to accept and enjoy the movies, television, and even the ever-present commercials. Parents everywhere find it difficult to prevent the influence on their children of the most powerful engine of mass education the West has yet produced: commercial advertising.

Global Audiences Growing. Each year many millions of people are drawn into the global audience, mainly through competing satellite and cable services of television as well as shortwave radio, which carry news as well as entertainment. With satellite dishes and antennas proliferating everywhere, even in the face of governmental opposition, the populous lands of Asia, particularly China and India, are flocking to join the global village.

Since the Tiananmen Square crisis, China has felt the impact of heightened international communications. Western television networks—CNN, ABC, NBC, CBS, BBC—carried words and pictures of the 1989 Beijing uprising to the world, while VOA and BBC reached hundreds of millions of rural Chinese with its Chinese language newscasts. After the crackdown on demonstrators when all Chinese media were brought under party control, shortwave radio continued to report news into China.

Since then, China has been facing a quieter but more serious challenge in the form of hundreds of thousands of satellite dishes. Millions of Chinese people can hook in via satellite to global television bypassing the Communist Party commissars. Some believe the information revolution threatens to supplant China's Communist Revolution, which was long sustained by the now crumbling government monopoly on news and propaganda. Besides shortwave radio, fax machines are widely available in private homes and direct-dial international phones and computers with modems are multiplying as well, enabling many Chinese to use e-mail and electronic bulletin boards.

In China and throughout Asia, Comsat-delivered television programming has been flooding in—Star TV in Hong Kong, HBO Asia, CNN, ESPN, MTV Asia, BBC World—bringing news, information, and entertainment to many millions for the first time. Some Asian nations welcome satellite television but others see it as a threat to their cultural identity and political stability.

Governments across the former Third World have tried to suppress global television with mixed success. Satellite services may be discouraged but educated Chinese can still get world news from BBC and VOA on shortwave radio. Governments are finding it nearly impossible to stop people from taking their news and entertainment from the skies. Dishes are easily put together from imported kits, which are growing smaller, cheaper, and more powerful.

Vast Audiences for Global Events. Great events—a regional war in the Persian Gulf or the quadrennial Olympic Games—can attract huge shares of the global audience. An estimated 2 billion people watched a Live Aid rock concert to help starving people in Africa. About 3 1/2 billion people watched some of the 1996 Olympics in Atlanta. The games were probably watched by more people in China than anywhere else, because more than 900 million Chinese had access to television sets, and three channels broadcast events all day long.

Some of the effects of heightened global news communication have subtle political and diplomatic effects.

History is accelerated. Nations and peoples react faster to important news because global television information moves so quickly and widely. War breaks out in the Middle East and the price of gas at the pump goes up immediately around the world. A bomb explodes in an airliner and security measures tighten in airports everwhere. Actions that would have been taken later are taken sooner, thus speeding up the pace of change—and of history.

"The whole world is watching." The reality that many millions around the world can watch on television as tanks rumble across national borders, or as troops storm ashore on an African coast, as police fire on peaceful protestors can give heightened consequences to a television report. For example, an amateur's camcorder tape of Los Angeles policemen beating Rodney King set off repercussions lasting for years. Vivid and dramatic video of several years of the tragic civil war in Bosnia and Croatia seared the world's conscience. Ditto for Tiananmen Square: The Chinese regime won the battle of ruthlessly squashing the demonstrators but lost greatly in the world court of public opinion for its abuse of human rights.

Diplomacy has changed. Foreign relations and the ways that nations react to each other are affected by public (and world) opinion, now often quickly formed by global communication. The editor of *Foreign Affairs* expressed concern about the dramatic increase in live television reporting of international crises. James F. Hoge (1994) wrote:

> These capabilities of modern media to be immediate, sensational and pervasive are unsettling the conduct of foreign affairs. . . . The technology that makes possible real-time, global coverage is truly revolutionary. Today's correspondents employ lap-top computers, wireless telephones that transmit directly to satellites and mobile satellite dishes to broadcast vivid pictures and commentary from the scenes of tragedy and disorder without the transmission delays, political obstructions or military censorship of old. (pp. 136–137)

Nonstop coverage by CNN and its new rivals, BBC and others, does provide the opportunity to constantly monitor news events and disseminate timely diplomatic information. However, Hoge believes politicians are more concerned than elated by global, real-time broadcasting. "They worry about a 'loss of control' and decry the absence of quiet time to deliberate choices, reach private agreements and mold the public's understanding" (p. 37).

Autocrats lose control. An authoritarian regime can no longer control and censor the news as completely as in the past. Shortwave radio, fax, direct-distance telephone, the Internet, and Comsats carrying CNN International or BBC World have changed all that and have blunted the power of censorship. The Chernobyl disaster in the USSR showed the impossibility of keeping a nation's bad news from its own people and the outside world. During times of crisis, dictators can no longer seal their borders and control information. The news will get out.

Surrogate media for fettered peoples. U.S. and other Western news media now provide news and information for people who are captives of their own governments. By publicizing human rights violations, torture, and political imprisonments, outside media often help victims to survive by reminding the outside world of their plight. It can be argued that a famine never occurs in a nation with a free press because the press by reporting incipient food shortages, will bring pressures on its government to act before people begin dying. During a famine in autocratic Ethiopia, the people endured suffering for many months as the world largely ignored their plight. But after dramatic BBC video reports appeared on the NBC evening news program night after night, Americans were galvanized to support relief efforts generously.

Reporting pariah nations. The Western press' persistent reporting about pariah states, such as South Africa under apartheid or the Philippines under Marcos, can help facilitate political change. Such reporting forms world opinion, which, in turn, can lead to actions by concerned nations. Persistent American and European press reporting of the civil war in Bosnia and the growing evidence of genocide by Bosnian Serbs undoubtedly pushed the Clinton Administration and NATO to intervene and impose a military truce.

Effects of no news. Sometimes the failure to report major news events can have political implications. Because Western journalists were largely barred from reporting the prolonged war in Afghanistan between Soviet forces and Afghan rebels, the impact of that major event on the world's awareness was minimized. In past years, numerous small wars and insurrections in Africa—Western Sahara, Angola, Sudan, and Algeria—

have passed largely unnoticed because the world's news media could not, or would not, report them. The prolonged war between Iran and Iraq was largely ignored because both sides barred Western reporters; yet the conflict lasted for years and had major significance.

Terrorism: news or theater? Global television, which is capable of bringing the world together to share a common grief, such as the death of a president, or exultation, as during Neil Armstrong's walk on the Moon, can also be manipulated to shock the world. Terrorism is still very much with us although the forms keep changing: plane bombings, hijackings, political kidnappings, assassinations, civilian bombings, and more recently, bombings of government buildings as in Oklahoma City and military housing as in Dhahran, Saudi Arabia.

Such acts are perpetuated, some feel, to capture time and space on the world's media. *Terrorism* has been called "propaganda of the deed"— violent criminal acts, usually against innocent people, performed by desperate people seeking a worldwide forum for their grievances.

Terrorists have learned a lesson of this media age: television news can be manipulated into becoming the final link between terrorist groups and their audiences, and as with sensational crimes, the more outrageous and heinous the act, the greater attention the media will give it.

Terrorism is news and poses worrisome questions for broadcast journalists: Does television coverage encourage and aid the terrorists' cause? Is censorship of such dramatic events ever desirable? Most journalists agree that terrorist acts are news and must be reported. Most believe that self-censorship is undesirable and usually not feasible. Some television organizations have established guidelines for reporting terrorism incidents in a more restrained and rational way. Journalists agree they should avoid giving sympathetic support or endorsement to the aims of terrorist organizations.

"Revolution" by personalized media. The spreading information revolution, characterized by personal computers, desktop publishing, CDs, VCRs, the Internet and World Wide Web (WWW), have turned individuals into communicators—even revolutionaries—who can reach out to others abroad. The overthrow of the Shah of Iran in the 1970s was substantially aided by photocopies and audio cassettes bringing in revolutionary messages from abroad. Now, the implications of the Internet for international journalism are just beginning to be realized. In East and Central Europe, personalized media—video and audio cassettes and shortwave radios—were key weapons in the overthrow of Communist regimes because they broke government communication monopolies and piped in the siren songs of the West.

Hachten (1996) quoted Peter Lewis who wrote:

Today, political dissidents of all nationalities are discovering a homeland in the worldwide web of communication known as cyberspace. . . . Today, many human rights advocates are exploring an even more powerful medium (than fax) the computer web called Internet, as a way of defying censorship. (p. 65)

Copy cat effects. With global news so pervasive and widely available, a particular occurrence can be imitated elsewhere. A terrorist's carbombing in one country, widely shown on television, is repeated 3,000 miles away. Somali clansmen defied U.S. soldiers in Mogadishu and a few days later, Haitian thugs were encouraged to stage a near riot as U.S. troops tried to land at Port-au-Prince, causing U.S. forces to withdraw.

Economic and financial considerations undergird the trans-national news system that has expanded so in recent years.

Profit-driven media. The fact that money was to be made has fueled the rapid expansion of international news and mass culture. INTELSAT, the communication satellite consortium that was such a crucial early component in extending the reach of global news, grew so quickly because of the profitability of a more efficient and cost-effective way to make international telephone calls. For whatever their shortcomings, the new media barons, Rupert Murdoch, Ted Turner, Silvio Berlusconi, and others, have been entrepreneurs who are risk-takers and innovators. Of course, news media have followed (and profited from) the expanding economy as it has become increasingly globalized.

Globalization of advertising and public relations. The two persuasive arms of Western mass communication, advertising and public relations (PR), have become globalized along with journalism. Here again, the Anglo-American model, speaking English, is the pacesetter. Although often criticized, advertising and PR are necessary and inevitable components of market economies and democratic governments. Moreover, advertising and PR often make news themselves and are an integral part of marketing.

DILEMMAS OF GLOBAL TV NEWS

If all politics is local, then it also may be true that all news is local, although most of the best journalists believe that foreign news is important and that the news media should carry more of it. Yet, U.S. journalism and that of other nations is clearly marked by provincialism. Unless there is a compelling story of global impact, most newspapers and broadcasters stress local news. Dennis (1992) reported that *InterMedia* published a global survey, "A Day in the Life of TV News," that measured country-by-country uses of domestic and foreign news on one day in 1991. The study found that 85% of television news in the Middle East was about the Middle East, 92% of Latin American news was about Latin America, 80% of the Eastern European news was about Eastern Europe, 78% of Japanese news was about Japan, and so on. The study illustrated the parochialism of news in most countries of the world.

A comparative study of television network news in Japan and the United States over 7 months between 1992–1993 found 1,121 reports from the United States on Japanese television and only 92 from Japan on American television. U.S. Ambassador Walter Mondale commented, "I thought our trade imbalance with Japan was bad, but now I see that the news imbalance is even worse" (Hess, 1996, p. 10).

This confirms the impression that most people abroad know more about Americans than American do about foreigners. But on the other hand, these distinctions may not be that significant if one accepts the view that the old distinctions between foreign and local news have largely disappeared. The fact that the best news media place high value on news from afar, whereas more entertainment-minded media do not, may indicate that it may be in our own self-interest to know more about the outside world.

As we have seen in this chapter, the flow of news and mass culture throughout the world has had a variety of important effects on our global community. Some of those effects have been due to the success of CNN. CNN became the first 24-hour cable news network and as such attracted news viewers away from the evening news shows of ABC, CBS, and NBC during the Gulf War and other periods of international crisis. When a big story breaks, CNN comes on the air and stays with the story. As a result, ABC, NBC, and CBS have become even more reluctant to interrupt scheduled programs with news bulletins or extended reporting.

From its beginning, CNN supplied television news to many foreign broadcast services, homes, and hotels via cable and direct broadcast satellites in many nations. CNN has provided independent Western news to many millions overseas, who previously had received only government-controlled information. CNN has had its great and not-so-great moments: live and global coverage of the Gulf War versus CNN's gavel-to-gavel coverage of the O.J. Simpson criminal trial, thus abdicating for many months its self-proclaimed role of reporting foreign news. CNN gets low marks on its programming and low ratings when crisis news is lacking.

Technologically speaking, however, CNN is a major innovation because of its ability to interconnect so many video sources, newsrooms, and foreign ministries to television sets in so many remote places in the world. In this way, CNN has certainly influenced diplomacy; coverage of a crisis in Bosnia or Zaire makes not only other journalists but diplomats everywhere tune in to get the latest.

A television news channel of true global reach was an innovation whose time had come, and CNN now has its imitators and competitors. In 1991, the BBC started its own World Service Television (WST), now called BBC World. Plans call for news and entertainment channels in Europe, Asia, and the United States. By mid-1997, BBC World had started to challenge the dominance of CNN International, which, according to CNN company figures, reaches 113 million homes in 210 countries and territories outside the United States, where the domestic services reaches another 71 million homes.

After 2 years in Europe, BBC World has gained an audience of 30 million homes outside of its worldwide viewership of 50 million homes in 174 countries and territories. BBC World is not yet received in Britain due to regulatory restrictions but is expected to soon start a 24-hour broadcast news operation in Britain. Following a $500 million agreement with Discovery Communications, BBC World is expected to be on the air in the United States in 1998 as part of a panoply of programs and channels provided by BBC Worldwide.

Another characteristic of the domestic CNN—as an around-the-clock, cable news channel—has elicited competition from other U.S. networks. In late 1995, ABC News announced plans for a 24-hour cable system to compete with CNN, but in May 1996, the idea was shelved by ABC's new owners, the Disney company. NBC, however, has moved ahead aggressively, launching MSNBC—a 24-hour cable news channel, owned jointly with Bill Gates' Microsoft—with great fanfare in July 1996. NBC's innovative effort is also available on the Internet and invites comments via e-mail.

Rupert Murdoch's Fox Network has joined the 24-hour cable news steeplechase with its own Fox News Channel or FNC. CBS was reportedly trying hard to get into cable news but, so far, has lagged behind the others.

Despite this headlong rush, there were serious reservations about whether even two, much less three or four, cable news channels could survive financially. CNN itself has not been very profitable lately. The average number of homes that tuned in to CNN, for instance, dropped from 572,000 in 1995 to 372,000 in 1996 and to 274,000 in 1997. CNN's prime time ratings sank 33% in 1996, in part because the O.J. Simpson trial ended.

In 1997, MSNBC's nightly cable news with Brian Williams averaged 27,000 households. Its rival, the Fox News Channel drew just 10,000 homes. In any case, this stampede to provide cable news channels probably reflects a sea change in broadcast news. People seem to be getting their electronic news more and more on the run in small snippets from car radios or at home (radio ratings have stayed high), or from cable news flicked on at odd hours. Less and less are people getting the news from the evening network news shows, which have been steadily losing viewers.

Multiple 24-hour cable TV news channels also have important implications for global television. Both Rupert Murdoch and NBC's Jack Welch have had their sights on global television networks similar to CNN Internatinal and BBC World. Murdoch is well on his way to achieving that goal with his existing Star TV satellite service based in Hong Kong for Asia and Sky Channel, a satellite TV service in England with a 24-hour news channel drawing on the staffs of his *Times* and *Sunday Times* of London. Murdoch's plans for a U.S. satellite TV service ran into problems in mid-1997 (see chap. 5).

NBC has similar global ambitions, and its well-regarded CNBC channel in Europe and the Middle East is widely available overseas. Emphasizing daily business news from New York, it is seen as a precursor for such a global network (Auletta, 1995a).

But again, reservations have been expressed about the economic feasibility for global television news at least along the lines envisaged by media tycoons Murdoch, Turner, and Welch. A careful and persuasive study by Richard Parker argues against the growth of more global television news. Citing the *InterMedia* study, just mentioned, Parker (1985) wrote:

> The overwhelming interest of audiences globally is not about global news per se but, rather in a much more focussed sense, of region as the relevant domain of concern. For organizations such as CNN International and other global broadcasters, this further erodes the mass-audience potential for a standardized global news wheel, and stresses the importance of national—and regional—broadcasters in delivering news to audiences that meet a broad audience interest. (p. 78)

Yet when the next major world crisis erupts, as it surely will, global television news will take center stage once again in reporting, explaining, and, yes, greatly influencing, if not manipulating, the world's response to those events.

CHAPTER

3

Freedom of the Press:
Theory and Values

The First Amendment reads more like a dream than a law,
and no other country, as far as I know, has been crazy enough
to include such a dream among its fundamental legal
documents. I defend it because it has been so successful for
two centuries in preserving our freedom and increasing our
vitality, knowing that all arguments in support of it are
certain to sound absurd.

—Kurt Vonnegut (1982)

Americans have long had lively, irreverent, rambunctious, and scurrilous newspapers, often disrespectful of authority and at times outrageous. People often despise newspapers, but they still value their right to freedom of the press.

Thomas Jefferson had strong and ambivalent feelings about the press, as his quoted words indicate: "Newspapers serve to carry off noxious vapors and smoke" (p. 85), and later, "Nothing can be believed which is seen in a newspaper" (p. 85). In addition, "The man who never looks into a newspaper is better informed than he who reads them, inasmuch as he who knows nothing is nearer the truth than he whose mind is filled with falsehoods and errors" (Rafferty, 1975, p. 26).

And yet, our most intellectual of presidents also wrote these words: "When the press is free and every man able to read, all is safe" (p. 61), and "No government ought to be without censors; and where the press is free none ever will" (p. 61), "The press is the best instrument for enlightening the mind of man, and improving him as a rational, moral, and social being" (Rafferty, 1975, p. 61).

Jefferson's ambivalence has been shared by other leaders because newspapers can sometimes be excellent, even indispensable to our political life, and at other times, of course, they can be offensive, dishonest, and hateful. Yet the importance of the concept of a free press as essential to a democratic republic has long been recognized, and the American press has been given more protection in our constitutional law than in any other democracy.

The First Amendment to the U.S. Constitution states clearly and unequivocally that "Congress Shall Make No Law . . . Abridging Freedom of Speech or of the Press."

Freedom of the press in the United States is more than a legal concept —it is almost a religious tenet. The Constitution, as interpreted by the Supreme Court of the United States is itself virtually a sacred text, and the First Amendment, which also protects religion, rights of assembly and association, and expression in many forms, is a central part of the value system proclaimed by most Americans (Soifer, 1985).

ORIGINS OF FIRST AMENDMENT

America's high regard for the principle of press freedom derives from the Enlightenment and the liberal political tradition reflected in the writings of John Milton, John Locke, Thomas Jefferson, James Madison, John Stuart Mill, and others. A democratic society, it is argued, requires a diversity of views and news sources available—a marketplace of ideas—from which the public can choose what is wishes to read and believe about public affairs. For no one or no authority, spiritual or temporal, has a monopoly on truth. Underlying this diversity of views is the faith that citizens will somehow make the right choices about what to believe if enough voices are heard and government keeps its hands off the press.

In American Constitutional theory, Blasi (1977) saw this libertarian view as based on certain values (and hopes) deemed inherent in a free press: (a) by gathering and publishing public information and scrutinizing government and politicians, the press makes self-government possible; (b) an unfettered press ensures that a diversity of views and news will be read and heard; (c) a system of free expression provides autonomy for individuals to lead free and productive lives; and (d) it enables an independent press to serve as a check on abuses of power by government.

Our press freedom, rooted in English Common Law, evolved slowly during England's long 17th- and 18th-century struggle between the crown, the courts, and Parliament; when none of the three could dominate the others, a free press slowly began to emerge. In the American colonies and later republic, a press relatively free from arbitrary government controls evolved as printers and editors asserted their freedoms and gradually established a tradition of a free press. Undoubtedly, the American press today is freer of legal constraints than is the press of other countries.

In American history, however, press freedom has suffered great gaps and defeats, especially at the state and local level. In fact, the key constitutional decisions supporting claims for press freedom have been decided almost entirely since the 1930s, beginning with the great Supreme Court decision on *Near v. Minnesota* (1931), which protected the press from prior restraint or censorship especially when involved reporting news of government.

How to define it? Our definition of *freedom of the press* means the right of the press to report, to comment on, and to criticize its own government without retaliation or threat of retaliation from that authority. This has been called the *right to talk politics.*

By this demanding test—the right to talk politics—press freedom is comparatively rare in today's world. A free or independent press is usually found in only a dozen or more Western nations that share these characteristics: a system of law that provides meaningful protection to civil liberties and property rights; high average levels of per capita income, education and literacy; legitimate political oppositions; sufficient capital or private enterprise to support news media; and an established tradition of independent journalism. In any case, freedom of the press really has meaning and can survive only within a framework of law.

Through the decisions of the courts in adjudicating legal disputes involving newspapers, pamphleteers, broadcasters, radical speakers, and others over basic conflicts between written, printed, oral expression and other competing claims, the framework of our system of press freedom has been delineated. In our law, free speech and free press are identical rights; only the form is different. Print and broadcasting are equally protected but radio and television seem less free because they are licensed by the Federal Communications Commission (FCC) and because broadcasters are not as assertive in demanding their rights as are the print media.

Great Supreme Court justices such as Oliver Wendell Holmes, Louis Brandeis, Charles Evans Hughes, Hugo Black, William Douglas, and William Brennan, in particular, have contributed to our expanding freedom of expression. Legal scholars Zechariah Chafee, Alexander Meiklejohn, Thomas I. Emerson, Vincent Blasi, and others in their commentaries have filled out the picture.

Some of the press-related issues decided by the courts have involved highly charged loyalty and national security issues; freedom from prior restraint and censorship; freedom to report legal proceedings and to criticize judges; libel immunity when criticizing public officials; freedom of distribution, pretrial publicity, and defendants rights; press rights versus right of privacy; freedom of expression versus obscenity; protection of confidential news sources; and access to information about public records and meetings. In most of these areas, press freedom has expanded significantly in this century.

ESSENTIAL TO DEMOCRACY

That the American press plays a key role in our democratic system, and in fact, is a central requirement for it, is due in part, Emerson (1985) believed, to several factors. First, instead of representing only private or partisan interests (as in the earlier days of the political party press and yellow journalism), the press has moved to representing the public interest. The growing stress on professionalism, the role of investigative reporting as a regular feature of serious newspapers, and even claims made for special treatment such as *shield laws* (protecting confidential news sources) are all indicators that the press perceives itself as serving the public interest. Certainly not all (or even many) of the news media share these goals (much less achieve them), but the mere existence of the concept is important.

Second, this concept of the press as serving the public interest has become the popular as well as legal justification for protecting freedom of the press. Despite widespread criticism of the media, residual support remains for this press tenet among the general public, opinion journals, and legislatures because the serious press does contribute independent and counterbalancing voices to public discourse.

Third, it can be argued that the press, as an institution, constitutes a viable base from which to stand up to government and concentrated corporate power. With the great expansion of state power and the proliferation of giant corporations, the serious press, despite its own links to many large corporations, still provides a significant potential for independence. So, if not constrained by government, the press in a general way, remains an important factor in generating political and social ideas and programs.

Finally, the constitutional and legal doctrines that protect the press are stated in general terms and are applicable to all sectors of the press. Freedom of the press is an individual right, we all are protected by it; it is misleading to hear, as is often stated, that newspapers are the only business specifically protected by the Constitution. Corporations are only claiming a right we all enjoy, including minorities, even especially unpopular ones. The First Amendment not only protects Time Warner and Gannett but also Noam Chomsky or any unpopular dissident or malcontent handing out inflammatory pamphlets in a mall.

In fact, the First Amendment and the rest of the Bill of Rights can be seen as primarily concerned with protecting minority or dissident rights. Thus a free society must tolerate irresponsible, reckless, and tasteless expression in order to protect the rights of all. The majority rarely feels the need for First Amendment protection, yet the survival of the First Amendment, as both Alexander Hamilton and Alexander Bickel averred, relies on the support of the people. That is the paradox of the First Amendment and a reason for its fragility.

VALUES OF THE FIRST AMENDMENT

Several scholars have elaborated on various values they deem central to the theory of the First Amendment.

Emerson (1966) saw four major values all of which stressed individual rights. The first was the right of an individual purely in his own capacity to seek his own self-fulfillment. "In the development of his own personality, every man has the right to form his own beliefs and opinions. Hence, suppression of belief, opinion and expression is an affront to the dignity of man, an affront to man's essential nature" (p. 5).

Second, free speech is the best method of searching for and attaining truth. This value is similar to values found in both academic freedom and the scientific method of inquiry. A journalist seeking important public information must be free to go wherever the leads take him or her to get the story, just as a scholar should be free to follow the indications of truth wherever they may lead.

Third, free speech makes self-government possible by encouraging the participation of citizens in social and political decision making. And fourth, by so doing, the system of free expression becomes a safety valve that helps maintain a balance between stability and change in an open, dynamic society. If people have access to information and are free to express their views and address their grievances to authority, they are less likely to take up arms against their rulers and resort to civil strife.

Diversity is a value directly relevant both to the ownership and performance of a free press. A related concept, the marketplace of ideas, which goes back to Milton, has come into some disrepute because critics say that truth does not always seem to come to the top and win out in the clash of ideas and programs. Propaganda, PR, and other persuasive and manipulative communications have made many of us skeptics.

Still, even if communication channels are polluted, diversity assures that press freedom is served if people are given a wide choice of information sources, as well as alternative proposals from which to choose rather than having an authoritarian selection imposed on them.

In an anti-trust case, *Associated Press v. United States* (1945), Judge Learned Hand expressed well the value of diversity:

> That (newspaper) industry serves one of the most vital of all general interests: the dissemination of news from as many different sources, and with as many different facets as possible. . . . It presupposes that right conclusions are more likely to be gathered out of a multitude of tongues than through any kind of authoritarian selection. To many this is, and always will be, folly; but we have staked upon it our all. (p. 20)

This view reflects Hand's skeptical view of free speech. The spirit of liberty, he said, is the spirit that is not too sure it is right. Therefore, many views must be available for consideration.

Diversity implies the necessity of competition and a variety of differing and even conflicting views. The steady decline of local newspaper competition coupled with the trends of concentration and monopoly of news media have placed this value in some jeopardy.

Another value, also directly linked to press performance, is the checking value, which sees the press as a watchdog on excesses and malfeasance of government. Blasi (1977) revived this neglected value, on which the drafters of the First Amendment had placed great stress, the ability of free expression to guard against breaches of trust by public officials.

Influenced by 20th-century wars, Blasi argued that government misconduct is a more serious evil than misconduct by private parties because there is no concentrated force available to check it. The potential impact of government on the lives of individuals is unique because of its capacity to use legitimized violence.

> No private party—not Lockheed, not United Fruit, not the Mafia — could ever have done what our government did to the Vietnamese people and the Vietnamese land. Private forces could never have exterminated such significant portions of the domestic population as did the Nazi and Soviet governments of the 1930s and 1940s. (Blasi, 1977, p. 527)

The checking value has been rarely invoked by the Supreme Court, but Justice Hugo Black did so in his last written opinion, in the Pentagon Papers case, *New York Times v. United States* (1971), giving it eloquent expression.

> In the First Amendment the Founding Fathers gave the free press the protection it must have to fulfill its essential role in our democracy. The

press was to serve the governed, not the governors. The Government's power to censor the press was abolished so that the press would remain free to censure the Government. The press was protected so that it could bare the secrets of government and inform the people. Only a free and unrestrained press can effectively oppose deception in government. And paramount among the responsibilities of a free press is the duty to prevent any part of the government from deceiving the people and sending them off to distant lands to die of foreign fevers and foreign shot and shell. (*New York Times v. United States*, 1971, p. 717)

KEY CONCEPTS OF FIRST AMENDMENT

The values of press freedom are further buttressed by several key concepts that are well established in constitutional law. One of the oldest—no prior restraint—means that government is barred from censoring any printed matter before its publication, a principle that goes back to Blackstone in 18th-century England. The landmark decision, *Near v. Minnesota* (1931), dealt with prior restraint or prior censorship and struck down a state statute that barred publication of a local smear sheet, *The Saturday Press*, which had been highly critical of Minnesota state officials. The key point about *Near* is that a publication was prohibited from future publication because it had criticized official conduct; the court found this to be an unacceptable restraint on a free press.

Chief Justice Charles Evans Hughes relied on Blackstone's rather narrow view of press freedom:

The liberty of the press is indeed essential to the nature of a free state; but this consists in laying no previous restraints upon publications, and not in freedom from censure for criminal matter when published. Every freeman has an undoubted right to lay what sentiments he pleases before the public; to forbid this, is to destroy the freedom of the press; but if he publishes what is improper, mischievous or illegal, he must take the consequences. (*Near v. Minnesota*, 1931, p. 702)

And in referring to the sleazy publication barred, Hughes wrote:

The fact that liberty of the press may be abused by miscreant purveyors of scandal does not make any the less necessary the immunity of the press from previous restraint in dealing with official misconduct. Subsequent punishment for such abuses as may exist is the appropriate remedy, consistent with constitutional privilege. (*Near v. Minnesota*, 1931, p. 705)

As *Near* and other cases demonstrated, press immunity from prior restraint in other situations such as obscenity or war-time security needs was not absolute, but the principle of no prior restraint of press criticism of government conduct (the right to talk politics) took on great and lasting importance from then on.

Another key concept, the press' right to criticize government, even wrongly, was spelled out in the celebrated *New York Times v. Sullivan (1964)* decision in the turbulent 1960s. The case involved a civil libel judgment against the *Times* for an advertisement, signed by civil rights supporters, critical of the conduct of public officials during civil rights demonstrations in Montgomery, Alabama. L. B. Sullivan, Montgomery police commissioner, sued for defamation, winning a $500,000 judgment. Upheld by the Alabama Supreme Court, the case went to the U.S. Supreme Court where it was unanimously reversed. The court famously announced a constitutional standard that a public official may not recover libel damages regarding official conduct unless he or she can prove actual malice —that is, knowledge on the part of the critic that the statement was false or "showed reckless disregard of whether it was false or not."

Justice William Brennan's decision stressed that Alabama's libel law was unconstitutional because it failed to protect freedom of the press. (Previously, no one ever thought civil libel had anything to do with the First Amendment.) Brennan said that at issue was: "a profound national commitment to the principle that debate on public issues should be uninhibited, robust, and wide-open, and that it may well include vehement, caustic, and sometimes unpleasantly sharp attacks on government and public officials." Brennan rejected the argument that falsity of some statements in the ad destroyed any protection the paper may have had. He said protection did not depend on the "truth, popularity, or social utility" of the ideas and beliefs expressed. He wrote: "A rule compelling the critic of official conduct to guarantee the truth of all his factual assertions —and to do so on paid libel judgements virtually unlimited in amount— leads to a comparable 'self censorship'" (*New York Times v. Sullivan*, 1964, p. 278).

Brennan pointed out a civil libel suit brought by a public official was as dangerous to press freedom as seditious libel. He added that "the court of history" had found that the Sedition Act of 1798 that had authorized punishment for criticism of public officials and government was inconsistent with the First Amendment. Professor Harry Kalven hailed the *Times* decision as a great constitutional event because the "touchstone of the First Amendment has become the abolition of seditious libel and what that implies about the function of free speech on public issues in American democracy." Kalven felt that the absence of seditious libel as a crime was the true pragmatic test of a nation's freedom of expression, because politically relevant speech is what press freedom is mostly about (Blasi, 1977, p. 568).

Another key concept of press freedom is the more general proposition that expression itself is protected and only actions can be proscribed. This is related to the view that there are no false ideas, that is, all views and ideas, however heretical or illogical they may seem, enjoy the same protection under the law. Only when the fighting words are closely linked to illegal action can the state step in.

In the long history of national security and sedition cases, the clear and present danger test and similar measures were devised to give as much protection as possible to political speech in the face of sedition laws. Since 1969, the Supreme Court has moved to an even more objective standard. In *Brandenburg v. Ohio* (1969), the court said a speaker could not be convicted for "mere advocacy" of illegal action; to be constitutional, a statute can only prohibit advocacy where it is "directed to inciting or producing *imminent* lawless action and is likely to incite or produce such actions" (p. 448). In so doing, the court reached back and adopted a standard used by Judge Learned Hand in the *Masses Publishing Co. v. Patten* (1917) case and greatly expanded freedom of political speech.

Of more direct interest to the news press is the key concept of the right to know which implies that the press not only can publish and comment on the news but also has the right of access to news itself at all levels of government. (One murky question is whether the right belongs to the press or to the public.)

Long ago, the press won the right to be present at open meetings of Parliament and legislatures, including Congress. The Fourth Amendment's guarantee of a fair and public trial has assured the right of a reporter, standing in for the public, to attend and report on public trials. Further, evolution of U.S. contempt-of-court law has given the American press broad powers to criticize judges, report on pretrial news and criticize the conduct of trials—as the O.J. Simpson trial so well demonstrated.

The right to know about the executive branch with its numerous bureaucracies and vast classified files and records has been a long and contentious problem for serious journalism. Some progress has been made, however, through the Freedom of Information Act and various sunset laws that require the release of classified government records after a specified time lapse.

The famous Pentagon Papers case, *New York Times v. United States* (1971), involved overclassification of government records—a secret history of the Vietnam War—and the alleged potential danger to national security posed by *The New York Times'* publication of them. U.S. Judge Murray Gurfein ruling for the *Times*, wrote:

If there be some embarrassment to the government in security aspects as remote as the general embarrassment that flows from any security breach, we must learn to live with it. The security of the nation is not at the barricades alone. Security also lies in the value of our free institutions. A cantankerous press, an obstinate press, a ubiquitous press must be suffered by those in authority in order to preserve the even greater values of freedom of expression and the right of the public to know. (p. 715)

The Supreme Court upheld the favorable ruling for the *Times*.

Another key concept, journalistic autonomy, supports the independence of newspapers from government intrusion into their operations. In *Miami Herald v. Tornillo* (1974), the Supreme Court said a right of reply requirement was unconstitutional when applied to the print media. The Court had ruled just the opposite in a broadcasting case, *Red Lion v. FCC* (1969). In *Tornillo, The Miami Herald* challenged a Florida statute that required newspapers to print free replies to political candidates that the papers had attacked. The Supreme Court ruled unanimously for the *Herald*, supporting editors and publishers. Chief Justice Warren Burger said it was unconstitutional to require a newspaper to print what it otherwise would not. Press responsibility, he said, was a desirable goal, but it was not mandated by the Constitution and "like many other virtues" could not be legislated. Burger said the law was unconstitutional simply because it intruded into the function of editors. He wrote:

The choice of material to go into a newspaper, and the decisions made as to limitations on the size and content of the paper, and the treatment of public issues and public officials—whether fair or unfair—constitute the exercise of editorial control and judgment. It has yet to be demonstrated how governmental regulation of this crucial process can be exercised consistent with First Amendment guarantees of a free press. (*Miami Herald v. Tornillo*, 1974, p. 248)

The values of U.S. press freedom may have influenced the professional values of journalists in other nations. One particularly influential concept is that of a free flow of news, which captures the spirit of the First Amendment. This concept refers to the need to report foreign news fully, accurately, and quickly across national borders and without interference from foreign governments. Timely and accurate news and other reliable information is deemed essential to the needs of an increasingly interdependent global political economy. This concept collides with the counterview that every nation has a sovereign right to control news and information passing back and forth across its borders. The free flow of news may be often one-sided, erratic, or delayed and, in some parts of the world, may seem a hopeless ideal. Yet the trend is favorable for more open and free journalism in more and more nations.

COMPARISONS WITH ENGLISH PRESS LAW

Although they have common roots and share similar values, the newspaper press of Great Britain today has significantly less freedom than that of the United States. A well-known editor, Harold Evans (1990), said flatly, "Britain has a half-free press and the ruling elites find nothing objectionable in that" (p. 192). British newspapers are much more closely controlled by specific legal restraints, especially in libel, contempt of court, and in national security. Britain has an Official Secrets Act and the D-Notices law, which directly and severely restrict the press on a wide range of military and intelligence needs. The United States, despite pressures to do so, has never adopted similar laws.

Our press freedom is specifically guaranteed in our written constitution; statutes challenging the First Amendment can be overturned by the courts. But without a written constitution, English law recognizes neither privileges nor special duties for the press. Rather, the ordinary law is applied equally to the press as it is to everyone else. Supperstone (1985) said the "rights of the press are no greater or no less than that of any English subject," and that an English newspaper is, "generally speaking, as protected as a letter—neither more than less" (p. 9).

CURRENT CHALLENGES TO PRESS FREEDOM

Most of the basic law protecting freedom of the press is considered settled, yet the news media have met several important challenges recently. Here are several:

• American news publications operating in Southeast Asia have been facing increased restrictions on distribution posed by authoritarian regimes, especially by the government of Lee Kuan Yew and his successor in Singapore. *The International Herald Tribune, The Asian Wall Street Journal, Time, Newsweek,* and *The Far Eastern Economic Review* have all been repressed at times by Singapore's authoritarianism and, sadly, the publications have not really fought back (more details on this in chap. 9).

• A rare case involving prior restraint of a publication, with echoes of *Near v. Minnesota* was settled in 1996 when a federal appeals court in Cincinnati threw out a lower court's ruling blocking *Business Week* magazine from publishing sealed court documents from a lawsuit brought by Procter & Gamble. The appellate court was somewhat incredulous that the trial judge seemed unaware he was engaged in the unconstitutional practice of preventing a news organization from publishing information in its possession on a matter of public concern.

• Two major confrontations between the news organizations of ABC and CBS with two tobacco giants, Philip Morris and Brown and Williamson, over broadcasts about the deadly effects of cigarette smoking had major press freedom implications. Neither network acquitted itself well (both controversies are discussed in chap. 5).

But here it should be noted that some critics are concerned that the ever-expanding media conglomerates are backing away from aggressive news coverage and subsequent legal challenges in order to placate their investors. Some media companies have taken legal actions that some analysts consider to be capitulation. These include ABC, NBC, *Business Week* and *The International Herald Tribune*. The national press, it is felt, may be backing away from a long-time principle: that the best way to ward off challenges to news coverage is to rigorously fight each and every one, particularly high profile cases. James Goodale, a First Amendment lawyer, said, "The press lawyers have lost sight of the fact that for press freedom to exist, it's a continuous, constant fight" (Glaberson, 1995b, p. A3). Some feared the effect it might have on journalism elsewhere. Jane Kirtley of the Reporters Committee for Freedom of the Press said:

> Never mind what happens to CBS, NBC, or CNN. What about the small news organizations all over the country? When the big guys won't fight those battles against the likes of the tobacco company, how can the small news organizations stand up to its local equivalent, or even more unthinkable, take on the tobacco industry? (Glaberson, 1995b, p. A3)

• Recently, television journalism has been facing a new form of legal attack, as individuals and corporations have been successful by charging that hidden cameras and other undercover reporting techniques trample on their rights. In January 1997, a jury found ABC News liable for $5.5 million in punitive damages for using deceptive research techniques, amounting to fraud, in a 1992 *Primetime Live* broadcast that accused Food Lion supermarket chain of selling spoiled food. The show's producers faked resumes to get jobs at Food Lion stores and used hidden cameras to show workers dealing with tainted meat. (In August 1997, a Federal judge reduced the punitive damages from $5.5 million to $315,000.)

ABC said the *Primetime* staffers were being punished for being journalists. Critics in journalism (and apparently the jury) said ABC was punished for trickery and deception. Increased use of hidden cameras by news magazine shows such as *Primetime Live* and NBC's *Dateline* was called part of a ratings-driven descent by major networks into the swamp of tabloid television. It was suggested that this and similar verdicts stem from a growing public skepticism about television. Jurors seemed to be showing more sympathy for the subjects of television news reports than for aggressive reporters.

One critic of ABC News said that such stunt journalism saps the credibility of the press and makes life more difficult for serious investigative journalism. Such rulings, however, certainly make it more difficult for smaller media, often the most visible comsumer watchdogs in their communities, but who can ill afford punitive damages, while reporting truthful information. These decisions can have a chilling effect on press freedom and may need to be adjudicated by the U.S. Supreme Court.

• A particularly disquieting decision for the press came in March 1997 when a Federal jury in Houston awarded $222.7 million to a local bond brokerage firm in a libel suit over a 1993 article in *The Wall Street Journal*, which the plaintiffs claimed was false and drove away customers, forcing the company to close. The *Journal* claimed it was just chronicling the difficulties of the company, not causing them.

The award was four times the next biggest libel award ever and shocked media lawyers who denounced the outsize award as dangerous to First Amendment rights. As with ABC News in the Food Lion case, the outsize award reflected public dissatisfaction with media performance. In May 1997, a U.S. judge threw out the $200 million in punitive damages but let stand the $22.7 million in actual damages.

• Finally, in 1996, after 4 years of legislative struggle, Congress rewrote the nation's communications laws, passing major legislation that would transform television, telephones, and the emerging frontiers of computer networks, but without much discussion in the nation's news media. It remains to be seen just how freedom of expression will be affected (see chap. 13 for details), but certainly the public as consumers are expected to gain in various ways.

Viewers will be offered attractive new choices for news and entertainment. They will be able to turn to their telephone company for cable service, to their cable company for telephone service, and to their electric facility for both kinds of service. The bill offers increased competition, which in turn should mean lower prices and innovation.

However, 1 year later the dilatory pace of competition concerned consumer advocates. Not only were cable television bills going up but cable companies were retreating from the phone business.

Nonetheless, overhaul of the nation's communication laws was long overdue to bring them in line for the competitive and technological needs of the 21st century. Because so much news and other public information is carried on television, cable, phone lines, and computer networks, it will be essential to keep track of how well journalism and press freedom fare in this rapidly changing information age.

CONCLUSION

As this overview of U.S. press law shows, our news media enjoy a wide range of legal rights and privileges enabling them to carry out their essential roles of providing meaningful news and commentary on public affairs. A free, vigorous, and outspoken press is indeed essential to a healthy society. It is important too that the principles and theory of our press are deeply embedded in our Constitutional law and are not just the yearnings of a handful of radicals and dissidents. All supporters of the U.S. Constitution, including the most conservative or reactionary judges, must support freedom of the press when they enforce the law.

Yet there remains the very real question of how well the American public understands and supports the First Amendment. The 1997 Roper poll, mentioned earlier, found that few Americans are familiar with the five rights guaranteed by the Constitution's First Amendment. Further, few believe that the right to freedom of the press should be guaranteed at all times. The poll found people see the role of news media as "crucial to the functioning of a free society," but the processes of press freedom are not understood. Eighty-five percent could not name press freedom as one of the five First Amendment freedoms. Nearly two thirds said "there are times when the press should not be allowed to publish or broadcast certain things." That, of course, would be prior restraint, illegal under the First Amendment.

One of our greatest judges, Learned Hand, in speaking of the spirit of liberty, sounded a cautionary note:

I often wonder whether we do not rest our hopes too much upon constitutions, upon laws and upon courts. These are false hopes. Believe me, these are false hopes. Liberty lies in the hearts of men and women. When it dies there, no constitution, no law, no court can even do much to help it. While it lies there it needs no constitution, no law, no court to save it." (Gunther, 1994, p. 548)

CHAPTER

4

Recent History
of the Press

*The press as it exists, is not, as our moralists sometimes seem
to assume, the willful product of any little group of living
men. On the contrary, it is the outcome of an historic process
in which many individuals participated without foreseeing
what the ultimate product of their labors was to be.*
                                                    —Robert Park (1923)

To understand the flaws of the press today, we must first examine several
trends in journalism during this century. The dismaying shortcomings as
well as the encouraging strengths we see in U.S. news media today have
their roots in the past.

The 20th-century history of American journalism has been dealt with
in all its complexity and fascination by numerous scholars and writers,
some of them journalists. Among other things, press history is a morality
tale with plenty of sinners and bad guys, some high-minded heros, and
even a few saints.

This historical overview, focuses on several topics related to the main
concerns of this book: the rise of the great metropolitan newspapers; trends
toward group or chain ownership of daily newspapers; roots of the gossip
or scandal-mongering tabloids and their obsession with celebrities; the
advent and growing influence of radio and television journalism; new
technologies for reporting the world; and criticism of the press.

BIG CITY NEWSPAPERS

By 1900, the press was poised to become big business—the leading papers
had attained large circulations, high capitalizations, and profits. High-
speed rotary presses that made possible automated printing on both sides
of the paper at once, the linotype machine, which speeded typesetting,
the typewriter, and the telephone helped create the big city dailies.

Important, too, was the telegraph, invented in 1844, which enabled newspeople to collect and send news from great distances.

These tools for putting out a newspaper were still in use well into the 1960s. Then another new technology of offset printing, computers (for writing, editing, and storing news), communication satellites, and high-speed data transfers (for instant global news distribution) again revolutionized journalism as well as telecommunications in general.

The great rivals of the 1890s, Joseph Pulitzer and William Randolph Hearst, set the tone for 20th-century journalism, especially for the more lurid and sensational variety. Pulitzer's *New York World* combined a crusading editorial page and thorough news coverage, along with some sensationalism for mass appeal. The *World* had the first sports section and comics, featured brightly illustrated pages and campaigned against corrupt public officials. By 1892, the *World* had reached a circulation of 374,000. (By 1900, the *Daily Mail* of London was selling 1 million copies day.) The first mass medium for a mass audience had truly arrived.

Pulitzer's success influenced the young Hearst who did the same thing with his father's *San Francisco Examiner*. In 1895, Hearst bought *The New York Journal* and began his famous circulation war with Pulitzer. Hearst hired away some of the *World's* staff, expanded the use of photography and introduced color printing to newspapers. The circulation competition led to lurid stories about sin and corruption, sensational pictures, and expanded use of the newly popular comics. The intense rivalry produced the shrill debate and jingoistic coverage of the Spanish American War. *Yellow journalism* was the term critics used for the formula of sensationalism that has persisted in varying forms to the present.

Interestingly, intense competition for circulation was a factor in the enduring tradition of objectivity as a standard for reporting. The papers, as well as the budding press associations—AP and later United Press— wanted all the readers they could possibly attract so it made sense not to turn off some customers with partisan or one-sided stories. Striving to be first—to get a "scoop"—was another enduring newspaper goal and a reason for extra editions to boost street sales. The UP motto of "get it first, but first get it right" animated journalists even after radio and television provided instantaneous delivery of spot news.

Democratization of news was also a hallmark of Pulitzer and Hearst, both of whom championed the little person. To maximize circulation meant targeting news to the masses, often recent immigrants, whose tastes and interests affected the newspapers' content. Despite its faults, *yellow journalism* did much to help the new arrivals off Ellis Island learn about and adjust to a strange, new land. Pulitzer's famous motto, "To comfort the afflicted and to afflict the comfortable," had an underlying commercial motive. Publishers like Hearst, Pulitzer, and E. W. Scripps also acquired readers through the inclusion of some serious social and political content. Bagdikian (1992) wrote, "They secured deep loyalties among readers because their papers crusaded in direct and unmistakable terms for reforms most needed by the powerless majority of the times" (p. 126). The young Hearst wrote, "I have only one principle and that is represented by the effort to make it harder for the rich to grow richer and easier for the poor to keep from growing poorer." Pulitzer's editorial position was "Tax luxuries, inheritances, monopolies . . . the privileged corporation" (p. 127). Such sentiments are rare in today's mainstream press.

The acquisition of *The New York Times* by Adolph S. Ochs more than 100 years ago in 1896 marked the real beginning of modern serious journalism and acceptance of a responsibility to stress news, not trivia and sensation. Ochs stated, "It will be my aim to give the news impartially, without fear or favor" (Johnson, 1979, p. 55). He eschewed yellow journalism and left out comics and other purely entertainment features. Ochs and his editor, Carr Van Anda, stressed persistent and full coverage of significant national and international events. The reporting was objective, the tone somber (some thought it dull) and the contents thorough enough for the *Times* to be considered a "newspaper of record" providing as its front page has long proclaimed, "All the News That's Fit to Print" (Johnston, 1979, p. 55). Following that approach, the *Times* outlived both the *World* and the *Journal* and prospered to become, 100 years later, perhaps today's leading newspaper.

After 1900, running a big city paper had become expensive and required revenue, not just from street sales but from advertising, which came from the newly arising department stores, like Macy's and Gimbel's. In circulation, number of pages per issue, and volume of advertising, the papers grew to sizes never dreamed of before, and the figures representing investments, costs, and revenues reached astonishing totals. Mott (1947) noted that the biggest U.S. paper, *The New York World,* had an annual expenditure of some $2 million and a full-time force of 1,300 men and women in the mid-1890s. Combined circulation of its morning and evening editions hit 1 million in March 1897. The *World* was said to be worth $10 million and earning 10% of that sum annually.

Mott (1947) quoted Lincoln Steffens in 1897:

> The magnitude of financial operations of the newspaper is turning journalism upside down. "Big business" was doing two things in general to journalism: it was completing the erection of the industrial institution upon what was once a personal organ; and it was buttressing and steadying the structure with financial conservatism. (p. 547)

Prophetic words indeed.

Corporate newspapers marked the end of the personal journalism of earlier America. As Mott (1947) wrote:

> The roar of double octuple presses drowned out the voice, often shrill and always insistent, of the old-time editor. . . . Yet, as was often said in this period, the soundly financed and well-established journal was in a far better position to resist undue interference with proper journalistic functions than the insecure sheet of an earlier day. Ochs of the *Times* could defy even an angry advertiser. And many of the papers of the period were inveterate crusaders against moneyed interests. (p. 548)

GROUP OWNERSHIP OF
DAILY NEWSPAPERS

Early in the century, New York City had 14 highly competitive dailies. Many papers lacked the money to compete and were forced to close down, consolidate with a rival, or be bought out. This was the beginning of *chain publishing* or later, *group publishing*, whereby several newspapers were owned and operated by one publisher or publishing corporation. (From a peak of 2,460 daily newspapers in 1916, the number of papers declined after World War I and levelled off at mid-century to around 1,750.)

Group ownership, although it made good business sense, was not necessarily good for democracy and the values of diversity and competing viewpoints. In 1900, 10 chains controlled 32 papers, just 1% of all dailies, and about 12–15% of total circulation. Chains boomed during the 1920s; the number of chain newspapers doubled between 1923 and 1933. By 1935, 63 groups controlled 328 papers and 41% of total circulation. In 1960, the figures were 1,098 groups with 560 papers (30%) and 46% of circulation. (Emery, Emery, & Roberts, 1996).

Around 1900, the eccentric E. W. Scripps was the first to establish a major U.S. newspaper chain, 34 papers in 15 states. Scripps broke all of the later rules for acquiring papers: he created new papers (sometimes in competition with existing ones) instead of acquiring established publications. He charged readers as little as he could and took in few ads. He crusaded for socialist reforms and against abuses of working people. Nevertheless, in 20 years, he was a major publisher worth about $50 million.

His success was followed by that of William Randolph Hearst, also a proclaimed socialist and populist early on. By the end of 1922, Hearst owned 20 dailies and 11 Sunday papers in 13 of the largest cities including New York, Chicago, Los Angeles, Baltimore, and San Francisco. By 1931, Hearst had taken control of 42 papers. With the largest chain in 1935, Hearst controlled 13% of daily circulation and 24.2% of Sunday sales.

Hearst was active in politics and used all his papers to push his own ambitions and favorite causes—he was opposed to entering World War I and later waged a long-time national campaign against radicals that was sometimes called "Hearst's red hunt." Mott (1947) noted that Hearst's vast empire, which included numerous major magazines, began to crumble during the 1930s. By 1986, Hearst had 14 dailies which represented only 1.6 per cent of daily circulation.

The press associations or wire services expanded during the rise of newspaper groups. The AP, which was started in 1848 by New York City papers to pool shipping news, expanded greatly in the new century, and although a cooperative, it mainly served morning papers in the larger cities. Scripps founded the United Press (UP) in 1907 because he feared an AP monopoly of news. Two years later, Hearst started the International News Service (INS) to serve his papers. (In 1958, UP and INS merged to form UPI, which today is nearly moribund.) Few papers could afford to station reporters in Washington or abroad or even to cover news outside their local regions. The wire services filled the gap by cooperative news gathering and distribution by telegraph or leased wires.

Group ownership of daily papers has flourished and expanded throughout this century. The expertise acquired in handling and merchandising news, boosting circulations, selling advertising space, and the promotion and marketing of their newspapers was, logically enough, carried over to other media—magazines, radio stations, book publishing, television stations, and in some cases, motion pictures. So after World War II, various newspaper chains, including Scripps' and Hearst's and others, were transformed into the great media conglomerates of today.

TABLOIDS: SCHOOLS FOR SCANDAL

The Roaring Twenties, following World War I, brought a revival of sensationalism in the form of tabloids patterned after the successful *Daily Mirror* of London. With pages half the size of broadsheet newspapers, which made them easier to read in subways or on buses, tabloids were intended for workers and the foreign-born and stressed crime and sex, ample photographs, and large eye-catching and irreverent headlines. (*Tabloid* refers to both the half-page format and the racy style of journalism.)

The most successful and enduring U.S. tabloid was *The New York Daily News* launched by Joseph Medill Patterson in 1919. Within 6 years, the *News* went to a million circulation, and before World War II had reached 2 million sales. Two competitors, Hearst's *Daily Mirror* and Bernarr Macfadden's *Evening Graphic*, which was the most lurid and irresponsible of the three, had joined in by 1924. In addition to stressing photos, the tabloids introduced *composographs* (i.e., faked photos), crime, and lurid stories of show business personalities. The intense circulation war led to what was called the battle of *gutter journalism*. The *Graphic* folded after 6 years and the *Daily News* gradually moved toward more straight news and less trivia and sensation.

Few tabloids in other cities were as racy as the New York tabloids, but the quest for sensational news did not end with the 1920s. Today's bawdy and irresponsible tabloids sold in supermarkets, such as *The National Inquirer* and *The Star*, continue the questionable practices of the 1920s tabs but are more directly related to the cynical Fleet Street practices of British journalism.

One tabloid journalist who left an indelible mark (or perhaps blemish) on American journalism was Walter Winchell, who wrote for *The New York Graphic* and then for *The Mirror* in the 1920s and early 1930s. Gabler (1994) wrote that Winchell invented the gossip column, breaking journalistic taboos in the process by chronicling the marital problems, peccadilloes, frailties, finances, and personal information about the prominent and famous, often basing his items on vague rumors or gossip. Winchell successfully kept at it for 40 years, and by one estimate, 50 million Americans either listened to his weekly Sunday radio broadcast or read his daily syndicated column in more than 2,000 newspapers. It was, according to one observer, "the largest continuous audience ever possessed by one man who was neither politician or divine" (Gabler, 1994, p. xi). Winchell's impact on journalism and mass culture was tremendous.

Frank Rich (1994) commented,

> The whole oppressive idea of celebrity as we know it today—a fame more often conferred by the press than earned by achievement—also owes its birth to Winchell. The Winchell column may have done more than any other single feature to spread tabloid journalism in its infancy and to speed the rise of the nascent public relations industry. (p. 1)

The way that Winchell and others reported the Hauptmann trial for the kidnapping of the Lindbergh baby in 1935 was a precursor, Rich believes, for the media circus of the O. J. Simpson criminal and civil trials.

In his fine biography, Gabler (1994) wrote (quoting columnist Leonard Lyons): "It was Walter Winchell who rewrote the rules for what was permissible in a major daily newspaper; it was Walter Winchell who first created a demand for juicy tidbits about celebrities and then spent 40 years trying to satisfy it" (p. 552). Gabler went on in his own words:

> If Winchell was responsible for having enlivened journalism, he was also responsible in the eyes of many for having debased it. Once loosed, gossip

refused to confine itself to columns. Once loosed, it danced all over the paper, sometimes seizing headlines, sometimes spawning whole publications and television programs, sometimes, and more insidiously, infecting reportage of so-called straight news by emphasizing gossip and personalities at the expense of objectivity and duller facts. Once gossip had been loosed, WE would become jaded. We would always want more and the media would bend to accommodate us . . . . The legacy remained. We would believe in our entitlement to know everything about our public figures. . . . Above all, we would believe in a culture of gossip and celebrity where entertainment takes primacy over every other value. (p. 553)

Winchell, of course, did not do it all alone. There were others—Broadway and Hollywood gossip columnists (Louella Parsons, Hedda Hopper) *Confidential* magazine, and a panoply of Hollywood fan magazines, as well as press agents and studio publicists, all working overtime to feed the public's appetite for gossip, rumor, and scandal. Winchell, of course, became a celebrity himself, and in part because of him, the circle of celebrities has been widened today to include many prominent journalists and broadcasters.

RISE OF BROADCAST JOURNALISM

In the 1920s, radio provided newspapers with a new form of competition in the news arena. At first, radio's offerings were limited. However, radio had the advantage of involving listeners with events taking places thousands of miles away with a flip of a switch. Also, radio could report news immediately and directly, many hours before newspapers could print and distribute their papers. Radio was the death knell for the extra edition; big city papers soon cut back on the number of editions published daily. (Although radio could get the news out faster, the newspapers still did—and do—gather most of the day's news.)

On November 2, 1920, the Westinghouse Electric Corporation inaugurated the first commercial radio station, KDKA in Pittsburgh. That day, a crackling KDKA kept a small number of listeners in a restricted area up to date on the tabulations of the presidential election of 1920. At that time, interested voters in remote rural regions of America far from telegraph lines, without telephones, and beyond population centers with daily papers, had to wait 2 weeks before news reached them that Warren K. Harding had defeated James M. Cox for the presidency. (Now, there is not a place in the United States where one cannot follow election night tabulations instantaneously and, indeed, be told the winner's name even before all the polls are closed. Broadcasters have been widely criticized for announcing winners before polls have closed in western states.)

By the end of 1922, 576 commercial radio stations were operating in America. Local stations started offering news summaries, often in cooperation with local newspapers. Johnson (1979) reported that in 1926, NBC, a subsidiary of David Sarnoff's pioneering Radio Corporation of America, initiated the first network with 24 stations interconnected; in the next year, the first coast-to-coast hookup was achieved with the broadcast of a football game. In 1927, CBS was organized, the Mutual Broadcasting System followed 6 years later.

For years, NBC operated two networks, the Red and the Blue, so dominating radio broadcasting that the FCC later forced the company to give up one. In 1943, NBC sold the Blue network which became the ABC. Significantly, the three major radio networks, NBC, CBS, and ABC, all moved on in postwar years to dominate the next medium, television, and today each are major parts of giant entertainment conglomerates. (Mutual opted not to go into television.)

Radio's entertainment shows—*Jack Benny, Amos 'n' Andy, Burns and Allen,* and others—drew large national audiences and interest in instantaneous, on-the-spot news reports became popular due to the Lindbergh kidnapping trial in 1934, presidential nominating conventions, and FDR's fireside chats. Radio commentators—H.V. Kaltenborn, Gabriel Heatter, and Lowell Thomas— became household names. Radio expanded greatly between 1935 and 1945, when commercial stations reached 900. Daily newscasts were routine and the networks and most major stations had news staffs and reporters in key cities.

Radio played a major role, of course, in reporting World War II with direct reports from the fronts and key cities abroad. Edward R. Murrow and his colleagues, William L. Shirer, Eric Sevareid, and Charles Collingwood, reported with distinction for CBS. Murrow became famous for his "This is London" broadcasts.

Radio as a news medium, however, was to be eclipsed a few years later by a new and more immediate broadcasting force. Television came in soon after World War II but it is often forgotten that television was an outgrowth of radio which provided the norms and the format for early television news as well as entertainment programming. Television took its viewers to the event itself—to show the President speaking, the touchdown being scored, or the sights and sounds of deadly combat. And from the 1950s, the news reports were in color.

The first regularly scheduled network newscasts began in 1948 with Douglas Edwards on CBS-TV and John Cameron Swayze on NBC. As on radio, these were only 15-minute newscasts with the "talking head" reading most of the news. Until the technology improved, live or taped video reports were slow in coming. When the television report finally did present the actual witnessing of an event on a screen, rather than reading a journalist's report, it had considerable impact.

Great social and political impact was felt throughout the nation by televised coverage of the Senate's McCarthy–Army hearings in the 1950s, space exploration, the Watergate hearings, the Vietnam War, and the tumultuous Democratic convention in Chicago of 1968. Americans felt these traumatic events deeply and viscerally because of what they saw and heard on that little screen.

The nightly newscasts expanded to 30 minutes and drew huge audiences. In the 1970s, an estimated 41 million Americans watched the 7 p.m. news on the three networks. The faces of the newscasters—Walter Cronkite, Chet Huntley, David Brinkley, Howard K. Smith, John Chancellor, and Harry Reasoner—became well-known and trusted. Broadcast journalists were on the way to becoming celebrities. For a time, television news was supplemented by some serious in-depth documentaries. Leading the way was the *See It Now* series and the later CBS Reports of Ed Murrow and Fred Friendly. Although technically better today, television news, and its familiar reporters, no longer enjoy the prestige they had in the 1960s and 1970s. Before they died, Murrow, Sevareid, and Chancellor all expressed disillusionment with current trends in television news.

Television news did not replace news on radio or in newspapers and news magazines; it supplemented them. Radio was hardest hit but slowly adapted to television news and has developed its own niche by adopting many new formats. Cronkite once called the evening television news a "headline service," and that is still the case.

Some big afternoon dailies were hard hit by television, but the press generally, especially the serious press, adapted and survived. Numbers of daily newspapers have been generally stable in recent times. However, several journalistic magazines, such as *Colliers*, *The Saturday Evening Post*, *Look*, and *Life* were electronically executed, not because their circulations declined, but because national advertising moved to television. Magazines generally prospered after television; the same can be said for books.

NEW TECHNOLOGY FOR REPORTING THE WORLD

From Gutenburg on, technology has always shaped the way that news is gathered and disseminated. The persistence of certain anachronistic terms attests to the importance of earlier mechanisms. The *foreign correspondent* was the journalist abroad who literally wrote letters transported by ship to his newspaper at home. The *wire editor* handled out-of-town stories that came clattering in over telegraph wires from around the country. The *cable editor* (not cable television) was the foreign news editor sifting through news reports coming from the underseas cable, mainly from London and the British Empire, which long controlled the cables. *Cablese* was a shorthand method used by news services to combine words to save on cable charges, which traditionally cost a British penny a word.

As mentioned, in the first half of the century, newspapers depended on the telegraph, the telephone, the typewriter, hot type (i.e., Linotypes), and the rotary press to get out the newspaper. But from about 1960, a wide range of innovations, loosely called the *new technology* came along and markedly affected journalism and especially news from abroad.

A much-deepened reservoir of information and its rapid dissemination among many more people are the hallmarks of this quiet revolution, which in its broader context, came to be called the *information revolution*. In the print media, high-speed transmission and electronic processing have accelerated and expanded the gathering, storing, and transferring of words for newspapers, magazines, and books. Computer composition and offset printing techniques have simplified production, leading to desktop publishing. (Today small newspapers exist that are published using a computer, printer, copying machine, and a staff of two or three people.) In broadcasting, minicams, videotape, and remote location transmissions have simplified the delivery of video to the television screen.

International journalism has been greatly facilitated by the vast improvement of telephone service, including fax, provided by the INTELSAT system. Foreign correspondents in remote places can be in close communication with their supervising editors.

A major innovation for global television reporting was the development of portable "satellite uplinks," which can be disassembled, checked as luggage, and flown to the site of a breaking story in order to send back live reports. Costing about $250,000 each, a flyaway dish can become a temporary CNN or ABC bureau in just the time it takes to get one on the scene.

Perhaps the major impact of communication satellites on the news industry has been the capability to relay color television reports instantly and globally, often significantly influencing world public opinion and understanding, as during the Gulf War or in Bosnia. The U.S. networks daily incorporate satellite news feeds from their correspondents in various parts of the world.

What are some of the implications for journalism of the four decades of innovations in communication technology? Here are some suggestions:

• The unit cost of communicating news will continue to drop as usage of world news systems increases and efficiency, speed, and reach of the hardware becomes greater. However, the same is not true for the print media due to the rising costs of newsprint.

• Technology has made it possible to send and receive news from almost anywhere in the world at increasing speed. Researchers have succeeded in transmitting information at a rate of 1 trillion bits per second through an optical fiber. That is the equivalent of sending the contents of 300 years of daily newspapers in a single second through a wire of glass. The continuing integration of computers with television means much more *interactive*, or *two-way*, communication will occur.

• The two-way capability of cablevision, tied in with Comsats and personal computers, means that information users can seek out or request specific kinds of news and not remain a passive audience.

• The two way capability of telecommunications means that a two-way flow of information and news is more likely, with consumers having more choice about what they receive.

CRITICISM OF THE PRESS

Criticizing the press has long been a favorite sport in America, if only because the press has long been so outspoken about our public officials and the establishment. H. L. Mencken once said, "The only way for a newsman to look on a politician is down." He also said: "All successful newspapers are ceaselessly querulous and bellicose. They never defend anyone or anything it they can help it" (Bartlett, 1992, p. 642). If so, they asked for it.

Like the government it supposedly keeps an eye on, the press itself needs watching and throughout this century, it has not lacked critics, including many from its own ranks. One of the earliest critiques was a series of articles titled "The American Newspaper" for *Colliers* written by Will Irwin in January–July 1911. *The Brass Check* by Upton Sinclair in 1919 pictured a false, cowardly press dominated by advertisers and business interests. Walter Lippmann's *Public Opinion* in 1922 raised serious questions about the validity of journalism itself.

Hearst and other press lords triggered a series of critical books, Oswald Garrison Villard's *Some Newspapers and Newspapermen* in 1923 and in the turbulent 1930s, George Seldes' *Liberty of the Press* and *Lords of the Press*, Harold Ickes' *America's House of Lords* in 1939, and Ferdinand Lundberg's *Imperial Hearst* in 1936. In those depression years, the largely Republican press was much on the defensive. Newspapers still endorsed political candidates and President Franklin Roosevelt claimed that 85% of the press opposed him; he blamed the owners, not the reporters.

A major effort to study the responsibilities and character of the U.S. press came from an academic study financed by *Time* publisher Henry Luce, headed by Chancellor Robert M. Hutchins of the University of Chicago and called the Commission on Freedom of the Press. Several books, but little research, by noted social scientists, came out of the effort. Its summary report, *A Free and Responsible Press*, in 1947, provided a statement of principles, which were largely rejected by newspapers but studied closely in journalism education programs.

Out of the tempestuous 1960s came a spate of journalism reviews, written by journalists themselves and highly critical of press performance. Before 1968, only two reviews existed, *The Montana Journalism Review* and *The Columbia Journalism Review*. *The Chicago Journalism Review*, published from 1968–1975, inspired about 40 or so similar publications, but fewer than a dozen survived after 1977, including *More*, a national review; *Accuracy in Media (AIM)* a conservative newsletter; *Media Report to Women*, *Twin Cities Journalism Review*, and *feed/back*.

Among newsmen who wrote for those reviews, the model of press critics was provided by A. J. Liebling, whose insightful "Wayward Press" pieces in *The New Yorker* entertained readers as he skewered newspaper errors and ethical lapses throughout the 1950s and 1960s. Throughout the considerable literature of press criticism, Johnston (1979) noted that certain themes have persisted: the media are too big and powerful, too tightly controlled by too few people, too standardized in their presentation of news and information; too much "managed" news; and too much attention is paid to gossip, trivia, sex, and violence and not enough attention to significant social, economic, and political trends.

As seen later, criticism of the press is alive and prospering, and there is some evidence that the news media heed their critics.

5

Bigger, Fewer,
and More
Like-Minded

Freedom of the press is guaranteed only to those who own one.
—A. J. Liebling (1960)

*Wall Street didn't give a damn if we put out a good paper in
Niagara Falls. They just wanted to know if our profits would
be in the 15–20 per cent range.*

—Allen Neuharth

A continuing and inexorable trend throughout 20th century America has
been for more and more newspapers, radio and television stations,
magazines, book publishers, and other media organizations to become
owned and controlled by corporate giants—usually called *conglomerates*
—that have become bigger, fewer, and, in significant ways, more like-
minded.

This thrust toward monopoly or concentration of ownership has
developed in stages, each of which represents potential threats to diversity
of ideas and views as well as to independent and vigorously competing
news media. First came the newspaper groups noted in the previous
chapter whereby a number of similar papers are held by one owner. The
Gannett Co., currently the largest, added 11 more papers in 1995 for a
total of 93 dailies and more than million circulation. Similar patterns of
group ownership of radio and television stations have characterized
broadcasting as well.

Next there were the increasingly common one-newspaper cities with
local media oligopolies whereby the only newspaper in a city also owned
local radio and television outlets. (The spread of national newspapers plus
more suburban papers has allayed somewhat this concern.)

Another stage was cross-media ownerships whereby one company—Tribune Co. of Chicago, Times Mirror of Los Angeles, Washington Post Co., and others—acquired newspapers, radio and television stations, book publishers, and magazines, scattered around the country. For example, the Times Mirror Co. has, at various times, besides *The Los Angeles Times*, owned *The Dallas Times Herald, Newsday, The Hartford Courant, The Denver Post, Baltimore Sunday papers;* the fourth largest college textbook publisher, magazines including *Field & Stream* and six other outdoor and sporting magazines, and cable television services. In such companies, media properties come and go as corporate strategies change. Recently, Times Mirror has been downsizing both staff and holdings to increase its profitability.

In broadcasting, groups of stations and networks have been swallowed by bigger fish. In 1986, the ABC network was acquired by the much smaller Capital Cities for $3.5 billion; General Electric, original owner of RCA, bought it back, including the NBC network, for $ 6.4 billion. In 1990, Rupert Murdoch assembled the Fox network out of the Metromedia television station chain and the film studio, 20th Century Fox. And in 1994, Hollywood film studios started two more networks—WB (Warner) and UPN (Universal and Paramount).

These various media companies have evolved to the most ominous creature on the media landscape: the giant conglomerate that owns not only news and entertainment media, but production and distribution companies as well. They deal in all of the products of entertainment and popular culture, including sometimes, over in one corner, news media.

The world's largest media company was, at a recent count, Time Warner, but others are in the chase, particularly Disney / ABC and the far-flung empire controlled by Rupert Murdoch operating under the misnomer of News Corporation.

No one has followed the continuing trends of media consolidation more closely than Bagdikian. Bagdikian (1992) has shown that ownership of most of the major media have been consolidated into fewer and fewer corporate hands—from 50 national and multinational corporations in 1983 to just 20 in 1992. In that 9-year period, the companies controlling most of the national daily circulation shrunk from 20 to just 11. Among magazines, a majority of the total annual industry revenues, he said, earned by 20 firms in 1983, was amassed by only 2 in 1992; in book publishing, revenues divided among 11 firms accrued to just 5 in that same 9-year period. This media merger frenzy has continued unabated with no end in sight.

The sheer size of media conglomerates makes them, as publicly held companies, active players in the financial markets, hence they are under pressure to compete for earnings with highly speculative investments.

Bagdikian (1992) commented,

> For the first time in the history of American journalism, news and public
> information have been integrated formally into the highest levels of
> financial and non-journalistic corporate control. Conflicts of interest
> between the public's need for information and corporate desires for
> "positive" information have been vastly increased. (p. xxx)

Driven by visions of expanding profits and ever-larger markets as well
as the opportunities created by new technologies of telecommunications,
the media giants have been acquiring each other at a quickened rate. Grow
or perish seems to be the credo; bigger is apparently better.

Several mergers of major U.S. media organizations occurred in 1995
with broad implications both for journalism and the entertainment business
here and abroad. The mergers also illustrated the complexity and global
reach of these behemoths.

DISNEY SWALLOWS ABC

In August 1995, the Walt Disney Company announced acquisition of
Capital Cities/ABC in a deal valued at $19 billion—the second largest
media takeover ever. The merged company brought together ABC, then
the most profitable television network, including its highly regarded
television news organization and its ESPN sports cable service, with an
entertainment giant—Disney's Hollywood film and television studios, its
theme parks and its repository of well-known cartoon characters and the
merchandise sales they generate. For example, in 1995, the Disney
Company sold more than $15 billion worth of Disney merchandise
worldwide—a figure more than seven times the global box office for Disney
movies (Auletta, 1996).

Both companies announced they would grow faster together. Disney/
ABC became the first media company to have a major presence in four
distribution systems: filmed entertainment, cable television, broadcasting,
and telephone wires through its connections with three regional phone
companies. So, ABC's news media operations, including its national news
shows, *World News Tonight with Peter Jennings*, *Nightline* with Ted Koppel
and the admirable ABC television news organization, plus 20 radio stations
and eight television stations, publishing operations, *The Kansas City Star*,
The Fort Worth Star Telegram, Fairchild and Chilton trade publications, and
international broadcasting interests were all merged, or better, submerged,
into an entertainment giant that generates about $17 billion in revenues
yearly. Heretofore, Disney had no involvement with any activity remotely

concerned with news or journalism. Now Peter Jennings and Ted Koppel and colleagues were all working for Mickey Mouse. At the time of the merger, no top executive from either Disney or ABC made any statement about how the merger would affect news media and journalists in the new company. (In early 1997, Disney announced it was putting up for sale the publishing businesses, including the newspapers, it acquired from ABC. *The Kansas City Star* and *The Fort Worth Star Telegram* were both purchased by Knight-Ridder.)

TIME WARNER BUYS TURNER

The next merger bombshell came 1 month later when Time Warner Inc. and Turner Broadcasting System announced they would merge their sprawling operations, reinforcing Time Warner's position as the world's largest communications giant. Time Warner said it would buy the 82% of Turner that it did not already own—at a price tag of $7.5 billion.

In this case, both companies had major news-related media. (Time Inc. and Warner Communications had merged in a $14 billion deal in 1989.) Time Warner's major publishing interests included *Time, Life, Money, Fortune, People,* and *Sports Illustrated* as well as Time-Life Books and Warner Books. However, just in money terms, these publications were overshadowed by the Warner Bros. film and television studios, television and cable channels such as HBO, Cinemax, and others, 50 record labels, the world's largest music publisher, film libraries and other businesses such as Six Flags theme parks, and so forth. The Turner company, of course, had CNN, CNN International, and Headline News channels, in addition to its film and television production, other television and cable channels, film libraries, and assorted sports franchises such as the Atlanta Braves baseball team, the Atlanta Hawks basketball team, and World Championship Wrestling. As with Disney/ABC, news and journalism opperations were in monetary terms a fraction of the corporate pie.

WESTINGHOUSE BUYS CBS

The next blockbuster merger also came in mid-1995 with Westinghouse Inc.'s takeover of CBS Inc., creating the nation's largest broadcast station group with 39 radio stations and 16 television stations reaching 32% of the nation. This merger brought together two pioneers of broadcasting— CBS started its radio network in 1927 and Westinghouse had launched KDKA Pittsburgh in 1920. However, today 90% of Westinghouse's sales are in manufacturing with only 10% in broadcasting. There were concerns about how well it could run a major network. CBS, once a leader in both ratings and quality of broadcast news, had slipped. The former Tiffany network had lost some important affiliates and had no holdings in cable. By the scale of today's mergers, once-mighty CBS was sold for an embarrassingly low price—*only* $5.4 billion.

Another significant merger was the marriage of a hot cable television company, Viacom, with a legendary Hollywood studio, Paramount Communications, Inc. for $8.2 billion in 1993. The new company, called Paramount Viacom International, fused Viacom's ubiquitous and Nickelodeon cable channels and Showtime pay television channel with Paramount's film company, Paramount television, and publishing firms —Simon & Schuster, Prentice-Hall, and Pocket Books—and several sports properties, Madison Square Garden, The New York Knicks, and The New York Rangers.

As deals come and go, the size and annual sales of the media giants rise and fall. The biggest in terms of estimated 1996 sales were: Time Warner, $23.9 billion; Disney/ABC, $21.9 billion; Viacom, $12.4 billion; and Rupert Murdoch's News Corporation, $9.7 billion (Fabricant, 1996).

MURDOCH ROLLS ONWARD

Although smaller than its rivals, News Corporation had expanded into satellite television and programming abroad and had global clout far beyond its size.

During these megamergers, Rupert Murdoch, the most conspicuous big roller among media owners, had not been idle. In July 1996, his News Corporation acquired the New World Communications Group, Inc. for $3.4 billion, making him the biggest owner of television stations in this country. The purchase gave Fox network ownership of television stations in 11 of 12 of the nation's largest television markets, extending the company's reach to 40% of American homes. Murdoch's reach extended even further in June 1997 when he agreed to pay $1.9 billion to acquire the cable channel controlled by Pat Robertson, the religious-right purveyor of programs reaching 67 million homes.

Since starting with a small group of Australian newspapers, Murdoch has been continually reshaping his media empire and juggling his considerable debts. Although long involved in journalism and newspapers, Murdoch has consistently shown a cynical and hypocritical disdain for responsible journalism, apparently considering news just another commodity to be sold. His Fox network has notably lacked respectable news programming and he has been criticized for using his news operations to satisfy his own political goals. One critic, Alex Jones, said of him,

News is a commodity that is of no more importance to Rupert Murdoch than a television sitcom. He crafts news for the audience, but in fact his sense of what the audience wants is skewed to sensation and a lowering, not an elevation, of standards.

Murdoch makes no excuses. "Look," he said, "the first thing you have to do in a public company is to survive, and I don't make any apology for a paper or a magazine" (Fabricant, 1996a, p. C6).

His current strategy apparently is to own every major form of programming—news, sports, films and children's shows—and beam them via satellites or television stations he owns or controls to homes in America, Europe, Asia, and South America. He recently said, "We want to put our programming everywhere and distribute everybody's product around the world" (Fabricant,1996b, p. C1). Some believe the recent media deals came about because Disney and Time Warner felt they had to catch up with Murdoch.

Murdoch has more than 150 media properties in his constantly shifting empire, based mainly in the United States, United Kingdom, and Australia, and with it, he has carefully put together a vertically integrated global media empire. In the United States, he owns the Fox television network, 20th Century Fox movies and television, *The New York Post*, *TV Guide*, *Weekly Standard*, and Harper Collins Publishers. In Britain, he owns *The Sunday Times*, *Times of London*, *The Sun*, *News of the World*, and other media companies. In Australia, he owns Fox Studios Australia for movies; seven television networks; one national newspaper, *The Australian*, and 117 other newspapers giving him two thirds of newspaper circulation; two magazines and other media-related companies. Further, through various holdings including ASkyB, SkyMCI, Fox News Cable, Sky Entertainment Latin America, British Sky Broadcasting, Sky TV in Asia, and Vox in Germany, he has satellite coverage of five continents.

Another key link in his quest for global television dominance was seemingly forged in January 1996 when Murdoch and MCI Communications, the long distance telephone company, agreed to pay the U.S. government $682 million for the last unclaimed orbital slot for a satellite to beam television to individual homes across America. Next, Murdoch announced in February 1997 that he was joining forces with MCI and Echostar's 430,000 U.S. subscribers to provide satellite delivery of television programming that promises serious competition to the cable television industry in America. In May 1997, the Echostar deal soured and was apparently dead as Murdoch seemed to be pulling back from the direct-broadcast satellite market.

THE RACE FOR GLOBAL MARKETS

These megamergers positioned the resulting giants—Disney/ABC, Time Warner/Turner, and Murdoch—to better penetrate and dominate the growing international markets for television, movies, news, sports, recordings, and other media products. At the time of the merger with ABC, Disney president Michael Eisner spoke glowingly of India's middle class of 250 million as a great potential audience for Disney/ABC movies, cartoons, news, and sports programs. NBA and NFL games have been gaining large audiences overseas, hence the importance of the ESPN networks.

The competition between CNN, MSNBC, and Murdoch's Fox network for a 24-hour cable news channel (see chap. 2) has strong international potential implications as well. Broadcast networks have been looking to international markets as a way of gaining hundreds of millions of new viewers. NBC's international holdings currently are about 20% of the network's worth of $10 to $12 billion; in 10 years, half of the network's value will come from international holdings. Asia is expected to be the main area of growth because about 25% of the continent's 400 million homes are expected to receive cable by the year 2000. By contrast, the U.S. market, with cable in 65 million of its 97 million households is nearing saturation. Numbers of cable viewers are expected to rise abroad in time for the start of NBC Europe and related NBC services in Latin America as well.

Other competitors in the global race after CNN and NBC are Disney, British Broadcasting Corporation, and NHK of Japan.

OTHER BIG MEDIA PLAYERS

Other overseas media barons are also competing for the growing international media markets. Among the bigger players are Bertelsmann A.G. of Germany, which built up a media giant with book and record clubs in Germany, Spain, United States, Brazil, and 18 other countries. Bertelsmann owns Bantam, Doubleday, and Dell book publishers in America, 37 magazines in five countries, and radio and television properties.

Possibly the most swashbuckling of the media tycoons is Silvio Berlusconi of Italy who built a multibillion dollar television and newspaper empire, Fininvest, of unusual power and influence. With 42% of Italy's advertising market and 16% of its daily newspaper circulation, ownership of Italy's three main private television channels, plus other properties, Berlusconi dominated Italy's media and influenced its politics. Using that power, he won election as prime minister in 1994. However, he was forced to resign after his media empire was linked to bribes of tax auditors. The future of his media empire has been somewhat uncertain.

Japanese corporations have invested heavily in Hollywood movie studios. MCA, owner of Universal Studios, Universal Pictures, MCA Records, theme parks, and Putnam's publishing firm, was acquired by Matsushita Electric Industrial Co. for $6.13 billion in 1990. Another Japanese giant, Sony, owner of CBS Records, Columbia Pictures and Tristar pictures, and Matsushita controlled more than a quarter of the U.S. motion picture market. However, the Japanese owners have not done well financially with these media properties.

Not many Americans are aware that the U.S. newspaper group with the largest number of daily papers, Thomson Newspapers, Inc. with 109 dailies, mostly small papers with about 2 million circulation, is Canadian-owned.

Such transnational acquisitive media activities are a natural and expected result of the globalization of the economy and the free flow of investment capital across borders. But the U.S. and other democracies may need to update and revise their own communications policies that were formulated before news, mass culture, entertainment, and other information moved so freely around the world.

IMPLICATIONS AND CONCERNS
FOR JOURNALISM

A principal concern for public affairs journalism is that the news operations —broadcast news divisions, newspapers, and news magazines—are just a small part of these giant entertainment companies. The future of independent news gathering appears threatened when news media are submerged into entertainment companies. An FCC commissioner, Andrew Barrett, predicted that by the year 2000 "we'll probably see ten to 12 companies controlling everything we see, hear, and convey in entertainment, voice, and data" (Hickey, 1995, p. 20).

Bill Kovach (1996), head of the Nieman Foundation at Harvard, wrote,

> Though the trend is not new, with the Disney / ABC merger the threat to a form of journalism that serves the interests of a self-governing people crosses a new threshold. Even with the best of intentions, owners and managers are influenced by the fact that they now preside over a corporation that, by the simple act of merger, has drastically reduced the proportionate importance of the news department. . . . ABC's news division will now have to compete with the enormous energy of Disney's entertainment productions in a company in which ABC's value as an outlet for entertainment is paramount. (p. A17)

The future of journalism as watchdog on the government is threatened when big organizations that do business with the U.S. government, like General Electric (NBC), and Westinghouse (CBS), have swallowed major news media. Communications companies in recent years have almost ingested most news organizations, yet these same companies are involved in lobbying government and buying government favors. In the 1994 elections, the communications industry was the sixth largest contributor to candidates, giving almost $10 million to political action committees.

A major concern is whether reporters within these entertainment giants will be permitted to objectively and critically report news about their own organizations. Lawrence Grossman, former head of news, reported that when the stock market crashed in 1987, he received a call from Jack Welch, chairman of General Electric, owner of NBC, telling him not to use words in NBC news reports that might adversely affect GE stock. Grossman said he did not tell his NBC news staff about the call (Bagdikian,1992).

"You cannot trust news organizations to cover themselves," said one critic, citing as example television's meager coverage of the telecommunications debate in Congress that led to major communications legislation in 1996 (Gunther,1995, p. 36).

Gunther (1995) raised these questions regarding megadeals:

> Will film critic Joel Siegel of ABC's *Good Morning America* feel free to deliver a withering critique of Disney's next big animated movie? Will CBS' *60 Minutes* investigate the nuclear industry's efforts to market "safe" plants abroad and at home, a drive led by Westinghouse? (p. 37)

Will ABC news be able to report critically about the Chinese government at a time that Disney may be trying to get its movies via satellite into China? We already know what Rupert Murdoch will do: In 1994, in an effort to curry favor with the Deng regime in China, which had criticized BBC news, Murdoch summarily dropped BBC's World from his Star TV satellite service in Hong Kong.

The word synergy has become a mantra for the CEOs of the recent mergers. When he bought ABC, Disney chief Michael Eisner used the term five times in four sentences to illustrate the advantages of merger. When Westinghouse purchased CBS, its CEO said that combining the two companies' broadcasting assets would save hundreds of millions of dollars a year and bring about "tremendous marketing synergies" (Auletta, 1995b, p. 31).

> Whether these wonders will come to pass remains to be seen. What is already apparent is that "synergy" is no friend of journalism. The business assumptions behind the word—cost savings, a "team culture," the "leverage" of size—can be actively hostile to the business of reporting. (p. 31)

Rich (1996) defined synergy as the "dedication of an entire, far-flung multimedia empire to selling its products with every means at its disposal." Another critic said, "When you hear the word synergy, you might as well read 'conflict of interest'" (p. 15).

When the Warner movie, *Twister*, was released, *Time* magazine just happened to run a cover story on tornados, and Time Warner was criticized for committing synergy. Another example: After joining with Disney, ABC broadcast a special on the making of *The Hunchback of Notre Dame* to coincide with the release of the animated Disney film. Several television stations owned by ABC also covered, as news, a gala celebration that Disney threw for the movie in New Orleans.

But some critics think the big problem is not compromised news coverage, but compromised news distribution, whether over radio, television, or satellite. On cable for instance, Time Warner, now owner of CNN, with 12 million cable subscribers, has effective control over 40% of U.S. households with cable. This is because TeleCommunications, Inc., another Turner shareholder, has over 14 million cable customers. Thus a rival for CNN could be shut out of this access unless the FCC intervenes.

A squabble between media barons over scarce television channel space came sooner than expected. In October 1996, Rupert Murdoch went to court in New York City charging that Time Warner was out to destroy his Fox network by refusing to offer Fox's new 24-hour news channel to Time Warner's New York cable subscribers. Instead, the cable channel went to MSNBC, the new Microsoft/NBC joint venture. New York's mayor, Rudolph Giuliani, got into the act, hoping to force Murdoch's news network onto the Time Warner channel, by trying to air it on a municipal channel. (Murdoch was a political ally of the mayor.) However, a Federal judge issued a broad ruling barring Giuliani from the action, rebuking the Mayor for what she said was a thinly disguised effort to help a political supporter. She said the mayor violated Time Warner's First Amendment right to choose the channel it transmits. At its simplest, it was a battle over a precious commodity in the information age, channel space, but it also raised questions about competition in the news business and relations between politicians and news organizations.

Synergy has a lot to do, of course, with marketing. Critic Edward Rothstein commented,

Disney can produce related movies, toys, books, videos, shows and infomercials so that each format feeds the others. A video game turns into a television show, a computer game into a novel. A newspaper reviews its own corporation's products; news shows promote made-for-TV movies with tie-ins. It can seem that much of culture has become a series of products being transported from one technological medium to another, with fewer and fewer hands manipulating the software. (Rothstein, 1996, p. B1)

The media giants' timidity and aversion to controversy was illustrated by recent legal clashes of both ABC and CBS news organizations with major tobacco corporations. In 1994, ABC on its *Day One* magazine show carried a hard-hitting investigative piece called "Smoke Screen" about the manipulation of nicotine in cigarettes and the behavior of tobacco companies. As a result, ABC spent 17 months and millions in legal fees fighting a potential $10 billion dollar lawsuit from Philip Morris. Both the producer and on-air correspondent said the story was accurate and ABC lawyers were confident they could win. But soon after the merger with Disney was announced, Capital Cities/ABC management forced the news division to issue a humiliating public apology, which Philip Morris reprinted in newspapers all over the nation. Many journalists were stunned. Why had ABC settled? Most agreed it was not a matter of journalistic ethics ("We were wrong") but more of corporate convenience ("We can't impede the merger"). Auletta called it "the logic of negative synergy" (Auletta, 1995b, p. 9).

A similar ethical embarrassment hit CBS' *60 Minutes* news program soon after and was even more of a cause celebre. In November 1995, in an atmosphere of increased tension between the tobacco companies and the press, CBS' lawyers ordered *60 Minutes* not to broadcast a planned on-the-record interview with a former tobacco company executive who was harshly critical of the industry. Many in journalism and the law felt that CBS, facing a multibillion-dollar lawsuit, had backed off from a fight it probably could have won. *60 Minutes* was faulted for not saying that the decision came at a time CBS stockholders were considering a merger with Westinghouse. *The New York Times* editorialized:

This act of self censorship by the country's most powerful and aggressive television news program sends a chilling message to journalists investigating industry practices everywhere. . . . But the most troubling part of CBS' decision is that it was made not by news executives but by corporate officers who may have their minds on money rather than public service these days. With a $5.4 billion merger deal with Westinghouse Electric Corp. about to be approved, a multi-billion dollar lawsuit would hardly have been a welcome development. Some of the executives who helped kill the *60 Minutes* interview, including the general counsel, stand to gain millions of dollars themselves in stock options and other payments once the deal is approved. . . . The network's action shows that media companies in play lose their journalistic aggressiveness when they let lawyers and corporate executives make decisions that ought to be the province of news executives. The same issue was raised when ABC settled its lawsuit with Philip Morris." ("Self-Censorship at CBS," 1995, p. 14E)

Both ABC and CBS took a critical lambasting from the press in general and from the journalism reviews, *Columbia Journalism Review* and *American Journalism Review.* Many in journalism were asking whether the corporate executives of the big conglomerates will back their in-house news media in future legal clashes with government or economic power as, for example, *The New York Times* and *The Washington Post* once did in the Pentagon Papers case. So far the outlook is not promising.

DOMINANCE OF GROUP OWNERSHIP IN DAILY NEWSPAPERS

The great majority of U.S. daily newspapers have not been swallowed by the huge entertainment conglomerates described earlier. This is important because the daily newspaper is a medium that is mainly involved with marketing news. However, more than 500 of the 1,516 dailies in 1997, including almost all of the largest and most influential, are owned by the 20 largest U.S. newspaper companies, that is, firms mainly concerned with putting out newspapers. Several are giants; three of them, Gannett, Times Mirror (*The Los Angeles Times,* etc.), and Knight-Ridder are among the top ten media companies in annual revenues (Emery et al., 1996).

The 12 largest groups, all with total daily circulations of more than 1 million, are in order of daily circulation: Gannett Co, 93 papers; Knight-Ridder Inc., 28 papers; Newhouse Newspapers, 26 papers; Times Mirror Co., 11 papers; New York Times Co., 25 papers; Dow Jones & Co, 22 papers; Thomson Newspapers Inc., 109 papers; (Chicago) Tribune Co., 6 papers; Cox Enterprises, 19 papers; Scripps Howard, 19 papers; Hearst Newspapers, 12 papers; and Media News Group, 17 papers.

In the aggregate, 455 individual companies own the nation's dailies. Of these, 129 owners now own 80% of the total.

In earlier days, the concept of several daily newspapers competing in one city for news and public support reflected the value of diversity and was considered essential for democratic government. New York City once had 14 dailies, whereas Omaha had 7. Today, only eight large American cities have more than one daily newspaper under separate ownership and are not involved in joint operating agreements: Boston, Chicago, Denver, Los Angeles, New York City, Trenton, NJ, Tucson, and Washington, DC.

However, in most larger communities, the presence of local radio, television, and cable outlets, suburban and weekly papers and local magazines, plus access to national papers, certainly contributes to diversity and a marketplace of ideas.

The steady, inexorable trend toward group ownership seems to go on unabated. The long-standing tradition of the family-owned newspaper may be ending. Media analyst John Morton (1995) said it cannot last because few family dynasties are left. In 1995, he counted only 77 independently owned, family-controlled newspapers of 30,000 circulation or more remaining; this represented about 5% of the 1,516 or so dailies still in business in the U.S.

According to Morton, the unusual thing about the growing concentration of ownership in the past 25 years, compared with other industries, is that it has come rather late to newspapers. Compared with auto makers, grocers, steel companies, and retailers, the newspaper industry remains diverse in ownership. Moreover, newspaper ownership is much more concentrated in other Western democracies such as Britain, France, Italy, Australia, and Germany.

When Gannett purchased 11 daily papers in July 1995, Eisendrath commented, "The war is over and the old guys lost" (Glaberson, 1995a, p.1, sec. 4). The "old guys" were independent newspaper publishers, many of whom had close ties to their communities. Gannett's earlier purchases of respected family-owned papers had raised the issue of whether good journalism and corporate ownership can coexist. Now the question does not seem to come up.

Some major newspapers have been able to withstand the pressure of potential buyers by either adopting a two-tier stock ownership plan, retaining voting power with the founding family, or by distributing the company to its employees through employee stock ownership plans. Several of the biggest companies in terms of circulation, New York Times Co., Tribune Co., Dow Jones, and Times Mirror (but not Gannett or Knight-Ridder) have such arrangements to ward off potential buyers.

At *The Milwaukee Journal*, an employee-owned trust was established in 1937 by publisher Harry Grant, who also acquired an ownership stake that his descendants control today. Grant felt that protecting the company from a buyout would promote superior journalism. In 1996, an offer of $1 billion was made for the Journal Co., which owns the recently merged *Milwaukee Journal Sentinel* and six subsidiaries. Although the offer was estimated to be twice the value of the company, the offer was rejected.

Whatever criticisms are made about their journalism, group ownership has often been very profitable. Here are the newspaper profit margins of some leading companies for 1994: Gannett Co., 23.1%; Knight-Ridder, 16.4%; Times Mirror, 9.4%; New York Times, 10%; Tribune Co, 22.3%; Dow Jones, 16%; Thomson Newspapers, 14.6%; Capital Cities/ABC, 14.4%; Washington Post Co., 18.7%; and Scripps Howard, 19.8%.

As noted earlier, most of best papers are in groups. The old days of William Randolph Hearst, sending out explicit orders from San Simeon regarding his pet campaigns and editorial positions to be carried in all his papers, are over. Most group-owned dailies enjoy considerable local autonomy with editors and publishers establishing their own news and editorial policies. Group ownership provides economic stability by efficient business policies that enable papers to survive where they might otherwise fold. The sharing of news through the group through news services and other cooperative efforts helps papers to survive. In its first years, *USA Today* was greatly assisted by the seconding of staff members from other Gannett papers who remained on the payrolls of their home papers. Nonetheless, papers within a group tend to look alike in format, typography, features, and editorial tone.

RESEARCH ON CHAIN OWNERSHIP

What does research say happens when a chain buys a highly regarded independent newspaper? The usual expectation is that the quality of the newspaper will deteriorate, the news hole and staff numbers will shrink, and the new corporate owners will squeeze as much profit as possible out of their new acquisition.This is not always the case.

Some research studies show a somewhat mixed picture. The independently owned *Louisville Courier-Journal* was purchased by Gannett in 1986. A careful longitudinal study of the news content of the Courier-Journal found a mixed commitment by Gannett to the editorial quality of the paper. Under the group owners, the Courier-Journal substantially increased the size of the news hole, but the average length of the stories dropped, coverage of hard news declined, and the number of wire-written stories exceeded staff-written pieces (Coulson & Hansen, 1995).

Another scholar used the recession of the late 1980s to compare how the different forms of newspaper ownership—chain and independent—responded to difficult economic conditions. Twenty-nine daily newspapers were studied from 1985–1992. Chain ownership showed modest and mixed effects.The chain papers had higher average profit margins, supporting a common accusation of their critics. Chains spent more on news editorial as a percentage of all expenditures and showed a consistently higher benefit ratio. The independents were higher on news hole and editorial pages (Blankenburg, 1995).

DECLINING PROFITS

In the past several years, although profits were still running at about 12%, or twice the Fortune 500 average, daily newspapers have not been as profitable as earlier. The industry has cut about 6,000 newsroom and production jobs and many others have gone unfilled. The Times Mirror Co. closed down its *Baltimore Evening Sun*, the paper of H. L. Mencken, as well as the New York City edition of *Newsday*—moves that sent a chill through the industry—in order to improve profit margins.

Some critics think that newspapers should be spending more, not less, on news gathering and publishing. Newspaper executives are understandably concerned about threats to the industry: advertising dollars moving away from newspapers, circulation slipping, an aging readership, and a younger generation with few of the newspaper habits of its parents. There seems little doubt that most newspapers publishers are more concerned with the bottom line than they are with exerting political influence and control.

For some time now, critics have predicted that the days of the daily newspaper are limited; that it is a sunset industry. Still, daily newspapers persist and provide more news and information today than ever before. For millions of educated and concerned Americans, their daily supplement of news and current specialized information supplied by either *The New York Times, The Washington Post, The Wall Street Journal, The Los Angeles Times*, or other metropolitan papers, is still essential to their public activities and private lives. On most days, news on commercial radio and television cannot compete with that.

Yet with proliferating new electronic and cable media, computers online, and Internet services providing outlets for clashing opinions and ideologies, the place of daily newspapers in the electronically expanded marketplace of ideas would seem to be diminished. Freedom of expression is much less dependent on the printing press than it has been in the past and that is a reason for concern.

Today's media mix presents a paradox. Sources of news and useful information, however wrapped and disguised in gaudy packages of entertainment and persuasive communication—marketing, advertising, propaganda and PR-driven messages—are greater than ever. This vast, expanding landscape also includes cable channels, magazines, and books (just visit a Border's or Barnes & Noble bookstore), the Internet, CD-ROM and other electronic outlets, and even mail order.

On the other hand, another reality is that the economic units—the media companies and organizations that produce, market, and distribute the news that enlightens us and the entertainment that diverts and beguiles us—are rapidly becoming gigantic, fewer in number, more remote, and more like-minded. That is certainly cause for concern.

CHAPTER
6

News on the Air:
A Sense of Decline

Radio, if it is to serve and survive, must hold a mirror behind the nation and the world. If the reflection shows radical intolerance, economic inequality, bigotry, unemployment or anything else—let the people see it, or rather hear it. The mirror must have no curves and must be held with a steady hand.

—Edward R. Murrow (1945)

For more than 40 years, television has been a powerful information force, focusing a nation's attention on great events—a presidential election, a disastrous war in Vietnam, an historic struggle in the 1960s for civil rights, and more recently, the fall of Communism and a prime time war in the Persian Gulf.

In 1963, the three networks began their 30-minute evening newscasts (originally 15 minutes as in radio) which became the "front page" from which most Americans got their news. But in recent years, things have changed. There has been a pervading atmosphere of unease about television news, a sense that broadcast journalism has lost its way and is in decline.

In addressing the shortcomings of today's journalism, it should be understood that some criticisms are peculiar to television news, others to news on radio, and still others to newspapers and magazines. Yet, many broad-brush indictments of poor press performance blame all news media equally. That is patently unfair. Some criticisms such as mixing entertainment with news may seem to cut across several media but not in the same ways. The problem of celebrity journalists is peculiar to television. Many media differences persist.

The media are not a monolith, but a complex and heterogeneous collection of diverse organizations and individuals often with quite different motivations and goals. Journalists, whether at *The Daily Chronicle* or ABC news or *The National Enquirer*, are members of a news organization and their performance is shaped by and is a reflection of where they work. Some journalists do their jobs well, not so well at times. So bear in mind that the criticisms that follow usually apply to only part of the news media. For clarity, television, radio, and the print media are analyzed separately as much as possible.

In its transition from radio to television, broadcast news was for many years a loss leader, a public service intended to attract serious viewers as well as prestige. Profits from newscasts were incidental. The best-known broadcasters—Edward R. Murrow, Eric Sevareid, Walter Cronkite, Chet Huntley and David Brinkley, Howard K. Smith, John Chancellor—enjoyed a stature and credibility with the public rarely found among today's anchors.

As the pioneering broadcast giants, William Paley at CBS and David Sarnoff at NBC, faded away, conventional corporate interests took control —General Electric at NBC, real estate magnate Lawrence Tisch (and later Westinghouse) at CBS, and Capital Cities (and later Disney Company) at ABC. News programs were increasingly expected to attract audiences and bring in revenue, and that required higher ratings.

The short television life of the early high-quality but low-rated documentaries soon ended, and the evening news broadcasts began to stress more crime, scandal, and celebrities, all of which tended to crowd out foreign and public affairs news.

After the ratings success of CBS' *60 Minutes* in the 1980s, the networks found money was to be made from the so-called newsmagazine shows. Imitators, such as *20\20*, *Prime Time Live, Turning Point, 48 Hours, Dateline NBC, Eye to Eye with Connie Chung*, and *Day One*, soon clogged the airways. The quality varied widely from the newsworthy to such trivia as Connie Chung seriously interviewing Tonya Harding, an Olympic skating hopeful who caused injury to a rival, and Heidi Fleiss, a Hollywood madam. These news magazines had a semblance of journalism, but were increasingly emulating the increasingly popular pseudojournalistic TV shows such as *Hard Copy, A Current Affair*, and the talk shows hosted by Oprah Winfrey, and Phil Donahue.

Veteran television anchors have expressed their concerns about all of this. Walter Cronkite, who anchored the CBS evening news for 17 years, wrote that in the face of rising competition from cable, VCRs, and more aggressive local newscasts and tabloid shows, the big three newscasts, he said, "frequently go soft. Their features aren't interpretive to the day's events, and the time could be better spent"(p. 34). Cronkite blamed two developments. First, the networks have cut news budgets "so practically an amputation has taken place. The reduction of the foreign bureaus is a crime. It is simply not possible for anybody to intelligently and adequately cover a distant foreign beat without living there"(p. 35). Second, Cronkite saw television news evolving away from the networks into something in the pattern of daily newspapers. That is, he said, "the local television station really does all the news—some international, some national, and some local. And many local journalists—smaller markets, smaller money—are not as good as those on the network" (Rottenberg, 1994, pp. 34–35).

John Chancellor, long-time NBC anchor and commentator, berated television for neglecting its coverage of politics. The networks, he said,

> are spending far less than they ever did on covering politics. I sense in the networks an unwillingness to go into much detail as far as politics is concerned. The people who run the news divisions feel that unless it's an unusual election, the public isn't all that interested. (p.1C)

Chancellor was the last news commentator on an evening network show. Daniel Schorr, NPR commentator, said, "Television deals badly with talking heads, especially when they are also thinking heads"(Glass, 1992, p.1C).

The decline of public affairs news on network news was further signaled by the decimation of network news staffs in Washington, DC., the major source for news of government and politics. In a 2-year study of 75 Washington correspondents and producers at ABC, CBS, and NBC, Kimball (1994) found not just a slump in coverage but "the end of an era in broadcast history"(p. 5). Overall, he found that the CBS and NBC Washington bureaus, which once had 30 correspondents each, were down to about 13 each; ABC had just eliminated seven reporters. The White House, Congress, and Supreme Court, and federal agencies all received diminished attention. Beats such as the environment and individual agencies were eliminated. Kimball found the networks relying more and more on shared pool coverage and *voiceovers*, or tape shot by a freelancer or syndicate and narrated by a home-based correspondent who had not been to the scene of the story. (Similar practices became prevalent in foreign news coverage.)

These cutbacks coincided with drops in the networks' share of viewers and advertisers and with the dramatic rise, most apparent in the 1992 presidential race, of alternative news outlets such as prime-time newsmagazines, radio talk shows and cable programming.

The soft news that has replaced public affairs news on network newscasts has been called "you news," "news lite," or "news you can use." A newspaper ad touted NBC's hottest story, "Marriage 'Boot Camp': Could It Save Your Relationship?" On any given evening, one third or more of the 21-minute news hole is given to features like "Sleepless in America (the growing problem of insomnia), " "Starting Over" (on keeping New Year's resolutions), "The Plane Truth" (airline safety), or "Going Home" (NBC journalists return to their roots). Currently the leader in ratings, NBC also puts soft news into regular segments like "In Their Own Words," "In Depth," "The Family," "The American Dream," and "Norman Schwarzkopf's America." ABC and CBS have similar nonnews segments.

With the downsizing of overseas and Washington bureaus, the networks seem to be losing their competency and interest in reporting public affairs news.

DECLINING VIEWERSHIP
OF TELEVISION NEWS

The changes and decline in quality of television news seems related to its continuing loss of viewers; as audiences evaporate, network producers seem to use more of these soft features, as well as sensational and entertainment-oriented news to attract a greater audience.

A study by the Pew Research Center for the People and the Press (1996) reported that television news is in trouble with the American public and especially with younger viewers. Fewer adults regularly watch it.

Viewership of evening network news was particularly hard hit. Less than half the public (42%) regularly watch one of the three nightly network broadcasts, down from 48% in 1995 and 60% in 1993. Among viewers under the age of 30, only 22% watch nightly network news, down from 36% the previous year. That is a drop of one third in just 12 months.

Local TV news broadcasts attracted more viewers over all, but their audience declines were also steep. Among all adults, 65% said they regularly watch local TV news; it was 72% the previous year. But among those under age 30, 51% said they watched local news, down from 64% 1 year before.

The Pew study reported that the public's opinion of network news had also eroded. A nationwide survey found that believability ratings for two of the four national networks declined significantly since 1993. Two of the three broadcast news anchors, Dan Rather of CBS and Peter Jennings of ABC, also received lower credibility ratings than they did in a 1993 Pew survey.

The networks also faired poorly in reporting results of the Clinton–Dole presidential vote on November 5, 1996. Combined ratings were only 28.7 points and a 42% share of the audience, a severe drop from 1976 when the networks commanded 51.6 points and a 74 share of the audience. (One ratings point represents 1% of all households with television sets.) In other words, only slightly more than one quarter of all television sets were tuned to election results, although admittedly the 1996 election lacked the suspense of the 1976 election between Ford and Carter.

Survey Director Andrew Kohut said, "The networks are facing a serious problem, with increased competition within their industry (from cable, VCRs, pay TV, etc.) and with a decreased appetite for news, especially among young people"(Mifflin, 1996b, p. C5.)

Network officials said the falloff is due to the fact that news is following the trend of cable—drawing viewers away from networks. As viewers grow older, these executives say, they will watch more news just as today's older viewers watch more news than younger ones do. Kohut partly agrees but is convinced they will be far fewer in number. "They will grow up and watch less news than the previous younger generation that is now middle-aged. I really think it's not a life-cyclical pattern, it's generational" (Mifflin, 1996b, p. C5).

The Pew study also found that people who use home personal computers more than 3 days a week said they watched less television news than people without computers. (Some, of course, may get news from online services such as CompuServe.)

The networks viewed these findings as part of a 10-year trend tied to overall television viewing patterns. Networks are facing more competition overall. Concomitantly, more outlets for news are available: expanded local news programs, CNN, and other cable news channels.

How does television news viewing compare with newspaper reading? Newspaper reading is a bit more stable. Half of those polled (50%) said they read a newspaper "yesterday," (compared to 52% a year earlier). In contrast, the percentage saying they watched TV news "yesterday" slipped to 59%, the percentage had been as high as 74% in 1994. Regular CNN-watching in 1996 was also less (26%) than in 1995 (30 per cent) and 1994 (33%). Interestingly, the Pew study found that listening to radio was largely unchanged in 1996, as it has been for more than 5 years.

As mentioned before, it is apparent that many people are getting their news on the run—from car radios, television news snippets, or newspaper headlines, but the disquieting trend is that young people do not include reading or listening to news in their lifestyle. Apparently a growing number of young people—tomorrow's leaders—are not interested in news.

IMPACT OF TELEVISION ON NEWS
AND ON JOURNALISTS

Newspapers and television both report the day's news, but, more and more, television news is becoming packaged entertainment with less hard news.

According to James Fallows, there are two significant differences in methods. In television, news becomes a kind of spectacle, designed to fully engage the viewers for a moment or longer but then move on to other discrete and separate spectacles. This contrasts with the press' view that news is a process and that events have a history that should be explained. Television's natural emphasis is on the *now*. Fallows (1996) said, "Part of the press's job is to keep things in proportion. TV's natural tendency is to see things in shards. It shows us one event with an air of utmost drama, then forgets about it and shows us the next"(p. 53).

Television's second impact concerns its effect on the concept of being a reporter. Television has shown that the most successful way to be a journalist is to give up most of what is involved in being a reporter. Fallows (1996) argued that "behind the term 'reporter' is the sense that the event matters most of all. Your role as a reporter is to go out, look, learn—and then report on what you have learned"(p. 53–54). Although TV journalists still call themselves "reporters," it is their personality (i.e., celebrity status) that is the real story they report. When Dan Rather travels to Afghanistan, the subject of the broadcast is not Afghanistan, it is Rather-in-Afghanistan. When Diane Sawyer conducts a high-profile interview, the real story is the interaction between two celebrities. One of them is a politician or movie star or athlete, but the other is a particular sort of TV "journalist." Diane Sawyer, Barbara Walters, Mike Wallace, and Sam Donaldson (among others) are not paid multimillon-dollar salaries because they are reporters in the traditional sense.

CREEPING TABLOIDIZATION

The changing definition of a journalist and other factors have made television news most vulnerable to charges of tabloidization. The term refers to the featuring of stories of crime, violence, or scandal in a sensational or lurid fashion as was the practice of some New York tabloid papers like *The Daily Mirror* and *Daily News* of the 1920s, or the supermarket tabloids of today such as *The Star* and *The National Enquirer.*

Of course, sensationalism and triviality have long been found in American journalism. But during the mid-1990s, television seemed to erupt with stories of sensation, bad taste, and lurid scandal, usually involving celebrities or notorious persons, appearing on the scheduled news programs as well as the newly popular newsmagazines like *Dateline* and *Prime Time Live.*

David Shaw (1994), the astute press critic of *The Los Angeles Times*, sounded the alarm.

Twenty years ago, there were essentially seven gatekeepers in the American news business—executive editors of the *New York Times* and *Washington Post*, executive producers or anchors of the CBS, NBC, and ABC evening news shows, and editors of *Time* and *Newsweek*. Occasionally, someone else—"60 Minutes," *Wall Street Journal, Los Angeles Times*, or the *New Yorker*—would break a big story that would force everyone to take notice. If a story didn't make it past one of these, it didn't fly and often the *New York Times* editor was the key one. Now, all of that has changed. Well, almost all. Now the *New York Times* and the other six no longer decide. There are dozens of gatekeepers or none at all. Today, there is a weekly network magazine show on every night— "60 Minutes," " Day One," "Turning Point," "Dateline," etc, plus syndicated magazine shows like "Inside Edition," "Hard Copy," "A Current Affair," "American Journal" are each on *every* night. That's a vast *maw* craving information, "infotainment," around the clock. Add to this CNN with its big appetite and once a CNN story comes on at any time, everyone scrambles for it. Once a story like the Clinton/Gennifer Flowers story gets on, it takes on a life of its own and the media succumb to it. The big seven cannot resist the pressure not to use it"(p. 4).

The fire walls that formerly separated the serious media from the trivial and sordid have disappeared. Another perceptive media critic, Howard Kurtz (1996) of *The Washington Post*, said we have become a talkshow nation,

> pulsating with opinions that are channeled though hosts and reverberate through the vast echo chamber of the airwaves. The Old Media—the big newspapers, magazines and network newscasts—still cling to some vestige of objectivity, the traditional notion that information must be checked and verified and balanced with opposing views before it can be disseminated to the public. (p. 3)

But talk shows, Kurtz said, revel in their one-sided pugnacity, spreading wild theories, delicious gossip, and angry denunciations with gleeful abandon. "Anyone can say anything at any time with little fear of contradiction. . . . The gatekeepers of the elite media have been cast aside and the floodgates thrown open" (p. 3).

Important news events are now discussed, analyzed, and snap judgments made as they are happening. Did Bob Dole win or lose in tonight's televised debate? When President Clinton ordered a bombing strike of Iraq in 1993, the White House was stunned to see pundits on *The Capital Gang* debating the political fallout before it was known whether the bombs had landed.

Kurtz (1996) believed the talk culture has been further vulgarized by the popularity of tabloid television which has increasingly set the agenda for mainstream media.

> Marla Maples discusses her love life with Diane Sawyer on *Prime Time Live.* Paula Jones dishes to Sam Donaldson. Gennifer Flowers is carried live on CNN. John Bobbitt does *American Journal* and *Now* with Tom Brokaw and Katie Couric. Even criminals become media celebrities: Diane Sawyer talks with Charles Manson on *Prime Time Live,* and *Dateline NBC* debriefs Jeffrey Dahmer. (p. 9)

Diane Sawyer was roundly criticized for her sympathetic and uncritical interview of just-married Michael Jackson and his wife on *Prime Time Live.* The show promoted Jackson's latest Sony album and attracted an audience of more than 60 million for the network. Walter Goodman (1995) wrote:

> It was an expertly modulated hour of synthetic collision and wholehearted collusion. Sony could be sure ABC's star would not put Sony's star in harm's way. Mr. Jackson did a little dance as the credits rolled. Why not? This hour meant millions for him. And then a voice announced, "This has been a presentation of ABC News." (p. B1)

ABC News considers Sawyer a journalist, and she often substitutes for Peter Jennings on the ABC newscast.

Earlier commentators at the time of Walter Lippmann or James Reston tried to influence informed readers on public issues, whereas the electronic talkers of today play to the audience. News of public issues is either pushed aside or trivialized in the new media mix of scandal, sensation, and commercial promotion carried on television and radio talk shows.

Clearly, the more or less respectable news programs or news magazines have often succumbed to the subjects and techniques of the gossip or tabloid shows—all done in the pursuit of ratings. Upscale news magazines such as *Dateline* and *Prime Time Live* have been infected with the viruses of *Hard Copy* and *A Current Affair.*

JOURNALISM TESTED BY
O.J. SIMPSON TRIAL

The O.J. Simpson criminal trial—the "trial of the century"—was a major cultural phenomenon that for a year and a half transfixed millions of viewers and raised continuing controversies. When the first verdict was announced at midday on October 5, 1995, about 107.7 million people, or 57% of the nation's adult population watched on live television. Another 62.4 million watched the recap later in the day.

The drawnout trial reflected and strained many aspects of American life—race relations, violence against women, the criminal justice system, and the integrity of the news media.

The continuing story had to be reported, of course, but did it have to dominate the news for so long? Coverage of the trial by the mainstream news media left much to be desired. CNN covered the entire trial from gavel to gavel for months and drew large audiences. Night after night, the network news shows on ABC, NBC, and CBS, as well as local TV news, led off with the day's developments and often devoted large chunks of their daily 22 minutes of news time to Johnnie Cochrane, Judge Lance Ito, Marcia Clark, Mark Fuhrman, and the other characters of the long-running soap opera. ABC News' highly regarded *Nightline* had aired 55 programs by the summer of 1995 on the Simpson trial—nearly half of its airtime during one 7-week period, boosting ratings 15%. "There's a point in journalism when you have to accede to the voracious appetite of the consumer," Ted Koppel explained. Koppel had acceded previously with two programs on Tonya Harding, two on Paula Jones, and one on child molestation charges against Michael Jackson (Hume, 1996, p. 54).

When he retired from public television's *MacNeil/Lehrer Newshour* after 20 years, Robert MacNeil had harsh words for the trend in television news toward ever more sensational stories. Singling out CBS and NBC coverage of the O.J. Simpson trial, MacNeil said,

> Here were these prestigious news organs saying in effect night after night last year, "Mr. and Mrs. America, this is the most important thing that happened today." The journalists knew perfectly well that O.J. Simpson was not the most important thing that happened that day. But they were scared to death—at least at CBS and NBC—that all the bottom feeders, as I call them, were going to steal more and more of their audience. (Kolbert, 1995, p. H39)

Newspapers and news magazines, including the most prestigious, were guilty of similar overcoverage, but a print medium still has space for other news stories; on television news shows, a great amount of significant news was barely mentioned or simply not reported during the trial. CNN, which prides itself on reporting news from abroad, turned its back on the world outside the Los Angeles courtroom. As a result of the Simpson trial, the public gained a new perspective on television news: some major events will be reported daily *unless* some sensational or titillating event comes along that will attract a larger audience. When that happens, important news will be ignored as some broadcasters cross the line and become mass entertainers.

The second Simpson trial, the wrongful death civil lawsuit brought and won by the families of Nicole Brown and Ronald Goldman, was a more moderate and lowkey media event, mainly because the judge banned television cameras from the courtroom. The trial was thoroughly reported, but this time, the media kept things more in proportion, generally avoided sensationalism, and managed to report other news as well.

During the trial, however, television news had little reason to be proud. Between June 17, 1994 and January 31, 1997, when the second trial ended, *NBC Nightly News* had devoted their lead story to O.J. Simpson 73 evenings, for *CBS Evening News*, it was 66 evenings, and for *ABC World News Tonight*, the O.J. trial led for 53 evenings. The three networks alone devoted 2,768 minutes or more than 46 hours of their weeknight newscasts during the same period to the story: forty-six hours that could have been devoted to important news (Carter, 1997).

GROWING INFLUENCE OF
LOCAL TELEVISION NEWS

As network television news has declined in both audiences and journalistic quality, local television news programs have gained in influence, especially in the metropolitan areas where local news shows are on the air one hour or more before the evening network shows start. Because of CNN, the networks are no longer first with breaking national and foreign stories.

According to Tom Rosenstiel (1994), CNN has significantly, if unintentionally, affected broadcast journalism's control over its own professional standards. In the mid-1980s, CNN, in order to generate more revenue, began selling its vast footage to hundreds of local news stations. Before that, the three networks had jealously protected their own footage, well-aware that exclusive coverage of the day's biggest story was one of their competitive advantages. CNN did not have that concern. In turn, CNN could make deals to acquire local footage from these subscribing stations, thus expanding its own coverage reach, even if CNN newscrews had not produced the pictures.

Next, the networks' local affiliates began pressuring the networks for more network footage so that they could compete in the local markets. Soon the networks' control over national and foreign footage had ended. In 1986, the three networks fed affiliates about 30 minutes of footage a day. By 1990, they had averaged about 8 hours a day. This greatly changed the business, and the networks became subservient to local stations. The network shows began doing more "you news" features and less hard-news reporting, as well as sending Tom Brokaw, Dan Rather, and Peter

Jennings off to cover floods, fires, and presidential trips live, thus hyping some stories beyond their importance.

Local television news, although often highly competitive, is usually less professional, less responsible, and more sensational then network news. The Rocky Mountain Media Watch in Denver analyzed the tapes of 100 programs in 58 cities on a single night, and found a disheartening sameness. The typical 30-minute program offered about 12 minutes of news, more than 40% of it depicting violent crimes or disasters. Commercials averaged more than 9 minutes and sports and weather nearly 7, leaving 2 minutes for promotions. Of the 100 programs, 37 led off with crime, 15 with disasters. On 70 stations, the favorite disaster that night was a mild California earthquake, one of 200 that month, which caused no injuries and little damage.

In commenting on the study, Max Frankel (1995) wrote: "Virtually, no station offers thoughtful coverage of important local issues, including crime. Few ever try to analyze the local economy or the school, transportation and welfare systems"(p. 46). About the late-evening local news, Frankel (1995) wrote:

> Their newscasts are distinguishable only by the speed and skill with which they drive the audience from rage and fear to fluff and banter, leading the way to long commercials that exploit aroused emotions. Sports results, too, are delivered at a manic pace, spiced with scenes of violence or pathetic pratfalls, and even the weather reports are used to drive our moods up and down, from alarm to calm and back again. (p. 47)

Production costs are the usual explanations for this kind of journalism. A television crew takes 1–2 hours to visit the scene of a murder or a fire; it may take days or weeks to report on the causes of crime or the poor state of housing.

> Murders, fires or accidents—the grist of today's local television news mill—are relatively simple stories to cover. It's not that local newsrooms have a built-in predilection for violence. It's just that it's there—easy to get—and it can be enhanced by production techniques. How many times have you seen on the 11 p.m. news on a New York City channel a reporter standing in front of a precinct house, reporting "live" on a murder that might have happened 15 hours earlier? It happens on Chicago television practically every night. (Frankel, 1995, p. 47)

In some cities, news on public television deviates from this pattern but still is criticized for not covering local news adequately.

PERSISTENCE AND STABILITY
OF RADIO NEWS

Although viewers for both network and local television news seem to be disappearing, many people are listening to the news on the radio. In the Pew Research Center for the People and the Press (1996) study cited earlier, the percentage of people who listen to radio news was largely unchanged in 1996, as it has been for the previous 5 years. Four in ten people (44%) said they listened to news on radio "yesterday" in the current survey, compared to 42% in 1995. The survey found 13% of respondents reporting they were regular (NPR) listeners, which was not significantly different than the 15% recorded in the 1995 study.

Yet radio news has been undergoing changes just as radio itself has. Developments in radio news have been both good and bad.

First, the positive. Lou Prato (1996) reported that an official at ABC News Radio said in 1996 that radio news overall was stronger than it has been in 15 to 20 years. "Radio is still the medium in which most American first hear a breaking news story. It's fast, ubiquitous, and a growing industry," Bernard Gershon said (Prato, l996, p. 52).

Not so positive was the news that Westinghouse has emerged as the biggest radio station owner of all time. When it acquired CBS, it added several major all-news stations and the CBS radio network to its holdings of all news and talk stations. In June 1996, Westinghouse offered $4 billion for Infinity Broadcasting, which owned dozens of stations and employed both Howard Stern and Don Imus. Westinghouse now owns over 150 radio stations with combined annual revenues of at least $l billion for 1996. The company owns two different all-news stations in the New York, Chicago, and Los Angeles markets.

Another stimulus for radio news came in 1994 when the AP launched a 24-hour all-news radio service to supplement its audio feed and newscast service. CNN Radio, with some 550 affiliates, was considering a new 6-hour morning drive-time news program to supplement its scheduled newscasts and impromptu updates.

Not so encouraging either is the trend of more and more radio stations to get out of the local news business altogether. In 1994, the percentage of commercial stations with no employees devoted to gathering local news increased to 16.9%. The survey also found that television news staffing had continued to grow modestly since 1987, even as radio news staffs declined at the steepest rate in more than 10 years. Since 1981, station owners no longer have been required to broadcast news and public interest programming in order to maintain operating licenses. Professor Vernon Stone, who did the research for the Radio-Television News Directors Association, reported that another 230 of the nation's 5,500 radio newsrooms went dark that year. Stone estimated that 1,100 radio news operations have ceased since 1981.

The radio industry increasingly relied on syndicated material—news, music, and talk shows—transmitted by satellite and offered by networks on a barter basis in exchange for commercial time. The decline in local news programming was also related to radio's move to specialized music formats ranging from bluegrass to polka; station owners have turned to narrow formats as a way to attract a specific audience desired by advertisers.

Neal J. Conan, of NPR, a noncommercial service that does report the news well, commented that the decline in local radio news does not mean that listeners are less well-informed. "I'm not sure a three-minute newscast was vastly informative. It's not a tremendous loss" (Adelson, 1994, p. C8).

A different litany of complaints and concerns from the public beset newspapers and magazines. These are discussed in chapter 7.

7

The Fading American Newspaper?

*The newspapers! Sir, they are the most villainous—licentious
—abominable—infernal—not that I ever read them—I make it
a rule never to look into a newspaper.*
—Richard Brinsley Sheridan (1779)

At this time of great change in public communication, newspapers, as well as news magazines, have been undergoing modifications similar to those of broadcast journalism. Publishers and editors of papers are increasingly under pressure to expand their profits and their attractiveness to Wall Street investors. As in other industries, many newspapers have been downsizing to increase their profitability. In addition, many editors, in pursuit of greater circulations, are stressing more entertainment-oriented, celebrity-soaked infotainment, as well as soft features that relate to the personal concerns of readers. Newspapers are not adverse to pick up on the sensational stories carried on television.

SLIPPING MORALE

Morale of reporters and editors on many newspapers is clearly low—a sense that working for a newspaper is no longer an exciting and respected calling. One former newsman, C. S. Stepp (1995) wrote:

> For all the trials of poor pay, lousy hours, and grinding pace, the payoff (in earlier times) was high: deference, entitlement, the buzz of recognition, the glory of it all. Readers grumbled but they paid attention. . . . These are different days. The newspaper person (today) is just one more harried

molecule in the maligned Media Horde. Newspapers are old news, byte-sized cogs in giant information conglomerates. . . . The criticisms were bearable, honorable scars from the ramparts. But irrelevance truly singes, the gnawing feeling that the spotlight has moved on forever. . . . The result: angst and anxiety are pandemic across American newsrooms, as newspaper people collectively sense the end of an era. (p.15)

Similar feelings were found in a 1995 survey ("Nieman poll finds decline in media quality," 1995) of 304 former Nieman Fellows—working journalists who had studied 1 year at Harvard. General findings were that:

- Overall quality of the media is declining and the basic principles of the journalism profession are being eroded.
- The distinction between news and entertainment is increasingly obscure.
- Television and radio are gaining in influence but declining in journalistic quality, whereas newspapers struggle to maintain quality and are losing ground.
- Media proprietors are more concerned with profits than product quality.
- The public is losing confidence in the media.

Although a good many newspapers, when viewed objectively, do a better job of reporting the day's news, many publications no longer enjoy the prestige and stature in their communities that they formerly did. Once great and highly regarded regional newspapers such as *The Minneapolis Star and Tribune*, *The St. Louis Post-Dispatch*, *The Milwaukee Journal*, *The Louisville Courier-Journal*, *The Atlanta Constitution*, *The Denver Post*, *San Francisco Chronicle*, and others are perceived by many as mere shells of their former selves.

Yet, daily newspapers remain going concerns and are more prosperous than most corporations. This fact, however, concerns many in the newsrooms who feel that public service and thorough news coverage are badly neglected in the scramble for profits.

"Job satisfaction in newspapering appears to be in significant decline," wrote David Weaver and Cleve Wilhoit in their recent survey of working journalists. "Only 25 percent say they are very satisfied with their job, about half the satisfaction rate of 20 years ago. . . . More than 20 percent . . . said they plan to leave the field within five years, double the figure of 1982-83" (Stepp, 1995, p. 17).

This crisis of confidence may be caused by a number of factors: declining number of independently owned papers; the slow but steady drop in newspaper readership and advertising revenue; less interest by the public in news; and competition from the varied electronic media— cable, VCRs, interactive computers, and the exciting prospects of cyberspace and the Internet. In university schools and departments of journalism, newspaper careers have been losing their appeal; the best students more often opt for careers in advertising and public relations.

Newspaper journalists have come to think of themselves as trapped in a sunset industry, and many are more concerned about protecting their financial interests and meager salaries than about serving the public interest. The long-term shift from family-owned to group-owned chains is probably the most demoralizing factor in the newspaper business today. Family-owned papers had their faults and would often play favorites and beat up on their enemies, yet much of the success of numerous great newspapers was due to their strong-willed and high-minded family owners. One thinks of the Sulzbergers of *The New York Times*, the Grahams and Meyers of *The Washington Post*, the Niemans and Harry Grant of *The Milwaukee Journal*, the Bingham family of *The Louisville Courier Journal*, John Cowles of *The Minneapolis Star and Tribune*, and the Pulitzers at *The St. Louis Post Dispatch*.

Group ownership brings the problem of a countinghouse mentality determined to downsize the newsroom and cut expenses to satisfy demands for quarterly earnings. The Gannett chain with its 93 newspapers and nearly 24 television and radio stations, has been very profitable ($800 million in 1994) and is considered a pacesetter in this trend.

Today, four widely admired dailies—*The New York Times, The Washington Post, The Los Angeles Times,* and *The Wall Street Journal*—are all protected in some way from the imperatives of quarterly reports. In the first three cases, original family members control enough stock to affect the newspaper's policies. *The Journal* is considered protected by its niche market for financial and industry readers and advertisers, but has been under some pressures from family stockholders to increase profits.

The most biting criticism of newspapers today often comes from journalists themselves. David Remnick wrote:

> With one eye on Wall Street and the other shut tight, newspaper owners everywhere except for a few . . . are following the path to deadening mediocrity. Everything that cannot be made blandly profitable is killed outright. Spoiled by the profits of the 1980s, the owners rarely have patience for a more modest future. . . . In a growing number of cities and regions newspaper owners have abused their franchise, slashing staff,

cutting the "news hole," dropping aggressive reporting and leaving little behind but wire-service copy, sports, and soft local stories designed to make readers feel all warm and fuzzy and inclined to place a classified ad. (Remnick, 1995, p. 82)

DECLINING READERSHIP
AMONG THE YOUNG

Newspaper reading has been on a long and steady decline. From 1972 to 1989, Walsh (1996) noted that Americans who read newspapers every day dropped from 69% to 50%. Most disquieting, the decline has been more pronounced among young people. Daily readership for those 18–23 years old dropped from 45% to 23%. Among those 24–29, the drop was from 48% to 26%. Among those 30–35 years, the decline was from 72% to 40%. Only the most elderly Americans, 60 and older, have remained faithful readers of dailies, increasing from 72% in 1972 to 73% in 1989.

Recently, however, newspaper readership seems to have stabilized. A survey of the Pew Research Center (Pew Research Center for the People and the Press, 1996) found no further decline in newspaper readership from the previous year or, for that matter, since 1989. Half of those polled (50%) said they read a newspaper the day prior to the survey interview. This was comparable to June 1995 (52%) and higher than March 1995 (45%). But most galling to many newspaper journalists was the finding that most print media were rated as less believable than television news.

FINDING A PRINT NICHE IN
A CHANGING ENVIRONMENT

At a time when news and entertainment seem inextricably mixed, newspapers have been constantly seeking a niche in the changing news picture. The decline of downtown department stores, and other changes in marketing from mail-order catalogues to Wal Mart, have led to cutbacks of retail advertising on metropolitan dailies.

After radio and television usurped the first reporting of breaking news, newspapers began offering more interpretive and analytical pieces, thus introducing more opinion into news columns. Professional standards have suffered because often the first news reports, as on CNN, are often fragmentary, lacking details and occasionally distorted or incorrect. Then, instead of waiting for fuller and more rounded reporting, both television and the print reporters immediately start interpreting the meaning of it all and offering opinions on the event's future impact.

Time, Newsweek, and other news magazines also have been struggling to find a role for themselves in an age of television saturation and more in-depth and opinionated newspaper stories. Talk radio, personified by Rush Limbaugh, Gordon Liddy, Don Imus, and Howard Stern, plus the television news magazines, have also skimmed off more and more news readers.

When television first appeared, newspapers tried to ignore it, in some cases not even carrying program logs, and by fully reporting stories television news did not cover. Now the printed press tends to report fully on television's big stories plus much news *about* television itself. A Super Bowl game seen by many millions on television will be fully reported and analyzed by newspapers, following the sound assumption that people like to read about events they already know about, whether it is a movie seen or a televised event or competition. Further, comings and goings of television's personalities, programs, gossip, and trends are reported as well. The British popular press carries this trend even further and has become, in effect, a mere adjunct of British television.

The print media have responded to television and radio talk shows' approach to the news by offering readers more and more of the news through the proliferation of signed columns or bylined interpretive pieces. In earlier times, few by-lines appeared in newspapers on hard news stories; the story itself was the important thing and the name of the reporter was incidental. In general, bylines were given out sparingly for unusually well-written features or soft news stories. Stories in *Time* and *Newsweek* rarely carried bylines.

Today, *Newsweek*, for example, presents its major news stories through the often lively, irreverent, breezy words of its stable of star writers— Howard Fineman, Jonathan Alter, Matthew Cooper, Robert Samuelson, George Will, Meg Greenfield, and others—who not only tell you their version of what happened last week and what it means for you, but what you should think about it. Often, the slant or spin on the story is more important than the content. *Newsweek* assumes most readers already know the basic facts but would still like to read something insightful or at least clever or funny about the story.

The New York Times has certainly joined the trend from mostly straight news to news liberally mixed with opinion. Diamond (1993) noted that until about 1960, there were never more than four or five columnists in the *Times*, one or two on the editorial page, a "Sports of the Times" columnist, and on the local page, Meyer Berger's "About New York" column. By the 1990s, the *Times* had about four dozen columnists scattered through the paper, who reported / commented on a much wider and softer variety of subjects than the traditional no nonsense hard news fit to print. In addition to signed editorials in "Editorial Notebook" and the op-ed page's regular columnists and guest writers, the proliferating columnists reflected a wide variety of reader interests: "The Practical Traveler"; four or more sports columns plus one of commentary on sports on television; "Peripherals" for computer users; "Personal Health"; "Pop View"; "Keeping Fit"; "Parent and Child"; "Runways" for fashion; "Patterns" for the garment industry; "Books of the Times"; "Media," and so on. Other newspapers, of course, have been following the trend; some like *The New York Daily News* and *The New York Post* have long been collections of signed columns. Small dailies rely heavily on syndicated columnists.

Proliferation of columns reflects a much more broadened approach to the news. This translates as less public affairs news (government, politics, and foreign affairs) and more news and useful information that, as on television news, people relate to personally such as personal health, medical advances, and sundry advice for coping with life's daily trends and challenges.

Daily newspapers have been greatly influenced in recent years by Gannett's *USA Today*. This innovative paper was launched in 1982 as a national daily available almost everywhere through satellite production and aimed at travelers. Taking its cue from television, the paper uses lots of color, imaginative graphics—graphs, maps, photos, and large, detailed national weather maps. Also it reports the news in the print equivalent of sound bites—short takes on complicated matters as well as on lighter themes and without jumps to inside pages. Sports are covered in great detail, but the paper maintains no foreign correspondents. Although criticized for reducing news to spoon-sized pellets, and called "McPaper" or "USA OK," many smaller dailies imitated its compacted news presentation and especially its color graphics.

Without a doubt, *USA Today* sells papers: Peterson, (1996c) reported the Friday edition, sold throughout the weekend, passed 2 million average circulation in 1996, while the Monday–Thursday editions have reached 1.6 million, making it second only to *The Wall Street Journal*. But 55% of sales come from newsstands and 25% is purchased in bulk for free distribution by hotels and airlines. Millions read the paper but not the same millions every week; hence, there is little reader loyalty, and as a result, advertising has been sparse. The paper finally began to turn a profit in 1993 after more than $250 million in losses since 1982. In 1996, the paper was under pressure to improve its scant profitability and began changing its news approach. Instead of its light, feel-good news, the paper began stressing more hard news in longer explanatory stories, including some important investigative stories. Said one newspaper editor, "Having ruined half of the rest of the newspaper industry with three-inch briefs, they're finally going the other way" (Peterson, 1996c, p. C8). Clearly, *USA Today* was moving back toward the mainstream.

Other newspapers are seeking more personal connections with their readers in order to reverse trends faced by most publishers and editors; an aging readership, declining circulations, and weaker ties between readers and their papers (Peterson, 1997). *The San Jose Mercury News* turns most of a weekly features section, called "Celebrations," over to articles written by readers; it is one of the paper's most popular features. Typical of the more popular articles were "Quotable Kids," "How I Met My True Love," and "The Seven Second Philosopher."

Earlier research found that most readers wanted more self-oriented features and local news. The need to reach young readers and develop future talents, prompted *The Kansas City Star* to create "Kidstar," a weekly half-page pullout section of news reporting and personal experiences by local teenagers. In an effort to attract more younger readers, *The Sacramento Bee* was recently looking for a second pop music critic.

GETTING INTO BED WITH
SUPERMARKET TABLOIDS

The relationship of mainstream newspapers with the so-called supermarket tabloids has been a reason for concern recently. Headlines for these lurid weeklies can be read at the checkout counters of 29,800 supermarkets in America—"Six Signs that PROVE the World is Coming to an End," "Liz's Hubby's Drug Bust," and so on. Most stories are not news by any definition.

Until a few years ago, most newspapers did not pay much attention. But nowadays, some of the stories that publications like *The Star, The National Enquirer,* and *The Globe* dig up on political and entertainment celebrities find their way to front pages of the better newspapers and on the networks evening news. These are stories that respectable journalists would not ferret out themselves, but once they are published, many editors and broadcasters believe they must go with the story or be left behind.

The National Enquirer's stories and pictures of Senator Gary Hart escapade with Donna Rice ended Hart's political career. The *Star's* stories on Gennifer Flowers threatened Clinton's political fortunes in the 1992 campaign. And in the O.J. Simpson criminal trial, the tabloids put out a string of scoops the more respectable media felt they had to follow. *The New York Times'* use of information first reported by *The National Enquire* about the Simpson case provoked journalistic criticism of the *Times.* But the *Times'* reporter, David Margolick (1994) said of the *Enquirer,* "Mainstream reporters may grumble about its checkbook journalism, laugh at its hyperbole, talk vaguely about its inaccuracies. But always, they look at it" (p. 6).

The 1996 political campaign was roiled briefly by *The Star's* revelations that President Clinton's closest political adviser, Dick Morris, had a year-long relationship with a prostitute. *The Star* paid the $200-a- night prostitute well for the expose. The story had short but intense coverage: CNN, ABC, and NBC gave it excited play the first day, and both *Time* and *Newsweek* put Morris on their covers. However, much press reporting was restrained in part because Morris was so quickly fired and the political impact was minimal.

But as Howard Kurtz noted, "The established media is increasingly covering the same sorts of things as the tabloids and finding that the supermarket papers are often better at the game" (Zane, 1996, p. 2 sec. 4). The paradox is that even as the mainstream media are inexorably moving toward the tabloid style of journalism, *The Enquirer* and *The Star* are gaining relevance and credibility by operating a bit more like their illustrious brethren. The tabloids are becoming more conventional in how they gather news and are entering into the political arena more often. Kurtz said the cross-pollination may be sowing the seeds of a new hybrid form of news. In another move to the mainstream, *The Enquirer* announced it was planning to open a Washington bureau.

Previously, the tabloids were staffed mainly by British journalists trained on the more egregious Fleet Street tabloids. More recently, current top editors have come from *The Washington Post* and *The New York Post*.

Interestingly, *The Star, The Globe,* and *The Enquirer* have each lost about 30% of their circulation in the past 5 years. Peterson (1996d) said that the tabloids are facing more competition from mainstream media. Their readership is aging and their approach and material are being stolen.

BRITISH INFLUENCE ON AMERICAN JOURNALISM

With a common language and shared culture, it is not surprising that there have been interchanges between British and American journalism. The first widely circulated tabloid was *The Daily Mirror*, which Lord Northcliffe started in London in 1903 as a "half-penny illustrated" that was small, sensational, and amusing. He convinced Captain Joseph Medill Patterson to try the same thing in New York City. Patterson took the advice, creating the *Illustrated Daily News*, later *The New York Daily News*.

As recently as 1992, the editors of the three leading supermarket tabloids here—*The Globe, The National Inquirer,* and *The Star*—and most of their reporters were British. It can be argued that the current supermarket tabloid genre is essentially a variation of Fleet Street journalism.

Journalist Tina Brown came over from London to edit *Vanity Fair* in 1984 and a few years later, became editor of *The New Yorker*, adding several British journalists to the magazine's staff. Critics have said that under Brown's editorship, the magazine is more concerned with the "buzz" or immediate public impact of articles than with their inherent worth.

Brown is married to Harold Evans, former editor of the *Times* and *Sunday Times* of London. Evans edited the *Conde Nast Traveler* here before becoming president of Random House book publishers. Both Evans and Brown bring the British journalistic approach of responding to headlines. Random House has offered three books relating to the O.J. Simpson trial, and Evans made headlines himself when he offered Dick Morris, Clinton's discredited campaign manager, a contract for $2.5 million for a campaign memoir. Critics thought he was responding more to the notoriety than the value of such a book. Evans also published *Primary Colors*, the campaign novel written "anonymously" by Joe Klein. Critics have noted a synergy between *The New Yorker* and Random House, both owned by the Newhouse conglomerate. The magazine frequently seems to promote Random House books and authors, and *New Yorker* writers' find a willing publisher at Random House.

Since Brown's arrival, British editors have taken over at times at *Vogue*, *The National Review, Details, The New Republic, TV Guide*, and *Harper's Bazaar*. *The Economist*, the highly regarded British financial magazine, has become successful in America, boosting its U.S. circulation to 221,000, about 45% of its total. It has been called "everyone's favorite magazine to call their favorite magazine."

Has the British influence been good or bad? British journalists seem to be well-qualified to edit high-culture, slick-paged, women's magazines. Further, British journalists, glib and articulate as they often are, seem suited for the lower end of journalism. Less concerned with accuracy and fairness, many see journalism as essentially a business, not as a calling or public service as many American journalists do.

BAD ATTITUDE: CYNICISM, ELITISM, AND OTHER COMPLAINTS

Fibich (1995) said tabloid journalism contributes to one of the press' major problems today—a feeling by the public, and many thoughtful journalists as well, that the press has become too cynical and negative. "Journalism is too negative, too negative, too negative," said Andrew Kohut, director of the Pew Research Center. "There's criticism of the way the press conducts its business, particularly its watchdog role. And the attitude is more fundamentally negative than in years"(Fibich, 1995, p. 17). Gallup surveys show that from 1981–1993, the share of Americans who felt that journalists had high ethical standards slid from 30% to 22%.

One survey by Kohut found the public had a favorable attitude toward the press but objected to some of its practices. The press was judged as too intrusive, too negative, driving controversies rather than just reporting them.

A 1997 Roper poll, commissioned by the Freedom Forum, found the public quite critical of journalists. People trust most or all of what ministers, priests, rabbis, and doctors say, but only 53% place similar trust in their local television anchors. Even fewer trust what network anchors say and just under a third trust newspaper reporters.

Ethically, people see journalists not as equals of teachers and doctors, but as being among those with agendas to advance—politicians, lawyers, and corporate officials. The public also believe, according to the poll, that special interests are pulling strings in newsrooms. The public believe that profit motives, politicians, big business, and advertisers, as well as media owners, influence the way the news is reported and presented. Also, a majority of those polled (64%) said a major problem with news is that it is too sensational.

According to Walsh (1996), President Clinton has been on the receiving end of harsh press judgments. The Center for Media and Public Affairs found that between Clinton's inauguration in January 1993 and June 1994, the President was the target of 2,400 negative comments on the evening news shows on ABC, CBS, and NBC. Sixty-percent of evaluations of Clinton by reporters and sources were negative. Some comments at that time pronounced the Clinton administration "a failed presidency" and predicted that he would not even be nominated in 1996. In contrast, only 51% of comparable evaluations of President George Bush were negative during a similar period 4 years earlier.

Sometimes the negative comments are entertaining and selectively true yet they show contempt for the political scene. Maureen Dowd's now famous page-one lead in *The New York Times* on Clinton's visit to Oxford in June 1994 illustrates the point: "President Clinton returned today for a sentimental journey to the university where he didn't inhale, didn't get drafted, and didn't get a degree"(Walsh, 1996, p. 286). Clever indeed, but did it belong on page one?

It should be noted, said Fibich (1996), that the press owns up to a lot of its criticisms. Kohut's study found that a majority of the news people surveyed thought that public anger with the press was justified, either totally or in part. A majority of journalists agreed about the validity of the charge that "the personal values of people in the news media often make it difficult for them to understand and cover such topics as religion and family values"(p. 19).

Joann Byrd said that during her three years as ombudsman for *The Washington Post* she received 45,000 telephone calls and she concluded that "people don't see journalism as public service anymore." Instead, they believe "that journalists are engaged in self service—getting ratings, selling newspapers, or making their careers . . . that our ideas about detachment are so much hog wash. . . . They feel cheated, I think, that the rules changed and nobody told them"(Fibich, 1996, p. 18).

Public annoyance at reporters and the bad news they bring is not new; it has a long history. However, there is the feeling that a healthy skepticism has crossed the line to a virulent cynicism that assumes all in public life are guilty until proven otherwise. Cynicism and negativism, some feel, has become a virus that has contributed to a decline in faith in democratic institutions.

A media reporter for *The New York Times,* Iver Peterson (1996a) wrote: "Nobody would dispute the importance of a skeptical mind and tough questioning, and few want reporters to be cheerleaders. What the critics are arguing is that newsroom cynicism has crossed the boundary between being tough and being mean" (p. C7).

The solution, according to Sig Gissler, a former editorial page editor of *The Milwaukee Journal* and now a journalism professor, is to strive for balance. He wrote: "We're great at raising people's anxieties but we don't leave them with much sense of hope or remedy. So I always thought it was a good idea to at least shade in some potential solutions to all those problems we see"(Peterson, 1996a, p. C4).

Elitism and a sense of being out of touch with the rest of the nation is another problem for journalists who work for the national news media. (Elitism is not a problem apparently on smaller newspapers and broadcast outlets.) Journalist Richard Harwood (1995) noted the elitist label is being pinned on journalists and journalism in unflattering ways:

> Journalism's ills are a symptom of a poison infecting all professional elites. Increasingly removed from the realities of manual labor, community ties, or ordinary life in general, professionals have disdain for those they see as inferiors and for any genuine achievement or heroism. Nothing is properly understood until it is exposed as corrupt, duplicitous, or hypocritical. (p. 27)

Journalists in New York City and Washington, DC. tend to identify with the affluent professional classes and follow their lifestyles. A 1995 survey found significant differences in attitudes between the mainstream media and the public. For example, more than 50% of the public said that homosexuality should be discouraged, whereas 8 out of 10 national journalists said it should be accepted. Two out of five Americans said they attended a church or synagogue regularly, compared with only one out of five national journalists.

Thirty-nine percent of Americans said they were politically conservative, compared with only 5% of national journalists. (Nearly 66% of national journalists identified themselves as moderates, and 22% said they were liberals.) More than 50% agreed that the press was too cynical and negative in covering Congress, whereas 8 out of 10 national journalists disagreed (Walsh, 1996).

Salaries clearly divide the elites of the national media from the "working stiffs" of regional and local media. Median pay for beginning newspaper reporters in 1994 was $19,240 with some beginners getting less than minimum wage. Experienced reporters averaged $23,300; senior reporters averaged $31,352.

Affluence is enjoyed in the top ranks of print and broadcast journalism. Across America, salaries of newspaper editors varied widely in 1994 from $19,000 to about $362,000. Harwood (1995) estimated that a majority of national newspaper and magazine correspondents have family incomes of $150,000 to $200,000 because journalists tend to choose spouses who earn as much or more than they do. Salaries for well-known television news personalities, still considered journalists by some, range from $5 million to $7 million for Diane Sawyer, and $6 million for Ted Koppel to $2 million for Tom Brokaw. Some media celebrities can earn $50,000 for one lecture—about twice the yearly salary of an average newspaper reporter.

LOSS OF CREDIBILITY

Many of the ethical problems faced by journalists today, including cynicism and elitism, relate to matters of credibility—the quality or power of inspiring belief, essential for public acceptance of serious journalism. Some say that credibility is the journalists' and the news media's most precious asset. Often, loss of press credibility is self-inflicted as two recent examples illustrate.

The first involved a best-selling novel, *Primary Colors,* a tale of political intrigue and deceit, whose author was identified only as anonymous. The book was a commercial success and after months of emphatic denials, Joe Klein, a political columnist for *Newsweek* and commentator on CBS News, admitted publicly that he was indeed the author. Klein offered no apologies for lying to friends and colleagues and said he guarded his secret the way journalists protect their news sources. *Newsweek's* editor, Maynard Parker, was privy to the secret and not only kept it out of his magazine but misdirected one of his own reporters who wrote a piece about the mystery in the magazine.

The response from the press was mixed. Stephen Hess (1994), a media expert at the Brookings Institution, was amused. "Look, people lie to reporters every day. What annoys journalists was that this was a member of their own community, a friend of theirs"(Peterson, 1996d, p.C5). Most were much tougher on Klein. Rem Rieder (1996), editor of *American Journalism Review,* wrote:

> Lying is lying. For a journalist, it is poison. Credibility is crucial. Why should *Newsweek's* readers believe what Klein writes when they know they can't believe what he says? And we're not talking little white lies here. No coy deceptions for Joe Klein. "For God's sakes, I didn't write it," he told the New York Times. (p. 6)

Editorially, *The New York Times* was critical of Klein, reflecting the views of many in the working press. The *Times* said:

> Their behavior (Klein and Parker) violates the fundamntal contract between journalists, serious publications and their readers. If journalists lie or publications knowingly publish deceptively incomplete stories, then readers who become aware of the deception will ever after ask the most damaging of all questions: How do I know you are telling me the whole truth as best you can determine it *at this time?* . . . Mr. Klein wants his colleagues to view his actions as a diverting and highly profitable whimsy. But he has held a prominent role in his generation of political journalists. For that reason, people interested in preserving the core values of serious journalism have to view his actions and words as corrupt and—if they become an example to others— corrupting. (*"Colors of Mendacity,"* 1996, p. A14)

Klein now writes for *The New Yorker.*

Press credibility took another hit a few weeks later amidst the media glare of the 1996 Olympic Games in Atlanta. After the bombing in Centennial Olympic Park, Richard A. Jewell, a security guard, was named in *The Atlanta Journal* as the focus of the FBI investigation because he fit the profile of the bomber. A blitz of media coverage raised all kinds of damaging questions about Jewell's possible guilt. Yet Jewell had not been accused by law authorities or charged with anything. The FBI had not spoken on record about their suspicions, nor had he been arraigned, arrested, or taken into custody. Why had the Atlanta paper gone with the story? Apparently, competitive concerns and police leaks of information were involved. The story was out there; people were talking about it and the paper was afraid that local television would get it first. Once the story was published, the feeding frenzy began in earnest, setting in motion worldwide coverage about a man who was never publicly implicated by officials or charged with the crime. The story led the evening news on all the networks and was regularly repeated by Tom Brokaw to the huge audience watching the Olympics on NBC. Major newspapers like *The Washington Post, USA Today, The Los Angeles Times,* and *The Chicago Tribune* all gave it front-page play.

Almost 3 months passed before the FBI held a press conference and announced that law enforcement officials had cleared Jewell and said it now believed he had nothing to do with the crime. Jewell sued the *Atlanta Journal-Constitution* for libel. NBC and CNN settled out of court to avoid litigation.

Media critics were livid about Jewell's manhandling by the press. Max Frankel wrote:

> Too easily overlooked among the athletic and political entertainments of the summer was the careless abandon with which this uncharged suspect (Jewell) in a murder case was identified, vilified, stalked, and stigmatized before the entire world without a shred of evidence. A journalistic industry that gradually learned to defend itself against the evils of McCarthyism urgently needs some new barriers against this comparable kind of slander. The barriers are best devised now, in the calmer moments between excitements. (Frankel, 1996, p. 60)

Unless such guidelines are established and enforced, the rule seems to be that the press will protect the rights of someone involved in a criminal case, unless there is such overwhelming media interest and competition that the story must be published anyway.

THE DUBIOUS PRACTICE OF
BUYING NEWS AND PHOTOS

The British press world of quasi-journalism has a long and dishonorable tradition of paying, and paying well, for scoops, exposes, and photos about the rich and famous, especially prominent politicians and the royal family. Fleet Street tabloids will pay $200,000 to $300,000 for a story that has lasting interest). Provocative pictures of Princess Diana commanded prices up to $6 million.

This practice, as much as anything, undermines the credibility of news because of the suspicion that sources will exaggerate to make a better—

and more profitable—story or photo. Unfortunately, although resisted by mainstream news media, paying for news has become more commonplace in U.S. journalism and its disreputable tabloid fringe. After the second Rodney King trial, *The Los Angeles Times* reporters found themselves excluded from posttrial interviews with certain jurors because they were not willing to pay them. Today, tabloid television shows such as *Inside Edition* routinely pay for interviews, whereas mainstream magazines like *Sports Illustrated* and *Redbook* have paid for news exclusives.

Bill O'Reilly, anchor of *Inside Edition*, defends the television show's payments: "The competition for ratings and stories is now so intense that "Inside Edition" must pay for some big scoops to survive. If we'd didn't pay, we'd be off the air. Simple as that" (O'Reilly, 1994).

The practice is not new; in the 1970s, *60 Minutes* paid Nixon-aide H. R. Haldeman $25,000 and Watergate burglar G. Gordon Liddy $15,000 for interviews. But the practice (and the prices) have escalated lately, even more bad news for journalism's slipping credibility with the public.

The violent death of Diana, Princess of Wales, in a high-speed car crash while being pursued by paparazzi photographers in Paris had ominous lessons not just for tabloid journalism but for the mainstream press as well. The immediate public reaction was revulsion aimed at the press, even though much of the public are eager consumers of scandal and gossip about the celebrities they have come to know well from tabloids and television.

Tabloids have little interest in serious news but will pay much more for intrusive and revealing photos of the rich and famous and hence have triggered intensive competition among the paparazzi, who use hidden vans, planes and motorboats to stalk and harass celebrities, often invading their privacy. The problem for mainstram journalism is that such lurid and distorted photos and the companion gossip and scandal their way into the more respectable publications and TV news. *Time* and *Newsweek* are regular users of tabloid by-products. *People* magazine ran 43 covers featuring Princess Diana. U.S. news media carry little serious news about the United Kingdom but most Americans are very well informed about the scandals and peccadilloes of the royal family. The unprecedented public grief and mourning in Britain at the Princess's funeral was stark evidence of the power of celebrity-driven gossip and scandal to affect the lives of many millions.

Journalism's credibility problems have been exacerbated as well by the antics of certain celebrity journalists whose names and faces, as well as incomes, are almost as well-known to the public as are rock stars or movie personalities. These are discussed in chapter 8.

CHAPTER

8

Why the Public
Hates (Some)
Journalists

*Whatever else one may say about the newspaper business,
self-examination is one of its virtues. Searching questions
about right conduct or wrong conduct are put whenever
journalists gather.*

—Marquis W. Childs (1970)

No question about it, many of the most prominent personalities in
journalism today have become unpopular with segments of the American
public. This is shown in public opinion surveys as well as in caustic
comments from a wide range of commentators including from within the
press itself. In general, many people feel that journalists, along with
politicians, are not dealing with the real concerns of the people. (This
chapter's title suggests that the perception of scorn is not directed at all
journalists, just mostly at one group—those on the highly visible national
media based in New York City and Washington, DC.)

Public affairs news, the heart of serious journalism, is the focus of this
criticism, striking most deeply at a press perceived as estranged from its
readers and viewers. Journalist J. Schell (1996) wrote:

On one side is the America of those who are political professionals. It
comprises politicians, their advisers and employees, and the news media.
Politicians waste little love on the newspeople who cover them, and the
newspeople display a surly skepticism towards politicians as a badge of
honor. Yet if the voters I met on the [1996] campaign trail are any
indication (and poll data suggest they are), much of the public has lumped
newspeople and politicians into a single class, which, increasingly, it

despises. Respect for the government and respect for the news media have declined in tandem. More and more the two appear to the public to be an undifferentiated establishment—a new Leviathan—composed of rich, famous, powerful people who are divorced from the lives of ordinary people and indifferent to their concerns. On the other side of the division is the America of political amateurs: ordinary voters. (p. 70)

Schell believes that the activity of politics has become an interaction between the media and people running campaigns. Everyone else is an onlooker.

Walsh (1996) believed good reasons exist for concern about the cultural chasm between the public and the Washington press corps. A 1996 survey for *U.S. News and World Report* found that 50% of Americans thought that the media were strongly or somewhat in conflict with the goals of ordinary citizens, whereas only 40% thought the media were strongly or somewhat friendly to their goals. This was the worst approval rating of any group measured—lower than prime-time television entertainment providers, welfare recipients, even lower than elected public officials, whose goals were judged to be in conflict with those of ordinary citizens by only 36%. Even lawyers did better, with 45% of Americans saying attorneys' goals conflicted with the public's.

Clearly, the media were seen as part of a strongly disliked governing elite. When asked about "the people running the government," 52% of those surveyed said they had little or nothing in common with them.

DEBASING PUBLIC AFFAIRS JOURNALISM?

Instead of reporting the news as carefully and fully as possible, many political journalists today are seen as too arrogant, opinionated, and biased in their comments on major issues, particularly when appearing on television. Rather than just telling the news straight, reporters often go beyond the news report itself and predict the future impact of the news. Needless to say, such predictions, so widely strewn on television talk shows, often prove wrong.

Newspaper reporters covering the 1996 presidential campaign were accused of letting opinion replace straight news. Because editors know that by morning most people learn from radio and television what the candidate had said the day before, the usual hardnews story was often replaced by an analytical or opinion piece. One critic said that one third to one half of every campaign story reflected some level of analysis. (But interpretive pieces, if carefully done can be free of opinion or bias. It is a fine line.)

Critical of the cozy relationship between journalists and Washington insiders, columnist David Broder calls this a "blurring of the line" when journalists become pseudoexperts on television talk shows. He told one audience, "On television, the 'punditocracy' has begun to look like the last scene from Orwell's Animal Farm. You can't tell the journalists from the politicians, the watch dog from the running dog. It's not just that they're in bed with each other. It's that they have become one and the same" (Fibison, 1996, p.1).

Matters are not helped when some journalists move back and forth between journalism and high political positions. David Gergen, for example, worked in the White House for both Presidents Reagan and Bush before joining *U.S. News* and *The MacNeil/Lehrer News Hour*. Then he joined the Clinton White House for a time and later returned to journalism. Pat Buchanan, once a Nixon White House aide, has used talk shows, especially CNN's *Crossfire* and his newspaper column, as springboards to his presidential campaigns of 1992 and 1996.

A recent high-profile political operator to leap into high-profile journalism was George Stephanopoulos. After 4 years of advising President Clinton on how to deal with and manipulate the press, Stephanopoulos suddenly became a political analyst and correspondent for ABC News and, as a journalist, he will now report on his former boss. ABC obviously believed that any conflict of interest of their new star reporter was more than balanced by his celebrity status and good looks. So much for the barriers that once separated news from propaganda.

CBS News joined the trend in 1997 by hiring Representative Susan Molinari to move directly from Congress to its anchor desk. Earlier, CBS hired Bill Bradley, the retired U.S. Senator, as a commentator.

Critics have long advocated that political journalism should get away from the insider game and move closer to the audience; that, however, is not where the rewards are these days for national journalists. A root cause of this animosity toward the press stems from the fact that due to exposure on television, many journalists have become well-known celebrities themselves and highly paid ones at that. Many of the public can instantly identify Barbara Walters, Tim Russert, Jane Pauley, Diane Sawyer, Sam Donaldson, or Mike Wallace, but they have no idea what the editors of the *Washington Post* or *Time* magazine look like, nor do they know their names.

As previously explained, news on television is becoming packaged entertainment. The role of celebrity journalists in such circumstances is not to report the news, but to embellish and "spin" the news with lively and entertaining commentary, most of it highly opinionated and speculative.

TALK SHOWS LEAD TO
LECTURES AND BIG BUCKS

Newspaper and magazine journalists in Washington, DC and New York City have learned that the way to become prominent and affluent in journalism is to appear on the weekend television talk shows such as *The Capital Gang, Washington Week in Review, McLaughlin Group, Inside Politics, Reliable Sources, Weekend Crossfire, Off the Record,* and others which have proliferated in the nation's capital since 1980. Some talk shows are carried nationally, but all are seen in Washington. Compared to prime-time network television or even the daytime talk shows, these political confabs attract scant audiences and are inexpensive to produce because participants receive little pay. But plenty of journalists want to be on them for the "visibility" and the leads that can result from their appearance.

Such talk shows have became known as "food fights" because the format requires guests to be opinionated, loud, witty, and, of course, disagreeable with other panelists. One participant said the less she knew about a topic, the better she was able to argue about it. These shows provide little time for measured and thoughtful comments on the news and public affairs. (Some journalists see these shows as pure entertainment but others considered them an embarrassment and disservice to serious journalism.)

But the talk shows provide visibility, and for many, they have been the path to affluence. Rem Rieder, editor of *American Journalism Review* commented: "It is a package. You say outrageous things to get attention on the shows so that you can become a regular, and once you become a regular you can get the speaking fees" (Fallows, 1996, p. 96).

For example, *Newsweek* reporter Howard Fineman, a regular on *Washington Week,* was hired to speak to a group of lawyers on a 12-day cruise from Holland to Russia. Margaret Carlson, the *Time* columnist, said her speaking fees doubled to approximately $10,000 after she became a regular member on *The Capital Gang.*

Kurtz (1996) said a partial sampling of journalists' speechmaking income from 1994 shows that Sam Donaldson got $30,000 a speech, Pat Buchanan received $10,000 and William Safire, *The New York Times* columnist and frequent *Meet the Press* panelist, pulled in $20,000 a talk. ABC's Cokie Roberts got at least $20,000 per lecture and was said to have earned $300,000 a year. Mike Wallace of CBS earned $25,000 an outing while CNN's Larry King received $50,000 for each appearance and was said to earn 1 million dollars per year.

David Gergen, a MacNeil/Lehrer regular and a *U.S. News* columnist, was paid $444,625 for 121 speeches in 1992. He earned another $239,460 for 50 speeches in the first half of 1993.

Because these hefty lecture fees usually come from a variety of for-profit organizations and interest groups, it is legitimate to ask whether ethical problems or conflicts of interest are involved here. According to Kurtz (1996), several prominent talk show regulars responded to his concerns this way:

"We are private citizens," said David Brinkley.
"I'm not an elected official," said Fred Barnes.
"I'm a totally private person," said Robert Novak.
"I'm not going to disclose it," said Al Hunt.
"I don't exercise the power of state," said George Will. (p. 205)

Some talks are given to educational or charitable groups but many viewers would be appalled at the web of potential conflicts of interest inherent in some of the relationships. Some members of Congress were annoyed. Senator Alan Simpson said: "Their audience deserves to know if they pick up a fat check from a group they report on. It applies to Congress, and it sure as hell ought to apply to this elite press corps in Washington." Representative David Obey of Wisconsin said: "What I find most offensive lately is that we get the Sanctimonious Sam defense: 'We're different because we don't write the laws.' Well, they have a hell of a lot more power than I do to affect the laws written" (Kurtz, 1996, p. 205).

CORRUPTION OR WHAT?

Many in the national press have been unhappy at the spectacle of this "buckraking" by so many of their colleagues. Fallows (1996) wrote:

The bluntest way to criticize journalists on the lecture trail is to say, simply, that they are corrupt. Some day, in some form, they may have to write about the groups they are addressing. If they have taken big money from these groups, they can't give the reader an honest—or as honest-sounding —assessment as if they had kept their distance. (p. 103)

He quotes Ben Bradlee, former *Washington Post* editor:

If the Insurance Institute of America, if there is such a thing, pays you $10,000 to make a speech, don't tell me you haven't been corrupted. You can say you haven't and you can say you will attack insurance issues in the same way, but you won't. You can't. (p. 103)

Similarly, Alan Murray of *The Wall Street Journal* said: "You tell me what is the difference between somebody who works full-time for the National Association of Realtors and somebody who takes $40,000 a year in speaking fees from realtor groups. It's not clear to me there's a big distinction"(p. 103).

"I call it white collar crime," Tom Brokaw of NBC has said. "That's just what I think it is." Other prominent television journalists who do not accept money for speeches include Peter Jennings of ABC News, Dan Rather of CBS, and Brian Lamb of C-SPAN. They make speeches but not for money. Ted Koppel of ABC's *Nightline* did something unusual. By the late 1980s, when he was getting $50,000 a speech, he stopped the practice. No matter how incorruptible he felt, he thought that the situation would look corrupt to members of the general public who found out about it, as they probably would (Fallows, 1996). Jim Lehrer of the PBS news show also no longer accepts speaking engagements.

The drumbeat of intramedia criticism of journalists speaking for lucrative fees has had an effect. In 1995, the ABC network drew up a restrictive policy drafted by Vice President Richard Wald. Before accepting a lecture engagement of any kind, ABC correspondents were ordered to check with their superiors and were specifically told not to accept a fee from a trade association or a for-profit business. Wald said,

We don't tilt what we say to please any special interest, we don't sell special access in the guise of fees—and we don't want to risk looking as though we do. It isn't just how big a fee is, it is also who gives it and what it might imply. (Kurtz, 1996, p. .218)

Later, NBC followed suit when it banned its journalists from accepting speaking fees from corporations and trade associations that lobby government or take public positions on issues. The NBC policy also prohibited staff members from speaking to any group they might cover and required that all paid appearances first be okayed by management. In April 1995, *Time* magazine adopted a similar policy that correspondents may not accept fees or expenses for outside speaking engagements or other kinds of sponsored events. If an appearance is in the magazine's interest, the magazine will pay for it from either the editorial or publishing budget. Referring to *Time* correspondents appearing on talk shows, the magazine was concerned about journalists saying things they would not be permitted to say in the magazine. Such policies cannot cover all contingencies and in some ways are probably unfair to some, but they show a concern about ethics which had been notably lacking for some years.

Kurtz (1996) summarized the ethical dilemma nicely:

The essence of journalism, even for the fiercest opinion-mongers, is professional detachment. The public has a right to expect that those who pontificate for a living are not in financial cahoots with the industries and lobbies they analyze on the air. Too many reporters and pundits simply have a blind spot on this issue. They have been seduced by the affluence and adulation that comes with television success. They are engaging in drive-by journalism, rushing from television studio to lecture hall with their palms outstretched. Perhaps when they mouth off on television, a caption should appear under their names: PAID $20,000 BY GROUP HEALTH ASSOCIATION OF AMERICA, TOOK $15,000 CHECK FROM AMERICAN MEDICAL ASSOCIATION. The talk show culture has made them rich, but, in a very real sense, left them bankrupt. (p. 227)

This problem is not the most serious challenge to journalism today (others are far more ominous), but it does point out the hubris of some national journalists. And it provides one more reason for the public to resent some journalists.

SELF-CRITICISM OF THE PRESS

Further, the continuing squabble over the pros and cons over money earned on television talk shows and the speaking circuit reminds us of the importance of self-criticism by the press. The news business does have recognized professional standards, and many in it are sensitive and often responsive to the criticisms of press performance that come from such highly regarded media critics as Howard Kurtz, James Fallows, Ken Auletta, David Shaw, Tom Rosenstiel, Edwin Diamond, Jeff Greenfield, Jonathan Alter, Tom Shales, and Jon Katz, among others, as well as from *American Journalism Review, Columbia Journalism Review,* and *Nieman Reports.*

A built-in problem for many of these critics—some who critique the media only part-time and do other kinds of editing or reporting—is that they have jobs with various news organizations. Hence, they never seem to zero in on the foible or errant behavior of their own paper, newspaper group, magazine, or broadcast station, much less the conglomerates of which they are a small part. Further, sometimes critics themselves can get crosswise on ethical concerns. For example, ABC media critic Jeff Greenfield opposed ABC's policy on speaking fees.

Incisive intramedia criticism is an important way the press improves itself at times. The talk show and lecture fee brouhaha struck a nerve with both management and individual journalists. Washington journalists are showing more sensitivity and have drawn back from some of the "food fight" shows and questionable lecture stints.

MORE PROFOUND CONCERNS
ABOUT JOURNALISM

The concerns already mentioned about the press' cynicism, negativism, trivialization of news, and decline of serious public affairs journalism have led to some somber assessments of today's journalism, originating from academics, both left and right, and from respected journalists.

Cynicism is at the heart of the new critique. Journalists, Glaberson (1994) reported, are bringing a self-canceling message: everything—from the O.J. Simpson case to the health care debate and on to journalism itself —is a game about nothing more than winning and losing. Thomas Mann of the Brookings Institution, said, "We're now at a point of believing it's all a scam, everyone is looking out for his own narrow interest and the job of the reporter is to reveal the scam"(Glaberson, 1994, p.1 ,sec. 4).

The longtime concern about liberal bias in the press has been replaced by a concern that a politically neutral bias now shapes news coverage by declaring that all public figures, indeed all people in the news, are suspect.

This journalism, it is felt, is undermining its own credibility. Jamieson said:

> Journalists are now creating the coverage that is going to lead to their own destruction.If you cover the world cynically and assume that everyone is Machiavellian and motivated by their own self-interest, you invite your readers and viewers to reject journalism as a mode of communication because it must be cynical, too. (Glaberson, 1994, p.1, sec. 4)

Studies, backed by statistics, strongly suggest that the press nearly always magnifies the bad and underplays the good. Since the 1960s, reporters have served America a steady diet of trends and events of such a fundamentally negative nature that we have undermined the country's faith in itself. Walsh wrote:

> Of course, the press has to report such stories but they have taken their toll. The media are no longer seen as society's truth-sayers. By embellishing the bad and filtering out the good, a negative picture emerges. It is understandable that Americans have come to associate the press with everything that has gone wrong. (p. 281)

Fallows (1996) thought the ascendancy of star-oriented, highly paid media personalities involves a terrible bargain.

> The more prominent today's star journalists become, the more they are forced to give up the essence of real journalism, which is the search for

information of use to the public. . . . The best-known and best-paid people in journalism now set an example that erodes the quality of the news we receive and threaten journalism's claim on public respect. (p. 7)

Further, Fallows sees an even more ominous future:

The harm actually goes much further than that, to threaten the long-term health of our political system. Step by step, mainstream journalism has fallen into the habit of portraying American public life as a race to the bottom, in which one group of conniving, insincere politicians ceaselessly tries to outmaneuver another. The great problem for American democracy in the 1990s is that people barely trust elected leaders or the entire legislative system to accomplish anything of value. (p. 7)

Other forces are involved, but Fallows believes the media's attitudes have played a surprisingly important and destructive role in public affairs.

Unless the press changes its ways, some feel that press protections will be rolled back within a decade. The public does not care anymore about protecting the press, it is argued, because most Americans no longer think it informs them well. Libel laws may be weakened and access laws tightened to make it more difficult for the press to cover news and investigate abuses in government and the private sector. In the 1990s, jury awards for libel soared as the public's trust in the press declined.

One solution to all these criticism problems is that journalists should keep on reporting the news and leave the task of assessing its impact to others. Criticism of investigative stories, such as Whitewater and White House fund-raising, some journalists say, suggests a naive belief that without the press, the news would somehow be better. Richard Wald of ABC thinks the current criticism is based on nostalgia for a past that never really existed. He thinks there is a broad societal skepticism today that erodes the influence of all institutions, including the press.

What may be significant, however, is that growing numbers of working journalists talk more and more about de-emphasizing coverage that focuses on conflict and scandal, and others say they are rethinking their aversions to positive news stories. These ideas are related to a significant but controversial trend in newspaper journalism today called public or civic journalism.

This approach is an attempt to help the public participate in public affairs without the press taking stands on issues. Instead of covering elections as contests or horse races that reduce citizens to mere bystanders, public journalism attempts to ground its coverage in a *citizen's agenda* or a list of problems and issues that citizens want discussed by the candidates.

The press is divided over public journalism but the controversy is a welcome sign of ferment in the news business.

Journalist Geneva Overholser, former editor of *The Des Moines Register*, said:

> The public is right to question whether newspapers are acting in the public interest. I think what readers are asking is "Are you really giving us a reflection of what is happening or are you just discouraging us?" We're so good at reporting all the negatives and all the infighting that we give people a sense it is all hopeless. (Glaberson, 1994, p. 1, sec. 4)

CHAPTER

9

Changes in
Foreign News
Coverage

*In an age of real-time, multimedia, interactive forms of
communication, there is a tendency to declare obsolete (or at
least dispensable) the diplomat and the foreign correspondent
in the field. We will do so at our peril. The myriad forms of
instantaneous communication threaten to substitute
immediacy for insight, reaction for reflection, sentiment for
judgment, hyperbole for reality and deniability for integrity.*
—Peter Krogh (1996)

*You know, being a foreign correspondent is like being a maitre
d' in a fine restaurant. You meet so many distinguished
people under such humiliating circumstances.*
—Quoted by Stephen Hess (1996)

International news gathered by foreign correspondents—that far-flung and
glamorous specialty of American journalism—has been undergoing some
basic change in recent times. Because of new technologies and financial
concerns, less news from abroad is reported and in very different ways
today. The correspondents are becoming a different breed of journalist
than in the bad (yet, journalistically, good) old days of the Cold War. Today
the American public seems a lot less interested in news from abroad, and
editors and broadcasters seem inclined to give the public less. Among the
print correspondents themselves, as with broadcast journalists, there is a
sense of decline. Things were better in earlier times—when *we* were young.
Serious journalists have long held that foreign news *is* important and

should be reported well and thoroughly. Much that happens overseas has a direct impact on American lives, as the rise of Hitler and Stalin, World War II, and the Korean and Vietnam wars amply demonstrated. In a democratic society, an interested public, it is argued, must know what is happening in the greater world in order to judge how well its own government responds to threats and challenges from abroad.

Further, foreign news is necessary to inform our leaders and decision makers about foreign dangers. (In his recent mea culpa on disasters in foreign affairs, Robert McNamara interestingly blamed the press for not better informing State Department officials about Vietnam.)

Yet for many, foreign news today does not seem as important. Who is to blame? The national press? The "media"—broadly speaking, with its pervasive cultural and social influences? Perhaps the public itself?

Without a crisis story intruding on the public's attention—famine and warfare in Zaire, civil strife and genocide in Bosnia, or terrorism in Israel or Ulster—the typical daily newspaper does not print much news from overseas—usually about 6 or more short items about 8 inches or less—unless American soldiers or hostages are involved. Anyone regularly watching network television is aware that foreign news has been typically reduced to several brief items ("And now the news from abroad"), unless some video with violent footage is available. (Fifty percent of television's foreign news does portray violence.) At the networks, foreign news has been pushed aside in favor of more personalized, self-help, and advice stories—so-called "you news."

Who cares? Apparently, not the public. The Pew Research Center for the People and the Press (1996) survey of the American public, found that among the regular users of the news media, the topics of most interest were crime, local news about people and events, and health news. International news ranked ninth, well behind sports, local government, science, religion, and political news.

One cross-national study found that 78% of Germans read a newspaper yesterday, whereas only 49% of Americans did so. When asked to identify the current secretary general of the United Nations at the time of the survey, 58% of Germans came up with his name, Boutros Boutros-Ghali, compared with only 13% of Americans.

This declining audience interest means that as a culture, we are missing the connective tissue that binds us to the rest of the world. The British have been long involved with far-off places, a legacy of their receding empire. For many Europeans, the consequences of two world wars are still keenly felt. For Americans, the experience of World War II, when everyone knew someone who was in it, and the aftermath of the rising Third World with its involvement with Soviet hegemony and the Cold

War, deeply affected two generations of readers concerned about the outside world.

Now the consensus in the news business appears to be that you can rely on international news to turn a profit only when it is actually domestic news. The most certain way to become domestic news is through a U.S. military intervention—when it is "our boys" who are "over there."

Others blame the news media. "A great shroud has been drawn across the mind of America to make it forget that there is a world beyond its borders," complained Frankel (1994), former editor of *The New York Times*,

> The three main television networks obsessively focus their cameras on domestic tales and dramas as if the end of the cold war rendered the rest of the planet irrelevant. Their news staffs occasionally visit some massacre, famine, or shipwreck and their anchors may parachute into Haiti or Kuwait for a photo op, but these spasms of interest only emphasize the networks' apparent belief that on most evenings the five billion folks out there don't matter one whit. (p. 42)

One indicator of this trend: in its heyday, CBS maintained 24 foreign bureaus, by 1995 it had reporters in only four capitals: London, Moscow, Tel Aviv, and Tokyo. (Miami was its base for covering all of Latin America.) Dan Rather has not hesitated to speak out. "Don't kid yourself," he told Harvard students,

> the trend line in American journalism is away from, not toward, increased foreign coverage. Foreign coverage is the most expensive. It requires the most space and the most time because you're dealing with complicated situations which you have to explain a lot. And then there's always somebody around you who says people don't really give a damn about this stuff anyway. . . . "if you have to do something foreign, Dan, for heaven's sake, keep it short." (Hess, 1996, p. 61)

FEWER COVER STORIES

The covers of the three major news magazines, each of which has long emphasized foreign news gathered by their numerous overseas correspondents, reflects the declining interest in international news. By late September 1996, *Time* had run five covers that year on international topics, versus 11 in 1995. *Newsweek* featured four international covers by September, compared to 11 in 1995. *U.S. News* published no international covers as of late 1996 but ran six in 1995.

Why the difference? The decline in interest surely was greatly accelerated by the major historic event of the late 20th century—the ending of the Cold War. In the dangerous and confusing post-Cold War period, foreign correspondents and news organizations have been going through an identity crisis over what is news and what is not news. The Cold War provided reporters with a coherent global road map, in terms of what to cover and how to cover it. Don Oberdorfer of *The Washington Post* added, "Since the fall of the Berlin Wall and the end of the Cold War news filter, the task of making sense of global events has become less manageable for the media." The press is not used to reacting to a world full of conflicts and violent encounters that, as George Kennan put it, offer no "great and absorbing focal points for American policy" (Hachten, 1996, p. 123). The American public has been confused as well and has turned inward.

Editors said that since Vietnam and the Cold War demise, there has been a gradual but significant lessening of interest in what happens abroad. "We no longer have enemies, we have dangers. And that obviously has less attraction for a large audience than what existed before 1990," said Morton Zuckerman of *U.S. News* (Pogrebin, 1996, p.C2).

Moreover, this trend has been a continuing one. Throughout 1995, *Time* devoted 385 pages to international news, or 14% of the magazine. *Newsweek* used 388 pages or 12% of its coverage and *U.S. News* had 386 pages on foreign news or 14%. This was a significant decline from 10 years earlier. In 1985,*Time* had 670 pages or 24% on foreign news, *Newsweek* had 590 pages or 22% and *U.S. News* had 588 or 22%.

Another view holds that only a very small portion of the American public is seriously interested and concerned about the outside world. These are mainly teachers and scholars, some business executives and travelers, and some public officials and journalists, especially those who have worked abroad. One editor said that at any given time, only about 2 million people in America are really interested in foreign affairs. The great majority of Americans are concerned about matters closer to home ("all news is local") just as people in other countries are. Hess (1996) said that "audiences with more cosmopolitan interests can find detailed information in the prestige press or outside the mainstream media" (p. 88). Maybe so, but that prestige press or national press is covering less and less foreign news. With the three television networks and the big news magazines continuing to slough off serious foreign news coverage, the major journalistic outlets seem to have narrowed down to a handful of papers—*The New York Times, The Washington Post, The Wall Street Journal, The Los Angeles Times,* and a few others. Their combined circulations of less than 5 million daily out of a total daily circulation of 63 million, will continue to inform that small group of serious thinkers who do affect public policy and our response to world news events, but they will not have much direct influence on the 250 million other Americans. Hence, knowledge and concern about global events has become one more of the separators between our two media systems. Foreign news may be a main dish for the elite media but is only an appetizer for the popular press.

HOW THE WORLD IS
COVERED BY THE PRESS

For many years, the prevailing pattern of international news has been an east–west–east flow across the northern hemisphere. Three cities—New York, London, and Tokyo—comprise the key centers of the axis. From those metropolises, news is relayed and returned from the southern regions: Latin American news to New York, European, Middle Eastern, and African news to London, and Asian news to Tokyo.

Needless to say, the news that Americans receive about most of 190 nations from Afghanistan to Zimbabwe is sporadic and uneven. In a sense, most news comes from where journalists are stationed, and the U.S. television networks keep their crews in residence in England, Japan, Germany, Russia, and Israel covering happenings in those areas. But because U.S. television crews are there, a certain amount of soft news comes out of these capitals as well; for example, one more story, picked up from Fleet Street tabloids about Britain's royal family.

From London, Tokyo, or Tel Aviv, reporters and cameras can be quickly dispatched elsewhere to a breaking story in crisis areas such as renewed violence in Ulster, a new dustup in Sarajevo, famine, genocide, and war in Central Africa. With modern air travel, broadcast journalists can quickly get to the scene and, standing before mobs of homeless Africans, can report back "live" from Goma, Zaire.

As regular television viewers know, most of the major foreign news seems to be coming from several chronic crisis areas: the former Soviet Union, especially Russia, Ukraine, Chechnya, and so forth, the Middle East generally, particularly Israel and its immediate neighbors, plus Iran and Iraq. The breakup of Yugoslavia and the ugly ethnic hostilities in Bosnia, Serbia, and Croatia set off a major running international story still continuing. China, with its economic expansion, uneasy relations with its neighbors, and persistent human rights abuses, has shared the Asian news spotlight with the region's amazing economic growth. Plus, any time the American military get involved overseas, it becomes major U.S. news.

In most of these crises, a case can be made that national interests of the United States were somehow involved. Other crisis stories—the prolonged struggle over apartheid in South Africa, unrest on the Korean peninsula, IRA terrorism in Northern Ireland, and political upheavals in the Philippines— appear erratically on the radar screens and then disappear for a time.

In his 7-year survey of network news, Hess (1996) found that among 190 countries, 6 were "constant (news) countries" (i.e., Russia, Germany, U.K., Israel, Japan, and France); 22 were "crisis countries" and 77 "others" rarely reported. His study looked at 2,300 stories from outside the United States. Most countries are rarely covered, particularly on television, and then only because they host an important event, have well-known tourists, or are the environment for the odd human interest story.

Confirming what other studies have shown, Hess (1996) found that 21 countries accounted for 79% of foreign dateline stories on network television from 1988–1992. Crisis journalism dominated the evening screens. For 16 nations, the news was wholly or mostly about serious unrest in their regions. A major effect of television news was the reinforcing of stereotypes: stories from Colombia were often about drugs; in Germany, about neo-Nazis; in Italy, the Mafia. Stories from England ignored business, focusing instead on somthing offbeat or the royal family.

A more disturbing but not surprising conclusion of Hess' survey was television's concern with violence. When combining the categories of combat (32.8%), human rights (13.7%), accident/disaster (2.3%), and crime (2.5%), the total showed that more than 50% of the television network news stories were concerned with some aspect of violence. Further, a correlation was found between violence and the distance of the story from New York City: the farther away from home, the more likely the cameras have been lured there by something violent.

TECHNOLOGY PRODUCES A NEW KIND OF CORRESPONDENT

For most of this century, the foreign correspondent was a journalist who was "posted" to a distant, foreign capital—Paris, Moscow, Cairo, Buenos Aires—often staying for several years, learning the language, making contacts, and closely following politics and various facets of the society. Some stayed a long time: Henry Shapiro of UPI covered Moscow for 40 years, but most reporters were rotated after 4–5 years. Because of poor communication, these reporters were pretty much on their own, and they liked it that way. They decided what to report and usually sent back their stories by cable or sometimes by erratic radio telephone, telex, and even by mail. Dispatches were often crafted in a more leisurely fashion with thought and reflection. Editors back home tended to go along with what their correspondent reported.

Foreign news enjoyed high credibility. A *New York Times* story from Moscow with Harrison Salisbury's byline really meant something as did a CBS television story from Berlin by Daniel Schorr.

Things have changed due to the revolutionary developments in telecommunications, particularly communication satellites, which make it possible to send a news story or video report instantly from one place to many others. The volume and speed of international news has been greatly accelerated. With the great improvement in telephone communication, thanks to INTELSAT, that lone foreign correspondent out there is no longer cut off from an editor, who now may be on the phone several times a day with advice and instructions, often when the reporter is on deadline.

With the availability of impressive gadgets—satellite telephones, lightweight versatile computers, reliable phone connections, faxes, and uplinks to send video reports via satellite—foreign reporting, when combined with air travel is made much easier and has become a lot different.

These technological advances have not always been for the better. Mifflin (1996a) quoted Dan Rather on how the traditional foreign correspondent's mobility has changed.

> Jet travel and technology—with smaller and better cameras, satellites, and cellular phones—have made it easier to send correspondents in and out of places swiftly. That means bureaus have been closed and correspondents, as well as anchors, make quick visits instead. . . . In 1996, I can literally go any place on the planet, hit the satellite and get up instantaneously. (p. C5)

[By "up" he meant on the air for a live transmission.] But what about thorough news gathering and reflection?

Foreign news gathering has always been expensive, and many foreign bureaus are being eliminated. Now broadcast news is being collected in other, less costly ways. Just a few years ago, if you saw a foreign news story on the NBC Evening News, chances are that it was reported by an NBC reporter at the scene and the film was shot by an NBC crew. Now, however, the networks are relying more on less expensive, and often less experienced, freelancers and independent contractors; their products are rarely identified on the air, leaving the impression the story was covered by networks staffers.

This practice gives rise to a growing concern about quality control. "By the time, the tape gets on the air, nobody has the foggiest idea who made it or whether the pictures were staged," contended Tom Wolzien, a former NBC News executive (Hess, 1996, p. 99).

More loss of quality or authenticity results when U.S. network correspondents, based in London, add voice-overs to stories they did not cover. Bert Quint, former CBS correspondent, said, "There's no reason to believe the person (doing the voice-over) because odds are he or she was not within 3,000 miles of where the story occurred"(Hess, 1996, p. 99). Martha Teichner of CBS's London bureau, recalled, "I was asked to do Somalia for the weekend news and I've never been to Somalia and I think, oh my God, what am I gonna do? I get every bit of research I can find, but even if I'm correct and accurate, I'm superficial. And I don't want to be superficial" (Hess, 1996, p. 100).

When a big story breaks, such as the plight of 500,000 Rwanda refugees in eastern Zaire, literally hundreds of journalists and camera crews, few of them knowledgeable about the area, quickly arrive, do their stories and video the reporters standing among the hungry mobs, and then just as quickly get out. Satellites and jet travel have made such *parachute journalism* not only feasible, but cost effective, often at the expense of serious news coverage.

Lack of follow-up and failure to provide context are two frequently heard criticisms of today's foreign coverage, according to Hickey (1996). The brilliant spotlight of powerful color television pictures of the 1989 Tiananmen Square uprising by student demonstrators played to millions around the world. During those dramatic days, CBS, NBC, and ABC aired 357 stories on China—more than they had done in the entire decade from 1972 (when China opened to the West) through 1981. Afterwards, China reportage plummeted from 14.6% of foreign news dateline stories in 1989 to 1.4% in 1990.

Foreign correspondents are changing in various ways. Fewer of the U.S. media's correspondents abroad are American citizens. Foreign journalists are not only less expensive but often have a grasp of local languages and knowledge of their countries that American journalists cannot match. The AP uses many locals—nationals of the countries they cover in their many foreign bureaus. Journalist Scott Schuster saw the trend as due to a global acceptance of English as a media language and the global influence of American journalistic methods. Schuster said, "American influence is most profound among broadcasters and foreign broadcast journalists need only turn on their TV sets (to CNN) to receive lessons on how to do the news American style" (Hachten, 1996, p. 125).

Increasingly, print has joined the broadcast media in relying more on stringers or freelancers to deal with rising costs and tighter budgets. Another survey by Hess (1994) found that 26% of 404 foreign correspondents working for U.S. news media were freelancers. Moreover, many of these were underemployed with 40% saying they do other work as well. All suffer the usual fate of freelancers: low pay, no benefits, and a precarious relationship with their employers. Hess found six types of stringers: "spouses" of other correspondents; "experts" who know languages and the area; "adventurers" like Oriana Fallaci, the Italian writer; "flingers," a person on a fling who may be starting a serious career; "ideologues" or "sympathizers" who are often British; and the "residents" who are often long-time residents and write occasional stories. Although stringers and freelancers remain marginal, many famous foreign correspondents started that way including Stanley Karnow, Elie Abel, Robert Kaiser, Elizabeth Pond, Caryle Murphy, and Daniel Schorr.

One of the significant changes has been the increased number of women among foreign correspondents, especially as war reporters. Before 1970, their numbers were small, although there had been a few outstanding reporters: Dorothy Thompson, Martha Gellhorn, Marguerite Higgins, and Gloria Emerson. Hess (1996) found that by the 1970s, about 16% of new foreign reporters were women; this doubled during the 1980s to about 33%. The total leveled off in the early 1990s. This ratio of two men for every woman was also found in Washington media as well as in U.S. journalism.

A number of women correspondents have established outstanding reputations. Among them are Caryle Murphy of *The Washington Post*, Robin Wright of *The Los Angeles Times*, syndicated columnist Georgia Ann Geyer, and Elaine Sciolino and Barbara Crossette of *The New York Times*.

Christiane Amanpour, who reported with distinction for CNN, has become something of a celebrity because of her aggressive and frankly committed reporting style. She listed the Gulf War, famine in Africa, and civil war in former Yugoslavia, as her most memorable stories. Other networks bid for her services. She agreed to do some foreign stories for CBS' *60 Minutes*, but decided to stay with CNN.

Foreign correspondents today are better educated and have higher status backgrounds than their predecessors. Current salaries for foreign correspondents range from about $50,000 to $90,000 with more experienced reporters earning even more.

PHYSICAL DANGERS FOR CORRESPONDENTS

Because much of foreign reporting deals with war, civil unrest, and other forms of violence, the work is dangerous, perhaps the most hazardous in journalism. Among the world's many troubled and unstable nations, journalists, both foreign and domestic, are frequently singled out as targets for arrest, beatings, or all too often, assassination. Sometimes they are just in the wrong place at the wrong time.

Algeria, beset by a long and deadly struggle between an authoritarian government and militant Islamic opposition, has proved a dangerous place to practice journalism. As of mid-1996, at least 59 journalists, mostly

Algerian nationals, have been slain since 1993; 7 in the first half of 1996. (In the same period, six Russian journalists were killed.) In Algeria, it has been estimated that 300 to 400 of the nation's 1,500 journalists have left the country at least temporarily.

The Committee to Protect Journalists keeps track of such violence worldwide and reported that in 1995 journalists were imprisoned in record numbers. Some 182 journalists were in jail because of their work at the end of 1995, compared to 173 the preceding year. The number killed in war or by authorities dropped to 51 in 1995, compared to 72 in 1994. Most of those were deliberately slain, the committee said, while others died accidentally covering wars or rebellions. Turkey had the highest number of journalists in jail, 53, with reporters there clashing with the government over efforts to suppress the Kurdish separatist movement. After Turkey, countries with the highest number of imprisoned journalists were Ethiopia with 31, China with 20, and Kuwait with 18. Largest number of journalists killed on the job, after Algeria, were the 45 who covered combat in 1995 in the former Yugoslavia (Peterson, 1996b).

TAMING THE WESTERN PRESS IN ASIA

As part of the trend toward a global economy, western news organizations are not only reporting the news, but distributing their news and advertising in the newly industrializing nations of Asia, however, not without considerable difficulties. For example, in India, the global television services, CNN International and BBC World have become targets for Indian politicians looking for scapegoats to blame for secessionist movements, religious strife, and even natural disasters. India's own television network, Doordarshan, owned and controlled by the government, is well-known for delaying and sanitizing news broadcasts. CNN International and BBC World came to India in 1991 and aggressively reported the razing of the Babri mosque in late 1993 by Hindu fundamentalists, an act that led to national riots in which 1,800 people died. In response, Indian leaders of both the left and right demanded strong action against the networks. However, when things go in favor of the politicians, they praise foreign coverage. (When CNN International reported the Gulf War to India, it was the first time that vast nation been exposed to independent television news from abroad.)

Southeast Asian governments have created the most problems for British and American publications. Because of the region's phenomenal economic expansion, the foreign press has been paying closer attention to business and political developments in Singapore, Malaysia, Hong Kong, Thailand, Taiwan, and South Korea. With increasing frequency, these Asian governments frown on independent news reports they feel tarnish their national image and diminish their attractiveness to foreign investors. Western publications, including *Time, IHT, Newsweek, The Financial Times,* and *The Economist,* all of which carry periodic stories from roving correspondents, have had run-ins with Asian governments. But two business publications, *The Asian Wall Street Journal,* a daily, and *The Far Eastern Economic Review,* a weekly, have had the most difficulty, particularly in Singapore. Why? Because each publication maintains a full-time resident correspondent who reports regularly and in depth about local business and politics in each major Asian nation. A series of incidents in recent years indicates that Lee Kuan Yew, longtime ruler of Singapore, who has the local Singapore media firmly under his control, has decided to neutralize the foreign press as well. These actions against the press have paralleled government suppression of domestic political opposition and dissent (Hachten, 1993).

One of Lee's primary weapons against the western media is Singapore's 1986 law permitting the government to cut the circulation of any publication "engaging in local politics." "Engaging in local politics" was interpreted by the authorities to mean any story that displeased Lee and/or the refusal to print in full any letter from government ministries refuting the offending report. Shortly after the law was enacted, *Time* became the first victim; its circulation was cut from 18,000 to 2,000.

In the following years, *The Asian Wall Street Journal's* 5,000 circulation was reduced to 400 and two Hong Kong-based publications suffered a similar fate—*The Far Eastern Economic Review* reduced from 10,000 to 500 and *Asiaweek* from 9,000 to 500.

Singapore's libel laws, similar to those of the British, have also been used to intimidate western media. The IHT, which prints an edition in Singapore for Asian distribution, was sued for libel by Lee Kuan Yew, Lee Hsien Loong (Lee's son), and the prime minister, Goh Chok Tong, for an article calling the island-state's succession policies "dynastic politics" rather than the officially espoused "meritocracy." The paper was found guilty and ordered to pay $678,000 in damages.

Some think Singapore's victories may be short-lived. Everette Dennis said, "The Singapore government is fighting a losing battle because the Internet, fax machines and other technologies have already rendered obsolete their ability to control all the information in their country. This is a last gasp. You cannot stop information" (Durocher, 1995, p. 11).

But the capitulation of the IHT (which chose not to appeal) to an authoritarian government for reasons of business expediency rather than fight for free press principles was disturbing. It is one more example of giant media corporations such as ABC, NBC, CNN, and *Business Week* (see chap. 3) proving themselves unwilling to fight for the principles of press freedom. Hong Kong, which returned to the control of Communist China on July 1, 1997, may soon be lost as the major base for western journalists covering Southeast Asia.

In conclusion, as international news and foreign correspondents continue to evolve due to the imperatives of instantaneous communication and financial pressures, there is real danger that our foreign news coverage may be losing something important. Dean Peter Krogh of the Georgetown School of Foreign Service, commented:

> Over the past 25 years, the numbers of foreign bureaus and foreign correspondents have declined. Deeply informed individual insight from the field is fast disappearing. News and media services compound the problem by making the news more homogeneous. The media are reduced to establishing a fleeting physical presence only after CNN announces there is a crisis abroad. . . . Yet CNN itself is, by its very nature, flawed. It provides unevaluated and sometimes exaggerated reports of developments abroad which drive a domestic rush to judgment and a correlated reaction. (Geyer, 1996, p. 10).

Krogh added:

> As the world gets bigger, the foreign policy agenda simultaneously grows longer. Replacing the set agenda of the Cold War is a veritable avalanche of pressing international issues. Our diplomats and journalists need to inhabit these issues where they reside in a far-flung world. (p. 10)

There still are a number of the traditional foreign correspondents sending in thorough and thoughtful news reports from distant capitals as Nairobi and Johannesburg but their influence may well be diminishing.

CHAPTER
10

In the Dark
About Africa

There is always something new out of Africa.
—Pliny the Elder (23–79 A.D.)

The only thing dark about the African continent is our understanding of it.
—Anonymous

In journalism's efforts to explain the world to the American public, no region presents more of a challenge than does sub-Saharan Africa. As a kind of case study, I consider how well this virtual terra incognita has been reported. First, some background.

It was only 110 years ago that great powers of Europe—Britain, France, Germany, Belgium, Portugal, Italy, and Spain—met in Berlin to carve up Africa, launching the modern colonial era. Without any Africans present, the European diplomats drew illogical boundaries that still frustrate African nations today. In the century that followed, Africa experienced 75 years of European colonial rule, and, since about 1960, over 40 years of political independence and self-determination.

The final years of colonialism, accelerated by dynamic nationalist and independence movements, were convulsive but hopeful times. Beginning with Ghana in 1957, more than 40 new African nations appeared. Observers expected that with self-rule, Africa would develop stable and prosperous nations. This has not happened. Instead came economic false starts and failures, frequent coups d'etat, persistent political instability, and usually one-party or military authoritarianism. During the first 25 years of independence, more than 70 leaders in 29 nations were deposed by assassinations, coups, or purges. The 44 new nations were rocked by 20 major wars and 40 successful coups between 1957 and 1981.

Africa's own news media, weak and fragmented under colonialism, were taken over by most of the new one-party states: newspapers, radio and television stations, news agencies, and information services were all brought under the direct control of governments. Hence, the African media have not been effective in reporting reliable news to Africans, much less to the outside world, and generally were not of much help to foreign journalists trying to report public affairs (Hachten, 1993).

During the 1960s and 1970s, Africa also received attention in the Western press for reasons other than crises: Nigeria, Ghana, Kenya, Ivory Coast, Tanzania, and others were exciting new nations with promising futures that were playing a prominent role in the rise of the Third World. But perhaps more consequentially, independent Africa was also caught in the crossfire of the Cold War competition between Western nations and the Soviet bloc. Hence, Africa's civil wars and wars of liberation as well as efforts at economic development had a U.S. angle—our security and foreign policy concerns were involved; the new African nations were important to us as friends and possible allies.

But as the new nations foundered and regressed, (Africa's standard of living actually declined in the first decade of independence), the Cold War waned and then ended, and the interest of U.S. news media in Africa dropped sharply with the exception of the special case of South Africa.

AMERICAN IGNORANCE OF AFRICA

Despite these events, the great majority of Americans, and the press to some extent, tended to see Africa as monolithic and homogeneous. Americans were (and generally still are) unaware of how varied and complex the continent of 800 million is and that these people, languages, and cultures are far more diverse than those of Europe. Journalist Howard French (1994) wrote, "For many Americans, the 'real Africa' is a blurred concatenation of game parks, starving infants and genocidal warfare—or it's a Disneyfied cradle of civilization"(p. 3, sec. 3). Although Africa does have 18 of the world's poorest nations and has been hard hit by AIDS, other diseases, and devastating famines, a number of nations are making progress after shedding one-party dictatorships and are opting for democracy. A good case can be made that many positive and constructive things are happening, most of which the outside world rarely hears about.

Educated Europeans, especially the British, French and Belgians, are better informed about Africa because of the close ties of their colonial pasts and more recent business involvements. For Americans to be interested in

Africa, some special relationship or involvement seems needed: teachers, scholars, or students who have studied Africa and learned Swahili or Hausa, or specialized in some aspect of Africa; diplomats and business people who have worked there; foreign correspondents and editors who reported from Africa or edited news about it; tourists who traveled there, or recent immigrants to America.

Recently, many African Americans who fit into any of the just-mentioned categories, have shown increasing concern about Africa. All told, the constituency that cares deeply about African news is not very large, but includes many articulate and knowledgeable people who feel strongly that African news gets short shrift in the U.S. press. Counted among them are opinion leaders and decision makers who decide how both the public and the private sectors will deal with the challenges presented by Africa.

In addition to the apathy of most Americans about sub-Sahara Africa, Hultman (1992) found a general consensus and grudging admission has developed among most journalists that Africa is badly neglected in the news. David Gergen said, "The history of the American media has been one of general inattention to Africa, except when there's been major famine or conflict" (p. 224).

Washington Post journalist Jim Hoagland said Africa has gotten short shrift in the media for a long time. "I was foreign editor and assistant managing editor of the Post for eight years and I would have to be honest in saying that Africa weighed relatively lightly on the scales of news worthiness. As a former correspondent in Africa, I regret that" (Hultman, 1992, p. 224).

Africa's Media Image (Hawk, 1992), with contributions by Africanists and journalists with African experience, provides detailed and informed analyses of the problems and shortcomings of western reporting of major African news stories over the past generation. The book confirms the near unanimous view of Africanists that American news media need to do better.

PATTERNS OF NEWS NEGLECT
OF AFRICA

The news flow out of Africa to America and Europe is somewhat similar to that from other poor, developing nations of Latin America, Asia, and the Middle East. The flow is characterized by the following examples:

Parachute Journalism. A story breaks that captures the world's attention: widespread famine in Ethiopia or Somalia, genocidal warfare in Rwanda, rioting in Soweto, South Africa. The foreign press arrive in great numbers, cover the story and shoot pictures, and leave. The 1983 civil war in Chad in Central Africa brought the largest number of journalists ever to gather in that impoverished former French colony. The Ministry of Information at N'Djamena, the capital, accredited 150 reporters, photographers, and television technicians from all over the world at the height of the Libyan intervention. Few of those reporters knew much about Chad itself. A few weeks later, almost all had departed, and Chad disappeared from the news.

This kind of reporting, so typically seen on television, fails to provide needed context and follow-up that such stories require. Often with more than 40 nations to cover, the majority of foreign reporters have been concentrated either in Nairobi, Kenya, or Johannesburg, South Africa, each with excellent air connections and good living conditions for reporters' families.

Declining Coverage of Africa. With the end of the Cold War, less and less news has been coming out of Africa. In the early 1980s, there were about 170 foreign correspondents stationed in Johannesburg covering both the continuing racial unrest in South Africa and the civil wars and upheavals in neighboring Zimbabwe, Namibia, Angola, and Mozambique. Many other nations of Africa, among them Benin, Botswana, Burkina Faso, Burundi, Guinea, Lesotho, and Sudan, not only have never had resident correspondents, but are rarely visited by western reporters passing through the region.

Further, the high-profile states have been given less and less attention. For example, a study of U.S. press reporting about two prominent nations, Ghana and Tanzania, as carried in *The New York Times, Times of London,* and *The Milwaukee Journal* for the years 1965–1982, found that more than half of the papers' coverage occurred in one just one year, 1965, although important events happened in these nations in following years. Ghana and Tanzania just disappeared from the news by the later 1960s. Another study by El Zein and Cooper (1992) corroborated these findings. In 15 years of sampled issues of *The New York Times,* only one story appeared about Ghana and none about Tanzania.

A few years ago, armed conflicts were going on at the same time in Angola, Chad, Djibouti, Ethiopia, Liberia, Rwanda, Somalia, Sudan, Western Sahara, and Zaire, yet little reporting about them appeared in U.S. news media.

In the trickle of news that does come out of Africa, most of it concerns violence and civil strife, as well as news about poverty and disease, giving the impression that most Africans are desperately poor, hungry, and incapable of improving their lot, which is not the case.

Barriers to African Coverage.   Reporters covering Africa face barriers not found elsewhere. Few correspondents know the local languages, but English and French are usually sufficient in dealing with officials and educated Africans. Logistics are formidable: distances are greater, communications are less reliable, and air travel is haphazard and inconvenient. Sometimes reporters have to fly through London or Paris to get from one African capital to another.

African governments treat the foreign press in a variety of ways. Some, at times, just bar all foreign reporters, as Guinea did for many years and Nigeria did for several years, or reporters may be permitted in but access to news sources or officials is severely limited.

Some African leaders feel strongly that they have a sovereign right to control information crossing their borders. In Africa, censorship may be achieved in a variety of ways. For example, a foreign journalist arriving at a national airport to investigate a rumor coup may be denied a visa to enter the country and thus miss the story. Or a foreign reporter may be denied the use of transmitting facilities; in many African nations, the telex or telephone facilities are only available in one government office. Some reporters believe that the inability to transmit a story out of Africa is a greater problem than direct censorship.

Failures to Report Bad News.   By seeking news that African authorities do not want reported, reporters face the threat of expulsion. Over the years, many Western reporters have been forced out of Africa and refused visas when they sought re-entry. Colin Legum, a leading British journalist, was barred from South Africa for many years because of his incisive reporting on apartheid. Because of this, some journalists believe that often the bad news does not get reported.Why? A British journalist, Xan Smiley, suggested that journalists who reported crisis events in places like Ghana and Tanzania in the early post-independence years soon found themselves in direct opposition to governments of these nations and, with the threat of expulsion hanging over their heads, decided that only the major crisis events were worth reporting. Smiley noted that heavy self-censorship is a standard feature of reporting by Western journalists throughout the Third World and that nowhere was it more rigorously observed than in Africa. Critics have charged that the U.S. television networks had softened their coverage of South Africa and avoided stories critical of the ruling Afrikaners during the turbulent 1980s in order to maintain their bureaus in Johannesburg (Hachten, 1992).

Because of this reluctance to report fully, a darker side of Africa may be ignored. Yes, the coverage has been thin and superficial, but the need is not to provide more positive, cheerful, and sympathetic coverage. The need may be for more honest and realistic coverage of the continent's deepening crisis. Not much of this gloomy scenario gets into daily news reports but it can be found in some magazines.

Robert Kaplan (1994) painted a dire and disturbing picture of West Africa which he said:

> is becoming the symbol of worldwide demographic, environmental, and societal stress, in which criminal anarchy emerges as the real "strategic" danger. Disease, overpopulation, unprovoked crime, scarcity of resources, refugee migrations, the increasing erosion of nation-states and international borders, and the empowerment of private armies, security firms, and international drug cartels are now most tellingly demonstrated through a West African prism.

These concerns were echoed by columnist William Pfaff (1995) who wrote:

> The destitution of Africa has been an all but forbidden topic in political discourse. . . . The time has arrived, however, for honest and dispassionate discussion of this immense human tragedy, for which the Western countries bear a grave, if partial, responsibility and which will worsen if not addressed. Much of Africa needs, to put it plainly, what one could call a disinterested neocolonialism.

A controversial proposal indeed and one endorsed by another journalist and historian, Paul Johnson, who called the United States and United Nations (UN) intervention in Somalia a return to colonialism that he applauded because, he argued, some African nations were not fit to govern themselves. Some Africanists disagree with such views saying they show a lack of belief in the survival skills of ordinary people and have the effect of convincing the educated and affluent classes to give up on the troubles of the developing world. Yet it is important that the press report Africa's problems more clearly and fully in its coverage and commentary, so that the concerned few will know what is happening.

This reflects a central quandary about reporting from Africa. Despite the steady decline in news from Africa, the U.S. news media's selective, violence-prone reporting has given the world a negative and discouraging picture of Africa. Yet, if what Kaplan, Pfaff, and Johnson said is true, the picture may be even bleaker than we have been led to believe, and there may be an imperative need for western nations to intervene. That is not something the American public wants to hear.

South Africa: The Exception.   One African news story that has been well-reported by U.S. media has been the long struggle for racial and political equality in South Africa—from the Soweto riots in 1976 to the inauguration of Nelson Mandela as president of the "new" South Africa in 1994. U.S. journalists covered the apartheid saga well while most of Black Africa was being ignored. During the 1980s, the number of accredited foreign journalists reached almost 200, mostly based in Johannesburg. The U.S. national media—the prestige dailies, major news magazines, and the big networks—all had reporters there. The story had a long-running fascination for American and Western publics: White on Black racism resonated with U.S. civil rights struggles and was more interesting than the Black on Black racism endemic throughout much of Africa. South Africa, too, was an unusual mixture of the First and Third Worlds, affluent Whites and poverty-stricken Africans, with social problems that other industrialized nations would soon face themselves. In South Africa, the Western press was reporting a low-level civil war of majority Blacks against entrenched Whites, and it made compelling television video.

Relentless U.S. and Western coverage helped make South Africa a pariah state, the "polecat of the world." Certainly the vivid television pictures of police attacking rioters and detailed reporting of the brutal and inhumane aspects of apartheid had great impact outside of Africa and eventually helped bring down the Nationalist party's control of the country.

But during the same years, as noted, the U.S. media essentially ignored what was happening in the other 40 countries of Africa. Nigeria, the giant of Africa with oil riches and more than 100 million people, was rarely seen on television except when President Carter visited in 1978 and Pope John Paul II came in 1982.

With the end of apartheid and its attendant violence, racism, and human pathos, South Africa has moved out of the news spotlight. Nation-building and reconciliation does not produce the kinds of dramatic television pictures that racial conflict did.

WHAT IS TO BE DONE?

Educated Americans with a special interest in Africa are not, of course, completely dependent on daily journalism, yet the news media, including public radio, can be an early warning device and serve the function of signaling that something important has happened in country X or to President Y.

Books, newsletters, specialized magazines, and academic journals are available for more thorough background and developments, but here the recent news was not good either. By November 1996, three definitive publications of African news and analysis in print—*Africa Report, Africa*

News Service, and *Africa Notes*—were defunct or about to be. However, although *Africa News Service,* which was started 30 years ago ceased its print version in 1993, the publication has been resurrected online and it is now available on the internet (http://www.africanews.org).

The other major print source for expert information on Africa was *Foreign Affairs,* which is only partly concerned with Africa, but reviews or mentions most newly published books on Africa. Interestingly, viable specialized magazines on Africa are published in both France and Britain, but they focus on economics, trade, and investment, not on policy analysis as in the American publications.

Further, considering the erratic and sparse coverage of Africa on television and in the news magazines, it becomes important that the handful of prestige papers not dilute their African coverage. One of those, *The New York Times,* still makes a serious attempt to cover Africa. In 1997, at least four resident *Times* correspondents were sending back full and timely stories. *The Washington Post* and *The Los Angeles Times* continue to produce superior daily reporting out of Africa.

The American public at large may not show much interest in distant and exotic places as such, but the media and the public do become very concerned when American soldiers, sailors, and airmen are sent off to those places. How the press reports our wars is discussed in chapter 11.

CHAPTER
11

The Press and
the Military

The first casualty when war comes is truth.
—Sen. Hiram Johnson (1917)

The Persian Gulf War—the short but intense conflict between Iraq and coalition Western forces led by the United States—lasted only 42 days, but it changed, for better or worse, the way that future wars will be reported. Television and especially CNN turned much of the world into a global community witnessing a televised real-time war as the brief struggle evolved from armed confrontation to spectacular aerial bombardment and finally to lightning ground action. The war became the biggest-running global news story in years, and the telling of it utilized the full resources of the U.S. news media and much of the international news system. More than 1,600 print and broadcast journalists and technicians were in Saudi Arabia along with many others in Amman, Baghdad, Tel Aviv, Nicosia, as well as Washington and London, two major news hubs.

It was a great television show. But this unprecedented news story provoked a bitter controversy among the U.S. press, the White House, and the Pentagon over how the war, any war, was to be reported.

The role of the war correspondent has changed greatly because of vastly improved communication technology, more skepticism of and abrasive relations with the military, and an increase in the number of reporters covering the same war.

War correspondents are a kind of specialized foreign correspondent —they work abroad under difficult and often dangerous conditions, and are often subject to restraint or censorship, often from their own government's military, not usually from a foreign regime. In the Gulf War, the press strongly believed that it had been barred from fully covering the war in the traditional ways of the past.

BACKGROUND OF PRESS RESTRICTIONS

How did the acerbic relations between American journalists and the military come to this point? During the two World Wars and the Korean conflict, the relationships had been generally good and mutually supportive. In World War I, some 500 American correspondents covered the conflict for newspapers, magazines, and press associations in France, and, unlike British and French reporters, they were free to go to the front lines without military escorts. Still, everything that well-known reporters like Richard Harding Davis, Will Irwin, or Floyd Gibbons wrote was passed through the censorship of the press section of the Military Intelligence Service. Details about specific battles, numbers of casualties, and names of units, could be released only after mention in official communiques.

U.S. military censorship followed the same general pattern in World War II with the added feature of controlling radio broadcasts. The Office of Censorship was headed by Byron Price, an AP editor, who handled with distinction the most difficult part of his job—the direction of voluntary press censorship—that applied to newspapers, magazines, and other printed materials outside the combat zones.

In scattered combat areas, reporters were generally free to move about and join military units, but were always subject to possible censorship. The U.S. Navy long withheld details of the Pearl Harbor disaster and of the sinking of ships in the Pacific, but in most theaters, the news was broadcast promptly. About 500 full-time American reporters were abroad at any one time and provided war coverage that many considered the best and fullest ever seen.

With mobile units and tape recordings, radio coverage greatly increased. Many broadcasts were memorable: Cecil Brown of CBS describing the fall of Singapore; Edward R. Murrow flying over Berlin in a hazardous 1943 bombing raid; George Hicks of ABC broadcasting under German fire from a landing craft on D-Day in Normandy. The best-known U.S. reporter of World War II was Ernie Pyle, a columnist for Scripps-Howard, who attached himself to U.S. combat troops and followed GIs through North Africa, Italy, France, and the Pacific, where he died in battle. Pyle was widely read and beloved by soldiers, the military brass, and the American public. No war correspondent has approached his stature. Relations between the military and correspondents were mutually trusting and supportive. Despite occasional conflicts over withheld information, everyone seemed to be on the same team.

The change began in the Vietnam War, when relations between the American journalists and the U.S. military soured and reached their lowest ebb. Reporters and camera crews, working within military guidelines, were given free access without field censorship to roam Vietnam; some called it the best reported war in history. Yet many in the U.S. military believed critical press reporting contributed to the defeat by overstressing negative aspects, including graphic pictures of dead and wounded, highlighting scandals such as the My Lai massacre, and misinterpreting key events such as the Tet offensive, which the military pronounced a defeat for North Vietnam, not a victory as the press reported. Such reports, the military argued, aided the antiwar movement at home and turned the American public against the war.

The press felt that the U.S. military had misled and lied to them in Vietnam and that officials consistently painted a much rosier picture of the war than the facts justified. Given the record of deception, the press, it was argued, was correct in being skeptical of the military.

A view prevailed within the military that the free rein given journalists in Vietnam led to reporting that seriously damaged morale and turned the country against its own troops. If news or information is a weapon, then, the generals argued, it should be controlled as a part of the war effort.

The brief war between Britain and Argentina over the Falkland Islands in the South Atlantic in 1982 provided a model for the Pentagon on how to manage the media during wartime. Only British reporters were permitted to accompany the task force, and these reporters were apparently carefully selected. The 17 finally accredited had to accept censorship at the source and were given a Ministry of Defense handbook telling them that they would be expected to "help in leading and steadying public opinion in times of national stress or crisis." The Ministry of Defense effectively imposed censorship at the source, and most war information followed a policy of suppression and subtle control of emphasis. Bad news was either not reported or delayed. After the war was over, the British press gave a very different picture of the war, detailing loses, mishaps, and failures previously unreported.

Philip Knightley (1982) wrote:

Vietnam was an aberration. The freedom given to correspondents to go anywhere, see everything, and write what they liked is not going to be given again. The Falklands was a model of how to make certain that government policy is not undermined by the way a war is reported. The rules turn out to be fairly simple: control access to the fighting, exclude neutral correspondents, censor your own, and muster support both on the field and at home, in the name of patriotism. Objectivity can come back in fashion after the shooting is over. (p. 54)

For America, the war news issue surfaced again on October 25, 1983 when U.S. forces invaded the tiny island of Grenada. The Defense Department barred all reporters from covering the initial invasion. After 2 days of vigorous protests by the press, a pool of 12 reporters was flown in with a military escort. By the end of 1 week with the fighting winding down, 150 reporters were ferried to the island and allowed to stay overnight. The press, however, was not mollified. Walter Cronkite said the Reagan administration had seriously erred, arguing "This is our foreign policy and we have a right to know what is happening, and there can be no excuse in denying the people that right"(Hachten, 1996, p. 154).

But, as in the later Gulf War, public opinion polls showed the American people generally supported the ban on press coverage. Max Frankel of *The New York Times* wrote, "The most astounding thing about the Grenada situation was the quick, facile assumption by some of the public that the press wanted to get in, not to witness the invasion on behalf of the people, but to sabotage it" (Hachten, 1996, p. 155).

As a result of the furor, the Defense Department appointed a commission that recommended a select pool of reporters be allowed to cover the early stages of any surprise operation and share its information with other news organizations. This seemed a fair compromise between the military's need for surprise and the public's need for information.

The new guidelines were first tested in December 1989 when U.S. forces invaded Panama. The press arrangements failed miserably. The Pentagon did not get the 16-reporter pool into Panama until 4 hours after fighting began, and reporters were not allowed to file stories until 6 hours later. Most critics blamed the White House for the mixup and for not insisting that the military facilitate press coverage. When the Gulf War loomed, the American generals, Colin Powell and Norman Schwarzkopf, and other Vietnam veterans, were ready to deal with the press.

AMERICA'S WAR WITH SADDAM HUSSEIN

Global television came into its own as CNN and other broadcasters stationed in Iraq reported a war as it was happening, or as it appeared to be happening. After hostilities began early on January 17, 1991, reporters described anti-aircraft tracers in the night sky of Baghdad and flashes of bomb explosions on the horizon. On succeeding nights, viewers were provided with live video reports from Tel Aviv and Riyadh of Scud missiles, some intercepted by Patriot missiles, exploding against the night sky and television reporters donning gas masks on camera.

The press talked of the "CNN effect"—millions anchored themselves to their television sets hour after hour lest they miss the latest dramatic developments. Restaurants, movies, hotels, and gaming establishments all suffered business losses. Ratings for CNN soared 5 to 10 times their prewar levels.

The Gulf War was a worldwide media event of astonishing proportions. Global television never had a larger or more interested audience for such a sustained period of time. Television became the first principal source of news for most people as well as a major source of military and political intelligence for both sides. CNN telecasts, including military briefings, were viewed in Baghdad as they were being received in Riyadh or Washington, DC—as well as in other non-Western countries.

The combatants, particularly the governments of Iraq and the United States, tried to control and manipulate the media with subtle and not-so-subtle propaganda and misinformation messages. Western journalists chafed at the restraints on news coverage of the war itself and complained that there was news they were not permitted to report. Most coalition news came from military briefings and from carefully controlled and escorted pools of reporters. Some official news released at the briefings was actually disinformation intended to mislead the enemy, not inform the public. For example, viewers were led to believe that Patriot missiles were invariably successful in neutralizing Scud missiles; such was not the case.

Information on the war was tightly controlled on television; one observer called it "the illusion of news." For their own self-defined security reasons, the military often held back or distorted the news they did release. In the opening days of the war, much was made of the smart bombs which allegedly hit their targets with about 90% accuracy. After the war, the U.S. Air Force admitted that smart bombs made up only 7% of all U.S. explosives dropped on Iraq and Kuwait. Television scenes, many of them realistic computer-generated re-creations, of precision-guided bombs going down chimneys or through the doors of targets, notwithstanding, the Air Force later said 70% of the 88,500 tons of bombs dropped on Kuwait and Iraq missed their targets (Wicker, 1991).

Peter Jennings of ABC News reminded viewers that much of what was revealed in the opening days of war was speculation, mixed with some hard facts and some rumors in the rushing river of information. But whether they were getting hard news or not, many millions of viewers stayed by their television sets, if only to find out what would happen next. Public opinion polls showed that the overwhelming majority of Americans supported both the war and the military's efforts to control the news; further, some favored more controls on press reporting. A Los Angeles Times Mirror poll found that 50% of the respondents considered themselves obsessed with war news, and nearly 80% felt the military was "telling as much as it can." About the same proportion thought that military censorship may be "a good idea."

But after the war, many in the American press felt that the traditional right of U.S. reporters to accompany their combat forces and report news of war had been severely circumscribed. Michael Getler of *The Washington Post* wrote:

> The Pentagon and U.S. Army Central Command conducted what is probably the most thorough and consistent wartime control of American reporters in modern times—a set of restrictions that in its totality and mindset seems to go beyond World War II, Korea and Vietnam. (Getler, 1991, p. 24)

President George Bush and the Pentagon followed a deliberate policy of keeping negative and unflattering news from the U.S. public lest it weaken support for the war. Long after the conflict the public learned that some Iraqi soldiers had been buried alive in trenches by U.S. plows and earthmovers and that the military had waited months to tell the families of 33 dead servicemen that their loved ones had been killed by friendly fire. Not until a year after the war did we learn that key weapons like the stealth bomber and the cruise missile had struck only about half of their targets, compared to the 85% to 90% rate claimed by the Pentagon at the time.

American casualties were reported, but there were few pictures of dead and wounded. Details of tactical failures and mishaps in the bombing campaign were not released, nor was the information that at least 24 female soldiers had been raped or sexually assaulted by American servicemen.

The older generation of military leaders felt strongly, despite evidence to the contrary, that unrestricted and critical press coverage in Vietnam, had contributed to the U.S. defeat there. They were determined it would not happen again. Some journalists blamed their own top editors and news executives for agreeing to the field censorship and pool arrangements ahead of time instead of vigorously opposing the issues.

COVERAGE BEFORE COMBAT

Each war is somewhat different and the particular conditions of the Gulf War affected the ways the war was reported and perceived by the public. Most Americans saw it as a "good war" with a quick, decisive victory with amazingly few U.S. and allied casualties. (Second thoughts about how "good" the war had been did not come until later.) Therefore, press concerns over restrictions on war coverage had little public impact and never became an important issue. Antiwar protests did not have time to develop.

For more than 5 months, from August 2, 1990, when Iraqi troops first invaded Kuwait to January 17, 1991 when the bombing of Iraq started, television news played a central role in reporting all aspects of the major international crisis—the first since the end of the Cold War. The press covered the rapid buildup of coalition forces in Saudi Arabia with television pictures of troops arriving with heavy armor and deploying in the desert. This enthusiastic coverage contributed to some Pentagon-inspired misinformation by exaggerating the ability of U.S. troops to repel an invasion. Later, 101st Airborne troops, first to arrive, admitted that during those first weeks they would have been mere road bumps for invading Iraqi forces.

Television also played a diplomatic role by reporting the fate of thousands of hostages held by Iraq and the international efforts to obtain their freedom. More important, the continuing diplomatic efforts by the UN and various foreign governments to resolve the conflict were fully aired and analyzed on television. Such international television reports accelerated the often cumbersome processes of diplomacy.

American and British television networks in particular swung into action, at great expense, to boost their ratings by getting their famous anchors into the Gulf, hoping to broadcast live from Baghdad and better yet, interview Saddam Hussein. Nonetheless, the press served the public interest at the same time it aggressively reported how its government conducts a foreign war. This time, television was better equipped to report a war. Television crews had the newest technology of small, lightweight cameras and portable uplinks that could transmit their video stories home via satellite. Print and radio reporters could call in stories to their newsrooms with suitcase-sized satellite telephones out in the field.

Probably never before have television viewers been exposed to such an endless array of experts—diplomatic, military, political, journalistic— who analyzed in excruciating detail each new phase of the unfolding drama. Journalist Elizabeth Drew (1990) commented, "Probably in no other prelude to a possible war has the media played such a prominent role as transmission belt—for feelers, for threats, for war scenarios designed to intimidate, and for military information perhaps designed to mislead" (p. 92)

Another impressive facet of network television coverage was its ability to interconnect with a variety of news sources thousands of miles apart. When, for example, a new peace proposal was announced in Moscow, Jennings on his ABC News program immediately obtained reactions and comments from ABC reporters and their news sources located at the White House, State Department, Pentagon, London, Tel Aviv, Amman, and Paris —another example of television's ability to speed the diplomatic process.

REPORTING THE SHOOTING WAR

All this was prelude to the shooting war that started just as the evening news programs were beginning at 6:30 p.m. Eastern Standard Time (January 16 in the United States, January 17 in the Middle East). The networks and CNN interrupted their prepared news shows to report that aerial bombing had begun in Baghdad. Then followed one of most memorable nights in television history: the opening phases of a major conflict reported in real time—as it actually happened—by reporters in Iraq, Saudi Arabia, and Washington.

CNN stole the show that night as three CNN correspondents, John Holliman, Peter Arnett, and Bernard Shaw, gave vivid eyewitness descriptions of the U.S. air attack from the windows of their Baghdad hotel room. As in old-time radio, reporters relied on words, not video, that first night. Other networks reported the fireworks, but CNN with its previously arranged leased lines stayed on the longest after the lines were cut for the other networks. Next day, General Colin Powell jokingly said the Pentagon was relying on CNN for military information.

The second night of the war gave prime-time viewers another long, absorbing evening as CNN and NBC television reporters in Tel Aviv reported live as Scud missiles landed. Reporters, often with gas masks on, put out raw and unevaluated information. At one point, NBC reported (erroneously) that nerve gas had been detected in one Scud attack. Tom Brokaw decried the situation for some minutes, but after the report proved false, NBC apologized. Networks expanded to near 24-hour coverage for the first 36 hours of fighting, and even the daytime soap operas were preempted briefly. There was not much to report at that point, and the same facts, theories, and speculations were repeated again and again. Nevertheless, the mesmerized public stayed tuned.

During this early bombing phase of the war, the Pentagon placed restrictions on interviews with troops and returning pilots. Reporters could go into the field only in designated pools. (One reporter likened a press pool to group of senior citizens on a conducted tour.) All interviews with soldiers were subject to censorship before they could be released.

Most information came from the daily briefings held by military spokesmen in both Riyadh and at the Pentagon but much of this information was rather general, vague, and deliberately incomplete. The military had coherent arguments for its restrictive policies. Destroying Iraq's military command and communications capability was a high priority of the bombing strategy, and it was important to withhold useful information, via the media, that would reveal troop movements and intentions of coalition forces. Keeping Iraq's forces off-balance and without reliable information was a key part of U.S. strategy.

However, some news executives and critics claimed the press restrictions went well beyond security concerns and were aimed at both preventing politically damaging disclosures by soldiers and shielding the American public from seeing the brutal aspects of war. If the war had been unsuccessful, the press would have had difficulty reporting the negative aspects. With more than 1,600 reporters in the theater only about 100 could be accommodated by the pools to report news about the 500,000 American force. As the ground war neared, the large press corps became increasingly restive and frustrated at this lack of access.

The response of some reporters was to freelance— to avoid the pools and go off on their own. Malcolm Browne (1991) reported,

> Some reporters were hiding out in American Marine or Army field units, given G.I. uniforms and gear to look inconspicuous, enjoying the affection (and protection of the units) they're trying to cover—concealed by the officers and troops from the handful of press-hating commanders who strive to keep the battle field free of wandering journalists. (p. 45)

Browne noted that nearly all reporters who tried to reach frontline U.S. troops were arrested at one time or another (including reporters for *The New York Times*, *The Washington Post*, *AP*, and Cox papers) and sometimes held in field jails for up to 12 hours and threatened with revocation of their press credentials. After the ground war began, these freelancers, particularly John Kifner and Chris Hedges of *The New York Times*, produced some outstanding reports. Forrest Sawyer of ABC News, who traveled unofficially with Saudi forces, provided some of the earliest and best reports on the freeing of Kuwait City.

Had the ground war been longer, more heavily contested, and taken a higher toll in U.S. casualties, relations between the military and the freelancing journalists probably would have turned quite acrimonious. But these journalists felt they were doing what they were supposed to do in time of war—maintaining the flow of information that Americans need to know when 500,000 of their countrymen are at risk in a foreign war.

THE PETER ARNETT CONTROVERSY

Television, and especially CNN, was the focus of some controversy over accusations that it was being "used" to further Saddam Hussein's propaganda goals. Heaviest criticism was aimed at CNN's Peter Arnett, who for a time was the only American reporter remaining in Baghdad.

The question was whether he was working as a professional journalist reporting under difficult conditions or whether he was mainly a conduit for enemy propaganda.

Arnett's televised interview with Saddam Hussein and his story about a bombed-out factory that Arnett said made powdered milk for infant formula were both controversial. The U.S. military charged the factory made biological weapons and that Arnett was aiding Iraqi misinformation because such CNN reports are widely viewed and believed throughout the Middle East. However, the U.S. press almost unanimously supported Arnett, a Pulitzer Prize winner for his AP coverage of Vietnam. Even under such restrictive conditions, it was argued, independent reports such as Arnett's widened the amount of information available, and censored reports are worth listening to if only to give the world an idea of what information Iraq wanted distributed. After reporters in Baghdad had left Iraq, they were free to write what they wished. Some criticism was directed at CNN for not providing more context and analysis of Arnett's Baghdad reports.

Some critics questioned Arnett's patriotism, implying that an American reporter should support U.S. war aims rather than report the facts as accurately as he could under the circumstances. Arnett's critics failed to understand that Arnett's CNN reports went to a widely dispersed international audience and that CNN's hopes for credibility and acceptance were dependent on the perception of objectivity and truthfulness of their reports.

TRIUMPH OF 24-HOUR GLOBAL NEWS

During the American Civil War in 1861–1865, the demand for news was so great that U.S. newspapers went to 7-day publication. During the 1963 Kennedy assassination, live television emerged as the preeminent medium for reporting breaking news. Such events positioned ABC, CBS, and NBC as major news gatherers but still essentially American media.

During the 42-day Gulf War, CNN established the importance of a 24-hour news network with true global reach. The concept has certainly changed the international news system—at least during times of international crisis and conflict.

The three major U.S. networks were shaken by CNN's success. After CNN's historic scoop on the first night of the war, a number of independent television stations, radio stations, and even several network affiliates relied on CNN in the crisis. Although the three networks had more talented and experienced reporters, they could not compete with CNN either in time on the air or the vast audiences CNN reached in about 100 countries. The success of CNN has encouraged similar services such as BBC's World television, but it remains to be seen how well any 24-hour global news network will do financially during quieter periods when interest in foreign news is low.

The Gulf War certainly conditioned viewers everywhere to keep their television sets tuned to CNN (or its future imitators) during times of high crisis. Perhaps the news today places too much emphasis on immediate and fast-breaking news "as it happens." Video shots of F15s roaring off runways, of smart bombs scoring direct hits, of Tomahawk missiles flying through Baghdad, and tank formations rolling through the desert made memorable viewing. Yet after the fog of war had cleared, the press and the public found that the Gulf War had not been quite what they thought it had been.

The tragic events in the volatile Middle East also reminded the public that wars and political crises are complex and intricate processes that can still best be reported and explained by the printed word. The best and most complete reporting of the Gulf War came ultimately from the print media, which rounded out the picture and gave the context and perspective necessary for understanding. During the first several weeks after the cease fire, it was the print reporters, not television anchors, who dug out and filled in the details of what actually happened during the air campaign and the brief ground war, information that the military on both sides had so effectively screened from public view.

LESSONS FOR THE PRESS

Wars between nations are major international news stories and should be reported by the press as completely and thoroughly as conditions permit. The American public may be blase about much foreign news, but it certainly pays close attention when its armed forces go to war and American lives are at risk. Yet governments at war, even the most democratic, will try to control and manipulate war news to their own strategic advantage. The Gulf War provided ample reminders of this generalization. Censorship and propaganda, the twin arms of political warfare, are integral components of modern warfare. Both sides often deny the press the opportunity to report what has occurred objectively.

In the Gulf War, more than 1,500 journalists were in the war theater, but were allowed little freedom to cover the actual fighting. On the Iraqi side, the few foreign reporters in Baghdad were severely restricted.

From all indications, both the U.S. military and the Bush Administration were pleased with the results of their media policy and would do the same thing again. But among the press, the general conclusion was that the press had been unduly and even illegally denied access to information about the war.

Five years later, much of the official version of the Gulf War was beginning to unravel, and it became clear that the war was a lot messier and less well-managed than the Pentagon would have the public believe. Further, there were considerable doubts as to whether the Pentagon actually was unaware of U.S. soldiers' exposure to chemical weapons.

After the war, a report calling military restrictions in the Gulf War "real censorship" that confirmed "the worst fears of reporters in a democracy" was delivered to Defense Secretary Dick Cheney. DeParle (1991) reported it was signed by 17 news executives representing the four networks, AP, UPI, and major newspapers, and news magazines. The report bitterly complained that the restrictions placed on reporters by the Pentagon were intended to promote a sanitized view of the war. The war was called the first in this century to restrict all official coverage to pools. "By controlling what reporters saw and when they saw it, the military exerted great power to shape and manage the news," the report said. Also criticized were the use of military escorts and "unwarranted delays in transmitting copy" (p. 4A).

After 8 months of talks with news executives, in May 1992 the Pentagon issued a set of principles intended to guarantee that journalists have greater access to future military operations than they had in the Gulf War. However, news media and the government could not agree on whether there should be any official security review of news reports before publication or broadcast. The statement affirmed that "open and independent reporting will be the principal means of coverage of U.S. military operations. The guidelines limited the role of military escorts and said that 'press pools' are not to serve as the standard means of covering operations" (Hachten, 1996, p. 151).

Subsequent military operations in Somalia, Haiti, and Bosnia have not provided an adequate test of these new principles. The Gulf War showed that despite all the wonders of rapid communication (and perhaps in part because of them), the Western news media still can be severely restricted by their own democratic governments in wartime.

MARINES' INCURSION INTO SOMALIA

The incursion of U.S. Marines into Somalia in December 1992 was intended to provide military protection to the relief organizations trying to feed starving Somalis caught in the crossfire of warring clans. Under these conditions, the Pentagon decided not to place any restraints on the media.

Kurtz (1993) called what happened the most embarrassing moment ever in media-military relations:

> the infamous night in December 1992 when Navy SEALS hitting the beach in Somalia were surrounded by a small army of reporters and photographers who blinded them with television lights, clamored for interviews, and generally acted like obnoxious adolescents. That sorry performance, turning a humanitarian mission to aid starving Africans into a Fellini-esque photo op, underscored what the Pentagon had been saying for years: that the press simply could not discipline itself, that reporters would blithely endanger the safety of American troops for the sake of journalistic drama. (p. 215)

It was not one of the media's finer days.

David Hackworth (1992) of *Newsweek* wrote, "to lurch from thought control to no control is plain stupid. When the press corps beats the Marine Corps to the beach, everyone loses" (p. 33). The Pentagon wanted full coverage of Somalia so no controls were placed on the press, and what resulted was a confused circus. There are those, however, who suspect that the Pentagon deliberately orchestrated the fiasco to make the media look bad.

The situation in Somalia raised the question of whether the media, by its heavy barrage of pictures and stories of starving Somalis, pushed President Bush to send troops on their humanitarian mission. The answer is unclear, but Bush did react by committing U.S. armed forces to a limited and supposedly doable assignment of famine relief. (On the other hand, despite horrific pictures of death, destruction, and "ethnic cleansing," from Bosnia the United States refused for many months to get involved militarily.)

When the Somalia assignment expanded in the early Clinton administration to include warlord hunting, it provoked a devastating firefight in the streets of Mogadishu. When 18 U.S. soldiers were killed and the pictures shown on U.S. television, the American public was unprepared to accept casualties when vital U.S. interests were not at stake. The White House soon announced the U.S. was getting out of Somalia. So it was said that television pictures got the Marines into Somalia and pictures got them abruptly out.

James Hoge, editor of *Foreign Affairs*, commented:

> From its understanding of Vietnam came the military's subsequent emphasis on quick solutions, limited media access and selective release of smart weapons imagery. The public, however, will not remain dazzled when interventions become difficult. As in Vietnam, public attitudes ultimately hinge on questions about the rightness, purpose and costs of policy—not television images. (Hoge, 1994, p. 139)

The "peaceful" landing in Haiti in September 1994 provided more perspective on military and media relations. When it appeared that a full-scale military invasion to oust the military rulers would take place, U.S. media were planning the most minutely documented war coverage ever. Several hundred reporters and photographers from television networks, newspapers, and magazines were already in Haiti, with the most advanced equipment ever brought to a war zone. The Pentagon had promised more cooperation than ever, and journalists said they would not be relying on the military for primary access.

However, White House and Pentagon officials, in a meeting with television representatives asked for a broadcast blackout of 8 hours. The Clinton Administration also wanted to restrict reporters to their hotels until military commanders gave them permission to go to the fighting.

The New York Times editorialized:

> Journalists and citizens who believe in the free flow of information should take note of this effort to blindfold the press and the public. It shows that the news-management policies that took root in the Reagan-Bush years and reached their full propagandistic flower during Operation Desert Storm are still in place at the Pentagon. Those policies represent a long-term danger to American troops and the ability of voters to judge the wisdom of elected officials who order military attacks. ("Military Censorship Lives," 1994, p. A18)

In this case, a press and military showdown was avoided when U.S. forces landed without incident in Haiti.

Nor were there any frictions between press and military in Bosnia when NATO imposed a military truce and thousands of U.S. and NATO peacekeeping troops occupied that troubled land in late 1995. There the Pentagon policy was to encourage friendly relations with reporters and broadcasters. GI's carried a 16-page guide to Bosnia with a section devoted to "Meeting the Media," which instructed a soldier that he or she "can be an excellent unofficial spokesperson."

More often though in recent times, the U.S. press has been inhibited or even barred from fully covering wars which it has historically and traditionally reported. So far, there are no real indications that the White House and Congress will modify those policies. This is important because the U.S. Supreme Court has ruled that the press, in order to inform the public, has a First Amendment right to be in those places that "historically" and "traditionally" it has had the right to cover such as trials and town meetings.

The Supreme Court has also ruled that the press has a First Amendment right to be present at all "public" events. Certainly an invasion by American forces lasting more than several hours or a full-scale war is a public event.

The press has no right to report sensitive military information that could aid an enemy and would not want to do so, but it does have a right to be there, to keep a watchful eye on the military just as it does on a criminal trial. No modern war has been fought as quickly and effectively and with as few allied casualties as by the American-led forces in the Gulf War, although we know now that much unflattering news was kept from the public. And when wars are unsuccessful, as they often are, with incompetent leadership, confused tactics, and unnecessary casualties, it is essential that the press, as independent representatives of the public and of the soldiers, be there to report what has occurred. The citizens of Iraq had no independent press reporting to them about the military disasters and political incompetence that led to the battlefield deaths of thousands of their young men—a basic difference between a democracy and a dictatorship.

The Supreme Court is unlikely to come to the defense of the U.S. press in this matter. Perhaps the best hope of the press is to protest and complain until a significant portion of the public supports the right to know. In the Gulf War, the U.S. news media and their owners did not complain loudly and vehemently enough about the pool and censorship restrictions before the bombs started dropping. A sitting president like George Bush or Bill Clinton is not likely to modify such restrictions of free expression in wartime until forced to by political pressure.

Ironically, the greatly expanded capability of global television to report instantly on a modern war provides another rationale for governments to control and censor war news. Yet when American or British journalists are denied access to war news, the rest of the world is denied access as well.

Reporting wars and our fast-changing world requires journalists who are resourceful and knowledgeable. The academic preparation of today's journalists is discussed in the next chapter.

12

Educating Journalists

*By maintaining close relations between journalism and liberal
arts , the [journalism] faculty hopes that the students will not
only come to see how much the exercise of their technique
depends on content but will habitually employ their human-
istic knowledge in their journalistic exercises.*
                                    —Professor David P. Host (1966)

Journalism has been taught at a number of colleges and universities for
about 100 years. Willard G. Bleyer began teaching a journalism course at
the University of Wisconsin in 1905, and his scholarly interests later greatly
influenced the field. The country's first separate School of Journalism, with
newspaperman Walter Williams as dean, began in 1908 at the University
of Missouri. The Pulitzer School of Journalism at Columbia University,
backed with a $2 million gift from the *New York World* publisher, enrolled
its first class in 1912.

There was a widespread belief that the nation's newspapers could be
improved and elevated if the journalists were better educated as well as
more ethical and public-spirited. Some impetus for journalism education
certainly came from public revulsion toward the sensationalism and
excesses of yellow journalism, which was so prominent at the time.

The growth of journalism education has been steady and at times
explosive, especially since broadening its curriculum to include radio and
television, advertising, PR, plus communication theory and processes. As
such, the field has paralleled and mirrored the growth of mass
communication in general.

In 1995, total enrollment in education for journalism and mass
communication stabilized at 141,167 students in programs at 427 colleges
and universities (Kosicki & Becker, 1996).

INFLUENCE OF WILLARD BLEYER

Journalism education generally had its beginnings in English departments with an emphasis on technique courses—reporting, news writing, editing, design, photography—often taught by former journalists. Among the pioneer teachers, perhaps the most influential was Bleyer of Wisconsin who was an English professor from a family of Milwaukee newspapermen. Bleyer advocated integrating journalism education with the social sciences, and, through his own history research, he provided an example and impetus for scholarly research about journalism. In 1906, he laid out a junior–senior curriculum of coursework in economics, political science, history, English, and journalism; he subsequently added sociology, psychology, and the natural sciences. He took journalism out of the humanities into social studies; in time, the new field followed his lead. He specified a 4-year bachelor's program of courses that would be one-fourth journalism and three fourths sciences and humanities. This became the model for many journalism programs and decades later became the basic command of accreditation, of which he was an early advocate.

Bleyer gave high priority to reporting of public affairs, was often critical of the press, and advocated academic study and research about the press and its interaction with politics and society. Besides techniques courses, Bleyer stressed the study of journalism history, legal aspects, ethics and professional concerns.

Like most of his colleagues, Bleyer thought journalism should be taught by teachers with professional newspaper experience, however, he wanted them to be scholars as well. During 1925–1935, he attracted a number of former journalists to do graduate work at Wisconsin—some took masters degrees, but others earned a doctorate degree in a social science discipline, often political science, combined with a double minor in journalism. A partial list of Bleyer's graduates who later greatly influenced programs at other universities include Chilton Bush of Stanford, Ralph Casey of Minnesota, Ralph Nafziger of Minnesota and Wisconsin, Robert Desmond of California–Berkeley, Kenneth Olson and Curtis MacDougall of Northwestern, Fred Siebert of Illinois and Michigan State, Henry Ladd Smith of Washington, Ray Nixon of Emory and Minnesota, and numerous others.

Bleyer believed in internships for students and that credits should be given for practical experience, as on a college newspaper. He was active as well in establishing a professional organization of teachers and scholarly publications such as *Journalism Quarterly*.

The focus on newspapers dominated journalism education through the 1940s at leading schools such as Missouri, Columbia, Northwestern,

Minnesota, Wisconsin, Illinois, Iowa, and others. But important changes were taking place in "J-schools" as radio and television emerged as major news and entertainment media. More courses and, in time, sequences of courses were offered on radio news, television news, and on broadcasting production techniques.

Speech departments, also offshoots of English departments, became involved in the preparation of students for careers in broadcasting. In some universities, the speech or communication arts departments were merged with the journalism programs, on some campuses, they were kept separate.

Concurrently, more and more journalism programs were offering courses in advertising and PR. Here, too, offerings proliferated, with some schools offering sequences in both specialties. Even separate departments of advertising appeared. Obviously, advertising and PR were distinct from journalism, giving rise increasingly to the term *mass communication* to describe this new amalgam of college courses on newspapers, radio, television, magazines, advertising, and PR, and an increasing involvement with the study of communication itself.

The Bleyer model of journalism education was particularly influenced by this closely related field—the study of communication, a new academic discipline in American higher education. Wilbur Schramm, who taught at Iowa, Illinois, and Stanford, was the leading scholar in communication studies and is credited with inventing as well as popularizing the field through his prolific writings as well as passing on the word to his graduate students.

The earlier strands of communication study are found in various social sciences. *Communication* can be defined as the study of mass media and other institutions dedicated to persuasion, communication processes and effects, audience studies, information interpretation, and interpersonal communication. Yet, it was more, because communication is one of the few fundamental processes through which virtually any social event can be portrayed. The field grew enormously because its perspective proved a useful one for perceiving society.

Rogers and Chaffee (1994) made a persuasive case that communication study found a lasting home in the branch of journalism education identified with Willard Bleyer and his proteges, Ralph Casey, Chilton Bush, Ralph Nafziger, and Fred Seibert, all administrators as well as scholars, whose journalism programs developed major components of communication studies, especially at the graduate level. The universities also produced the new PhDs who staffed the next generation of journalism and (mass) communication faculties from the 1950s onward. Increasingly, graduate work was concerned with communication theory whereas undergraduate courses stressed preprofessional training for careers in news media, advertising, and PR.

By the 1960s, many of the former journalism departments and schools had been transformed and acquired new names such as School of Journalism and Mass Communication, Department of Communication, School of Communications, College of Communication Arts, and other variations. Some did not change their names: At Missouri, it was (and is still) the School of Journalism and at Columbia, the Graduate Department of Journalism.

EDUCATION FOR JOURNALISM AND MASS COMMUNICATION TODAY

As Professor Lee Becker's annual reports suggest—some 140,000 students in 427 programs—this has become a giant academic field, yet a somewhat amorphous one with great variations in quality, size, and focus. More than 3,200 journalism and mass communication educators in higher education are members of the Association for Education in Journalism and Mass Communication (AEJMC) founded in 1912 (Kosicki & Becker, 1996).

Today, there are some excellent programs and others that can only be described as marginal and weak. (Becker's surveys do not include another flock of related programs, some with such names as Speech Communications, Communication Arts, or Media Studies, which have come out of the speech departments and study aspects of communication as well.)

A variety of journalism and mass communications-related subjects is taught in today's universities. In the Department of Journalism at the University of Texas' College of Communication, sequences (related courses) are offered in broadcast news, magazine journalism, news and public affairs reporting, public relations, photojournalism, media skills, and media studies. The University of Florida, which granted 604 undergraduate degrees in 1995 and has a regular faculty of around 55 instructors, grants separate BS degrees in advertising, journalism, PR, and telecommunication, as well as masters and doctoral degrees in mass communication.

By whatever name, journalism and mass communication study is not a discipline in the sense that political science and history is but a rather loose interdisciplinary field covering a wide range of concerns somehow related to public communication.

The various research and teaching interests of today's faculties are reflected in the names of the divisions or interest groups within their professional organization, the AEJMC—advertising, communication technology and policy, communication theory and method, history, international communication, law, magazine, mass communication and society, media management and economics, minorities and communication, newspaper, PR, qualitative study, radio-television journalism, scholastic journalism (high school), and visual communication. In addition, there are other interest groups on gay, lesbian, and family diversity, media and disability, religion and media, and civic journalism.

BACK TO EDUCATION FOR JOURNALISM

Journalism education, in the narrow sense of preprofessional training and education for careers on newspapers, broadcast news, news services, magazines, or other publications, has become a diminishing fraction of what goes on in today's academic programs just as news operations are a small fraction what goes on at the giant media conglomerates.

A high school graduate intent on a career in news journalism usually has three options. First, look carefully at the journalism programs offered at well-regarded universities and select one that fits your needs; pick your courses carefully, work on the college newspaper, and try to get an internship or two while still in school. A second option is to obtain a BA degree in a social science and then go on for a professional masters degree in journalism at, say, Columbia, University of California–Berkeley, or Northwestern. Finally, get a good college education and perhaps work on a college paper. After graduation, look for a news job. Graduates of Ivy League and Big Ten schools without journalism degrees often have been hired on the national media in the East.

There are several advantages in studying journalism in college. Clearly it is a path to a news career that many thousands of professional journalists have followed. A student learns about the field—its relevant history, legal controls on the press, ethical and social concerns—and also acquires the basic skills of reporting, writing, and editing news. In most programs, the student also studies social science courses relevant to journalism—history, political science, economics, and sociology. One pitfall for some students is spending too much time on techniques courses—how to run a video camera or radio broadcast gadgets—to the neglect of substantive courses that develop critical and informed thinking. Many journalism teachers believe that a university degree should prepare a student for lifelong learning and not just for the first few weeks on a job. In other words, for a career and not a vocation.

Should a student interested in journalism take communication theory courses in college? Yes and no. Communication and media studies, it has been argued, have very little to do with the practice of journalism. On the other hand, many top communication scholars had newspaper or magazine backgrounds, scholars such as Wilbur Schramm, Paul Deutschmann, Ralph Nafziger, John McNelly, and Philip Meyer.

CONTROVERSIES AND PROBLEMS
WITHIN THE FIELD

The evolution from small, newspaper-oriented departments of journalism to larger schools, and even colleges of journalism and mass communication has engendered a number of controversies.

Some journalism professors as well as newspaper executives have been suspicious of academic research, especially the more theoretical communication variety, feeling with some justification that it has little to do with training tomorrow's journalists and in fact impedes the process.

This controversy been around a long time; 40 or more years ago, it was characterized as the "green eyeshades" who thought journalism could only be learned on the job or from ex-journalists versus the "chi squares," the college teachers who measured and counted phenomena but could not teach a student how to cover a police beat.

More and more, the professors on journalism faculties doing the most research usually have PhDs in communication and have lacked significant professional media experience. Yet these professors or their teaching assistants have been teaching undergrads how to report and write the news.

This controversy surfaced again in a 1996 report of a year-long survey by Betty Medsger, a former journalism teacher and ex-*Washington Post* reporter. Medsger argued that journalism schools need a major overhaul, including changes in the curricula and the credentials that they require of new faculty hires.

Medsger found that journalism students are being trained by people with doctorates but little or no experience as reporters or editors. She also reported that journalism courses are giving way to generic communication courses, a trend opposed by news professionals and many journalism educators. The increased emphasis on communication theory at the expense of basic reporting and writing skills has been accompanied by the elimination of journalism as a stand-alone major at some schools.

Some journalism educators agreed with the Medsger report, but noted that a number of schools have resisted the trend and have continued to emphasize news reporting and writing "from the sidewalk up."

More than half of the journalism educators that Medsger polled reported the number of students intending to become journalists was declining. Most students were heading instead for a related field.

Low beginning salaries for journalists was certainly part of the problem. She cited an annual survey on job recruiting on the Michigan State University campus as evidence. There the starting journalist's average salary of $20,154 was the lowest of any college-educated workers entering the workforce. In December 1996, the same Michigan State survey found that the salaries for all 1997 BA graduates were expected to increase by 6%. Highest beginning salaries were $43,000 for chemical engineers; again, lowest reported were for beginning journalists at $22,000. However, it should be added that journalism salaries tend to increase quickly with experience.

Journalism schools cannot be blamed for low starting salaries. Instead, the responsibility lies with the news media themselves who place so little value on their new hires and make so little effort to attract the best and brightest of college graduates. It is a reflection on our society's values that a Washington media star like Cokie Roberts or Sam Donaldson can make twice as much money for one public appearance as a new reporter can earn in a year.

In general, financial support for journalism education by major media organizations has, with a few exceptions, been tentative and reluctant. Still, over the years there have been some major benefactors: The philanthropic foundations associated with Gannett, Knight-Ridder, Dow Jones Newspaper Fund, Cox Newspapers and others. The largest financial contributions to journalism education have come from Gannett's Freedom Forum which has supported the Media Studies Center at Columbia (since moved) and other activities for journalism education and free press concerns. Some critics regard the Gannett influence on journalism education as too heavy-handed and intrusive into academic prerogatives at times and as such, created resentment among some journalism professors.

DECLINE AND FALL OF THE
BLEYER MODEL

The model of journalism education forged by Willard Bleyer and followed by so many colleges is clearly in decline, particularly at the major universities where it once florished. A number of reasons account for this shift.

First were changes in higher education. Before World War II, universities were primarily concerned with teaching, which journalism departments stressed. Since then, we have seen the rise of the research university and the primacy of research over undergraduate teaching. The better the college or university, the greater the rewards—higher salaries, research grants, research leaves, named professorships, lighter teaching loads—go to professors who can get grants and their results published.

To keep abreast of this trend, universities and even small colleges have placed high priority on hiring new faculty with doctorates. In journalism education this has meant hiring PhDs in communication or other social sciences. Significant professional media experience—5 or more years—is no longer a prerequisite and in fact may be considered a drawback because those years might have been better spent doing advanced graduate work.

It is ironic that at the universities where Bleyer's proteges had the greatest influence—Stanford, Wisconsin, Minnesota, Michigan State, and Illinois—have produced many of the scholars and PhDs who have rejected Bleyer's ideas about the importance of preparing young people for news careers.

Further, the research university has often been dubious of any kind of professional training at the undergraduate level whether it be journalism, social work, or library science. For this reason, California–Berkeley, Columbia, and Michigan have stressed journalism training at the masters level. The Ivy League universities never taught undergraduate journalism. The University of Pennsylvania's Annenberg School has focused on communication studies. Big Ten universities with their land grant tradition of public service were early leaders in journalism education because of a perceived need to provide trained graduates for a state's dailies and weeklies.

In today's research-oriented universities, journalism faculties are expected to do more than teach beginning reporting classes. In fact, in some schools, these basic courses are often taught by teaching assistants with slight or no media experience. Most professors prefer to teach substantive or theoretical courses, or better yet, seminars for graduate students that relate to their own research specializations.

Today, the faculties of a number of well-known schools and departments of journalism and communication are really collections of diverse social science scholars, each with his or her own research interests and priorities. One excellent journalism faculty at the University of Wisconsin-Madison, pursues such diverse scholarly interests as history of media and popular culture, communication theory, communication of science news, feminist studies relating to Africa, radical political economy and the media, media in developing countries, history of motion pictures and movie censorship, economics of newspaper publishing, communications law, and problems of misleading advertising among other interests. Understandably, this talented faculty, as do others, lacks both the professional background and apparently much interest in preparing undergraduate students for jobs with the news media.

ACCOMPLISHMENTS OF JOURNALISM / COMMUNICATION EDUCATION

What then has the field of journalism and communications education accomplished in the past 100 years? In short, a great deal.

Literally thousands of would-be journalists and communicators have been prepared for careers in news and other related fields of advertising, PR, specialized publications. Some editors believe that those who study journalism in college tend to be more committed to the field as a career than those who enter it casually. A list of distinguished journalists and public communicators can be compiled from the journalism alumni of Missouri, Columbia, and Minnesota over the years. (Much the same can be said of students who studied advertising and PR.)

Of course, anyone is free to enter and practice journalism. No license or certification is needed; the First Amendment prohibits that, however, a century of journalism education deserves credit for establishing the precept that anyone in journalism or media occupations should have a college education or better, a masters degree.

In the specific field of journalism, many useful textbooks, monographs, and journal articles, including a great deal of press analysis and criticism have been written by journalism faculties. Much of this work on the history, legal aspects, social, political, and economic aspects of journalism has found its way into journalism courses and everyday journalistic practices. Many of the numerous books and articles by practicing journalists and broadcasters also are used in journalism courses and reading rooms.

A careful look at the impressive *Mass Media Bibliography: Reference, Research, and Reading* by Eleanor Blum and Frances Wilhoit (1988), with its 1,200 annotations, gives an idea what has been accomplished. Published by the University of Illinois Press, it covers all fields except communication law.

Research by journalism and communication professors has contributed substantially as well to a long list of pressing public issues, such as the effects of television on children, improved public opinion polling, media relationships with politics, and a variety of legal issues such as pornography, access to government news, free press and fair trial, privacy, and so on.

A bibliography of the books, monographs, textbooks, and major journal and magazine articles produced in the past 40 years by the faculties of the leading 24 journalism faculties would be impressive.

In the much broader realm of mass communication and communication studies and research, similar contributions by faculty members have added to our knowledge of persuasive communication, including advertising, PR, public opinion, and propaganda, as well as on other facets of communication processes and effects. The academic study of communication, as described earlier, also has had interactions and mutual benefits from like-minded scholars in political science, sociology, history, economics, and education.

The whole field of international communications studies has had global impact in Europe, Asia, and Africa due to work done by American scholars in journalism schools. In fact, the American concepts of journalism education and communication research have been widely emulated in many nations.

Journalism and communications programs have helped, too, to educate the public—the consumers of mass media—to be better informed and more critical of the media. Many nonjournalism students in colleges, as well as journalism dropouts, have taken journalism courses, such as introduction to mass communication or mass communications and society. Of course, it will take far more than this to build a critical and concerned public at a time when young people are reading less and paying less attention to the news media.

MID-CAREER EDUCATION FOR JOURNALISTS

Mid-career working journalists who wish to broaden their expertise into new areas have ample opportunities to return to college campuses for specialized study. At least 20 such programs are available, including the John S. Knight Fellowships at Stanford, Michigan Journalism Fellows at Ann Arbor, Fellowships in Law for Journalists at Yale, the National Arts Journalism Program Fellowships at Northwestern, and the progenitor, the Nieman Journalism Fellowships at Harvard since the 1930s. Participating journalists are well remunerated: At Stanford they get a $40,000 stipend and benefits; at Michigan, they get a $30,000 stipend, plus tuition and a travel allowance. Surprisingly, applications for these programs have been dropping off in recent years, yet such programs certainly have had an impact on journalism. For example, the Knight Center for Specialized Journalism at the University of Maryland offers intensive week-long seminars on science, technology, business, economics, law, and social issues. More than 950 journalists from some 250 news organizations, both print and broadcast, have attended the 43 courses since 1988.

CONCLUSIONS AND COMMENTS

Education for both journalism and the broader area of mass communication has both considerable strengths and dismaying weaknesses. The outside critics, for example, fail to understand its research and other contributions of the academy; on the other hand, many professors arrogantly ignore the real concerns of news media about the way students are being prepared to enter the field.

We need fewer and better schools of journalism, yet the same thing can be said about law schools, business schools, and schools of social work. Some downsizing seems to be going on with several universities such as the University of Michigan, University of Washington, Ohio State, and University of Arizona among others who are reevaluating and modifying their journalism and mass communication programs.

Gene Roberts, former managing editor of *The New York Times* has a good perspective because he taught journalism at the University of Maryland. Roberts sees no problem with the disappearance of some programs as long as an adequate number of good ones remain.

> The country probably needs 30 or 40 or 50—some reasonable number of journalism schools that are really good at what they do. . . . They should emphasize writing but also emphasize enough of a history of journalism that people really emerge with some sense of where we've been and how we developed as newspapers—and that is missing even more than writing. (Kees, 1996, p. 6)

Important as that view is, the field is changing rapidly, and the academic community can play a helpful role in dealing with the challenges and opportunities presented by online publications and other innovations. The implications of such new media for news journalism is discussed in chapter 12.

A curriculum task force was appointed by AEJMC in 1993 to look at the mission and purpose of journalism and mass communication education. The final report, "Challenge: Responding to the Challenge of Change" (1996), showed that much more consensus than contention exists in the field.

Here are some of the highlights:

> The purpose of media education is to produce well-rounded graduates who have critical-thinking skills and who have an understanding of the philosophy of the media and a dedication to the public service role that the media have in our society.

> Media education has at least five objectives: (1) to provide students the competencies they need for successful careers in media-related professions, (2) to educate non-majors about the role of the media in society, (3) to prepare students to become teachers or to undertake graduate work, (4) to prepare liberally educated graduate students to become media analysts and critics, and (5) to provide mid-career education for media professionals. (Challenge: Responding to the Challenge of Change, 1996, p. 102)

Change, after all, is what journalism and education for journalism are all about. At the same time, I personally regret the decline in the teaching of journalism as such.

More than any other sequence such as advertising, PR, communication, or media studies, journalism has the greatest claim on being a profession. By objectively and dispassionately gathering all the important news of the day and making it available to the public, journalism performs an essential public service for our democracy. Advertising and PR do not meet this test and could just as easily be taught in a business school.

Technological changes in the media have long provided a rationale for academic concerns about journalism and mass communications. The most recent innovation—cyberspace and the Internet—are discussed in the next chapter.

13

News on
the Internet

*Today, having reached the age of 21, the personal computer is
only now beginning to reveal its true value and greatest
potential, not as an engine for crunching numbers and
processing words, but rather as a communication device that
lets people share ideas freely on a global network.*
—Peter H. Lewis (1996)

In this latest facet of the ongoing information revolution, millions of
personal computers are connected by the Internet and other computer
networks and have started a global revolution in business and
interpersonal communications. The personal computer today functions
as a combination personal printing press, radio, telephone, post office,
and television set. Lewis (1996) argued that the computer may not replace
any of these media, which are, of course, heavily involved in journalism.
Still, the Internet has the potential to transcend them all, providing not
just one-to-one communications, or one to many, but the creation of whole
new communities of people sharing ideas and interests regardless of where
they live.

The stunning possibilities of the Internet for journalism and the news
business are somewhat obvious. Publishers, broadcasters, and journalists
are aware of this explosive information revolution and believe they should
be involved. However, neither they, nor anyone else, seem to know where
this brave new world of communication is headed. (A few years ago, no
one had foreseen the potential of the Internet.)

No consensus exists as to when and how journalism as we know it
will get involved and be changed by the Internet, but no one doubts that

change is coming—and fast. The future of cyberspace is murky and yet exciting. (This chapter examines some implications of the Internet for the news media, particularly newspapers.)

A newspaper is, of course, a business operation. At a time when some publishers are downsizing staffs and trimming costs to increase profitability, other papers are investing heavily in the new electronic or interactive journalism. Although no one seems to know whether they will ever make money on the WWW, the Internet multimedia information retrieval system is on the verge of becoming a mass medium itself.

In early 1996, the National Newspaper Association listed 162 newspapers that had electronic pages on the Web, triple the number in 1994. By early 1997, another source reported the number of online newspapers to be about 700. These numbers will only go up and to date include such heavy hitters as *The New York Times, The Chicago Tribune,* and *The Wall Street Journal.*

A web site can be simply a screen or two of information, or it can be an extensive and complex number of offerings, with news items plus advertisements, illustrations, documents, and background stories not included in a printed daily.

FEAR AND GREED

For newspapers, two basic uncertainties currently exist about interactive journalism: first, will the public pay for electronic news on a medium where information, after a basic user's fee, is free? Second, will advertising displayed on web pages "sell" on a medium that so far lacks both an effective way to count the number of people who eyeball web pages or to ascertain the demographics of those viewers.

Hence, the press' rush to online services is seen as driven by both fear and greed. The fear comes from the threat to the newspapers' advertising base, especially classified advertisements, from the computer's point-and-click technology and the ease of getting answers quickly, complete with pictures and sound from great amounts of electronic information. By 1997, about $200 million was being spent annually on advertising on the web; a significant amount but a tiny fraction of total newspaper advertising.

Greed is stimulated by the possibility of large sums to be made if a system is developed that counts and categorizes every visitor to a web site. If this happens, Internet publishing could be a profitable marriage of newspapers' advertising bases with franchise strengths. Publishers also hope to attract the younger users who no longer read newspapers.

So far, the numbers of potential users of interactive newspapers are still small compared with total newspaper readership but the numbers are growing fast. Currently about one fifth of adults (not counting teenagers) use computers, and research indicates that about 21 million users seek news from the various online services and web sites. Supporting this trend, the Pew Research Center for the People and the Press (1996) study on media usage found that watching TV news "yesterday" fell more among people who use computers and go online than among people who do not. Also, reading a newspaper "yesterday" also declined to a greater extent among computer users who go on-line. Computer users with modems have easy access to current daily and updated news from AP, Reuters, *The Wall Street Journal*, *The Los Angeles Times*, *The Washington Post*, and the numerous other papers and magazines through such online services as CompuServe, America Online, Prodigy, and Microsoft Network (MSN). The access for this fledgling news source is established, but so far the numbers of news readers is small and no one is making much money out of providing the news. Researchers estimated that *The Los Angeles Times'* interactive edition gets an estimated 50,000 visitors daily, a number that doubles every 6 months. Online news users tend to be young male adults who log on from office computers.

The only certainty, promoters of electronic publishing say, is that the breakthrough to make the Internet economically viable for the newspaper business will come someday.

Prospects for profits, of course, have long driven the development of new media in our free enterprise system.

The competition to (potentially) make money on the Internet is lively. *The Wall Street Journal* has been trying to determine if a significant number of Internet viewers will pay to receive its interactive edition. By the end of 1996, the *Journal* had signed up 30,000 people who were paying $49.50 annually to receive the interactive edition. Another 100,000 people were receiving free access to WSJ.com via MSN. On January 1, 1997, after extending the grace periods four times, the WSJ Interactive Edition cut off the freeloaders who were asked to start paying. Only a minority were expected to start paying. Other interactive newspapers were watching the *Journal's* efforts closely. If the *Journal*, despite its prominence and its high number of business users, does not succeed, other publishers may feel they will not have success in charging users—at least, not yet.

The web site of *The New York Times* requires users to register but does not charge them. Nine months after it opened in January 1996, about 600,000 users had signed up to use it. The other best known news sites—CNN, *USA Today*, *The Washington Post*, *The Chicago Tribune*, and *The Los Angeles Times*—were open to all.

THE INTERNET AS THE NEXT MASS MEDIUM?

In November 1995, the AP announced that it would adopt the WWW to begin distributing its articles and photographs over the global Internet. In so doing, AP followed other old-line media organizations onto the Web. The Web incorporates many elements of various print and electronic media that have preceded it; computers can be used to send and receive text, sound, still images, and video clips. Yet for all its versatility, the Web is not expected to replace its predecessors but to take a place alongside them as a social, cultural, and economic force in its own right. The history of mass communication has taught us that new media do not replace old media, but instead supplement and complement them; radio did not replace newspapers and television did not replace radio.

The Web's complementary role is already evident: Along with steadily increasing numbers of newspapers and magazines with web sites, many radio stations and all the major television networks have web sites, publicizing their programs and stars. One of the big players is NBC, which with its partner, Microsoft, puts out an elaborate online version of MSNBC, its 24-hour cable news channel.

Few movies are released without a promotional web site and prime-time television commercials by major advertisers routinely include a web address.

Virtually all of the hundreds of journalistic web sites do not take full advantage of the Internet's unique characteristic: its immediacy. So far, the general practice for online newspapers and news magazines has been to withhold their exclusive breaking stories from the Web until their published editions come out. Instead, online newspapers use breaking and updating news from the AP and other news agencies but will not put out their own important stories developed by their own staffers. So far, the papers do not like the idea of scooping themselves because the printed product brings in the money whereas web sites do not. Magazines also hold back their best stories until the print editions appear. *Time, Newsweek,* and *U.S. News & World Report* do the same as the dailies (Zuckerman, 1997).

Instead, many publications prefer to take advantage of the Internet's limitless space and interactivity by posting transcripts, documents, and other supporting information about the articles published and by playing host to online discussions.

Although online readers must now seek out web sites to read news, some software products have come along to deliver web news pages directly to readers' computers. Pointcast, the largest such system, has nearly two million users and carries articles from *The Los Angeles Times, The San Jose Mercury News, The New York Times,* and others. In addition, *The Mercury*

News, the *Times,* and others have been offering special services that transmit their articles directly to readers daily via electronic mail.

NEW JOURNALISM CAREERS ONLINE

Interactive journalism is already developing a new generation of young journalists who are attracted to online jobs for the money, opportunity, excitement, and a way to avoid unpaid internships and small-town newspaper jobs. *The Chicago Tribune,* for example, has a staff of 20 who work exclusively for the Internet edition—writing stories, taking pictures, using video cameras, and even creating digital pages.

Many of today's journalism graduates are heading for such jobs because that is where the opportunities are. Michael Hoeferlin, placement director at the University of Missouri's journalism school, said, "Online publications are generating more jobs at higher salaries than we have seen for a long time" (Jacobson, 1996, p. C7). At online publications, entry level jobs approach $30,000 compared with about $20,000 for most beginning newspaper jobs. In 1995, 5% of Northwestern University's journalism graduates took jobs with online publications or services and the numbers are expected to keep increasing.

The young people entering the murky world of digital journalism now are the ones who will bring about the great changes later. The older generation of journalists who wonder whether it is really journalism, have been much slower to recognize the changes that are coming.

WHAT ABOUT THE INFORMATION UNDERCLASS?

Interactive journalism is just one aspect of what has been called the information revolution and the information superhighway. One nagging question has been: who will participate in this revolution and who will be left behind? From a global perspective, the information revolution has been mainly in the United States, Japan, Western Europe, and other industrialized nations. These information societies, mostly in the rich, industrialized north, are further widening the gap between themselves and less-developed nations. A highly industrialized nation like Japan can utilize any new technological innovation much faster or more completely than say, Pakistan or Nigeria, hence resentments by developing nations over information inequities persist and are exacerbated. Poorer nations want the new media, but lack the economic and social bases to utilize and sustain them.

Only 12 of Africa's 54 countries are linked to the Internet and international experts warn that unless Africa gets online quickly, what is already the poorest continent risks ever greater marginalization. "Everyone realizes that Africa is lagging, that it is the only part of the world that does not have network connectivity," said Lawrence Lanweber, president of the Internet Society, which aims to promote the network's development.

> Latin America and all but a very few Asian nations are on the Internet. But then you look at the map of Africa and you seek huge gaps all over that will prevent this continent from participating in so many aspects of life on this planet as it is developing. (French, 1995, p.A8)

Within this country, concern is expressed that the rapid expansion of our telecommunications systems will follow the logical economic path of going to the people who can afford to pay for the computers, telephones, and varied electronics services. No technological reason exists why the information superhighway should not reach every home, yet private companies will not voluntarily provide service to all homes, schools, hospitals, libraries, and universities. Some commentators feel that where financial rewards are not great enough to drive free market investment, the government should require every company in the industry—from programmers to information providers—to subsidize the people who otherwise would be overlooked (Forester, 1993).

In the fast-moving world of cyberspace, it is far too early to predict the role that journalism will play, but there is at least the hope that interactive or digital journalism will reach and influence many millions of young Americans who do not follow serious news.

CHALLENGES TO PRESS FREEDOM

On its 21st birthday in 1996, the personal computer's potential as a medium for ideas, information, and news flowing freely around the globe were being recognized. At the same time, the virtual press was already facing serious legal challenges over what could and could not be transmitted over computer networks. Legal restrictions, imposed here or abroad, could very well prevent the personal computer from reaching its full potential.

The sweeping communications bill passed by Congress in February 1996 banned pornography over computer networks and set penalties for those convicted of distributing indecent material to minors. Civil liberties groups quickly vowed a court battle over the provisions that would block the free flow of material, even smut, over computer networks.

Congressional committees debating the communications bill rejected the idea that the Internet is the electronic equivalent of the printing press, thus enjoying the full freespeech protections of the First Amendment. Instead, Congress opted to regard the Internet as a broadcast medium, subject to Government regulation and eligible for only some of the Constitutional rights given to newspapers.

The irony is that the same words, printed on ink and paper are fully protected by the First Amendment, but once those words go on the Internet and become bits traveling in packets over wires and fibers, they lose their protection. But the protection returns when the words are reprinted on paper.

The potential erosion of free speech is due in part to sincere efforts to protect children from pornography being transmitted over the Internet and online services. Despite the existence of current laws punishing those who make and distribute child pornography in any medium, some saw the opportunity in this new medium to banish words and images that heretofore had been considered indecent but not illegal expression.

At about the same time, CompuServe voluntarily denied its 4 million subscribers access to over 200 newsgroups, because a prosecutor in Germany found them offensive and had threatened legal action. Many technologies already exist to let parents restrict areas of the Internet and online services that children can visit. But these are only partial solutions.

Some advocates of the Internet fear the possibility that this freest and most open of all media may be restricted to carrying ideas and information only suitable for children. It may be years and many hard-fought legal battles before guidelines defining legal protections for the Internet are firmly established.

However, a major advance for free speech occurred in June 1997 when the U.S. Supreme Court declared unconstitutional the Communications Decency Act which made it a crime to send or display "indecent" material online in a way available to minors. The unanimous decision was the court's first effort to extend First Amendment principles into cyberspace. The court held that speech on the Internet is entitled to the highest level of First Amendment protection, similar to that given to newspapers and books. This is in contrast to more limited First Amendment rights accorded to expression on broadcast and cable television, where the court has tolerated a wide amount of government regulation.

This decision, of course, was not the final word. Other legal challenges are still to come. But the decision bodes well for the future of the Internet as a purveyor of serious news and information on what is being recognized as the most participatory marketplace of mass expression the world has yet seen.

INTERNET VERSUS FOREIGN DESPOTS

The potential of the Internet as a technology of freedom has been demonstrated in recent years by clashes between computer users and authoritarian regimes in Serbia, Singapore, and China.

In Belgrade, President Slobadan Milosevic, faced with large anti-government demonstrations, forced the last of the independent media, the station Radio B92, off the air and thus set off a technological revolt in December 1996. Tens of thousands of students, professors, professionals, and journalists connected their computers to Internet web sites around the world. B92 soon began digital broadcasts in Serbo-Croatian and English over audio Internet links, and its web site took over the reporting of the protests that had been triggered by annulled elections.

Milosevic quickly backed off, and the radio station was soon back on the air, but the event showed the protesters the potential for bypassing government transmitters, news agencies, and television studios to get their message out across Serbia and abroad.

On the other side of the world, the small, affluent, and authoritarian nation of Singapore thinks it can control the technologies of freedom that threaten its one-party rule. To control television, satellites dishes have been banned and the country has been wired for cable television, which enables the government to screen out objectionable material.

Controlling cyberspace will be harder, but Singapore is trying. Use of the Internet is encouraged by equipping schools with computers and urging Singaporeans to link up with the computer network by dialing a local telephone number. Thus, the government is able to monitor use of the Internet that goes through the local servers. Singapore has already blocked material it considers pornographic. Local officials concede that some users can bypass this system by dialing into the Internet through foreign phone systems. In the future, however, Singapore is not expected to be able to maintain controls over the flow of electronic information.

The People's Republic of China is also trying to regulate and monitor the Internet, which has been used by human rights groups to communicate with dissidents within China. In February 1996, China issued a new set of regulations for Internet use. Rather than cutting off access, the rules steer the flow of electronic information through officially controlled ports so that it can be better monitored. Any network offering Internet service is subject to close supervision of the Ministry of Post and Telecommunications or one of three other agencies. The rules were clearly concerned with information the government considers threatening. China's security apparatus is believed to monitor a tremendous volume of telephone and fax traffic and is expected to do the same with the Internet.

Access to the Internet, however, is limited to a relative few in a country where few homes have a private telephone much less a computer. Unofficially, about 50,000 to 100,000 Chinese use the Internet, many of them university students with irregular access because of limited computer time and others who privately pay a registered user to share an e-mail address. In any case, the elusive and free flowing ways of the Internet present far more of a challenge to authoritarian regimes than they do to open, democratic societies.

RUMORS AND CONSPIRACY THEORIES

One of the strongest arguments for increasing the presence of serious journalism on the Internet concerns the wild rumors and unfounded conspiracy theories that often fly through cyberspace in an age of easy global communication. Often mainstream media reports are distorted and gross assumptions are made about the government's capacity for malevolence; on occasion, stories and theories are just fabricated.

When TWA Flight 800 exploded off Long Island in July 1996 killing everyone on board, investigators focused on three possible causes: a bomb, mechanical failure, or a terrorist missile. Within 36 hours after the disaster, a message posted on an Internet discussion site suggested a darker possibility: "Did the Navy do it? It is interesting how much evidence there is that it was hit by a missile." Within days, numerous Net writers speculated that the jet was downed by accidental friendly fire from a U.S. Navy ship on a training cruise. Such a blunder, according to the evolving theory, was quickly covered up by a conspiracy involving U.S. investigators, the military, and President Clinton. Although it was weak, the rumor hung around despite official efforts to discredit it.

Four months later, the theory came to life when Pierre Salinger, a veteran journalist and former spokesman for President John Kennedy, told an audience in France that he had a document showing that Flight 800 had been shot down by the Navy. Because of Salinger's reputation, the theory once again bounced around the news media, particularly on television news. The story had a familiar ring to it, so CNN called Salinger and confirmed that Salinger's document was a printout of the Internet message posted anonymously 4 months earlier.

What formerly was considered just gossip takes on a new credibility when it appears on the Internet. Clifford Stoll, an Internet critic, said "Gossip's been blessed by the computer and sprinkled with techno holy water. The gossip that comes across the Internet comes in precisely the same format as does professional news, Wall Street reports, and other important factual information" (Wald, 1996, p. 5). Net watchers say that such wild, unfounded rumors and conspiracy theories run into the hundreds at any one time.

Obviously, the news media can play an important role by providing reliable, disinterested, and professionally sound news and information to counter and shoot down some of the wild rumors or just plain gossip on the Internet.

In conclusion, one thing that can be said with some certainty about the future of journalism on the Internet is that changes are coming fast, but no one can say with much confidence what those changes will be. Stay tuned. Or better yet, stay logged on.

Reporting news is mostly about recording change and, as the final chapter suggests, many of journalism's troubles are an outgrowth of a dynamic society.

CHAPTER
14

Conclusion: Journalism at a Time of Change

In this question, therefore, there is no medium between servitude and license; in order to enjoy the inestimable benefits that the liberty of the press ensures, it is necessary to submit to the inevitable evils that it creates.
—Alexis de Tocqueville (1835)

For journalism in America today, the news has been both encouraging and dispiriting. At its very best, during a time of crisis or a momentous event, the news media can do a marvelous job of telling the news thoroughly, yet quickly, then following up with needed interpretation and explanation to inform and reassure the public. For example, on the day of the death of China's top leader, Deng Xiaoping, in February 1997 *The New York Times* provided five full pages of news and informed analysis. Several days later, *Newsweek* published a 25-page special report, "China After Deng" written by eleven experts.

But at their worst, even the best news media, when caught up with a riveting but essentially trivial story that may combine varying elements of celebrity, sex, crime, or scandal (preferably all four) can compete vigorously with the bottom-feeding tabloids for tidbits of scandal. The long-running saga of O.J. Simpson was only the most glaring example of many journalistic excesses. This kind of journalism has turned much of the public against the news media.

REASONS FOR CONCERN

This volume has been concerned about the fate of serious news and public information at a time when our vast popular culture apparatus has engulfed

174

legitimate journalism into a churning melange of entertainment, celebrity, sensation, self-help, and merchandising—most of which is driven by corporate entities devoted to advertising, promotion, PR, marketing, and above all, a healthy bottom line.

News media have always reported frivolous stories or gossip that intrigue the public but were without serious consequence. Reporters are always alert for the good story that will appeal to a wide swath of readers or listeners—regardless of its true merit. The history of journalism reminds us that newspapers and journalists concerned with reporting significant news have always been a minority.

Further, since the time of Gutenberg, the press has always had its critics and enemies, beginning with kings and other autocrats who controlled the printing press ruthlessly for several centuries. Yet today, a widespread feeling exists that serious journalism is in trouble not because of a threat of censorship, but because the news iself—hard and informative—has become a smaller portion of what Americans glean daily from their television sets, newspapers and magazines, radios, computers, and other electronic means. Further, news as public knowledge seems all wrapped up in a shiny package of entertainment and diversion. It has become trivialized.

Equally distressing is the trend that a smaller portion of Americans, especially young people, are paying attention to news from any medium in their reach. Serious news about the public sector and the world beyond our borders does not seem as important and relevant to the public anymore. Polls show that fewer Americans are paying attention to the news—whether on broadcasts or in print. Even if the media provided more serious news, it is questionable whether the public would pay more attention.

There is ample evidence that much of the public holds the press in diminished regard and when asked, expresses animosity and irritation toward journalists. Journalists are not trusted by the public and are equated in their ethical standards above lawyers, elected officials, and corporate officials—all with self-serving interests. The public views the press as part of the political elite, not their independent representatives.

Television news, with its tremendous power to inform, educate, and influence public opinion, has largely failed to report significant news beyond providing an erratic headline service. Among the print media, a few of the national publications still do a competent job of reporting a comparatively wide range of news developments, but news coverage in many newspapers is bland, unimaginative, and incomplete.

Probably the principal concern the news media face, then, is the increasing intermixing of news with entertainment in various forms—gossip and scandal, promotion of pop culture products (movies, television programs, etc.), publicity about celebrities, and eye-catching self-help features.

Public affairs journalism—the life blood of democracy—has been particularly trivialized and corrupted. Top-of-the-head opinions and predictions, whether on television talk shows or in signed columns, have often replaced careful reporting and cautious interpretation, particularly during political campaigns. Journalists see a deterioration of their professional standards. Celebrity journalists are perceived by the public as cynical, arrogant, and out of touch with the needs and interests of the average citizen.

Another cause for concern has been the persistent trend toward larger media conglomerates primarily concerned with providing entertainment and diversion for a mass public. News organizations within such behemoths represent a small part of those diverse companies whose main concern is to make profits for their stockholders.

The corporate mentality of these megacorporations seems at odds with vigorous efforts to aggressively report the news and defend freedom of the press, as did *The Washington Post* during its confrontations with the Nixon White House in the Watergate and Pentagon Papers affairs. The majority of the biggest and best news organizations are controlled by these large corporations that seem to put profitability ahead of public service. Further, corporate journalism, with some exceptions, seems less able or willing to counter the overwhelming influence of great corporations on public policy here and abroad.

WHAT IS TO BE DONE?

Here are several prescriptions for reversing some of the discouraging trends discussed throughout this volume.

First, most critics believe the immediate problem is somehow to restore the well-known fire wall that separated news from entertainment and sensation on most responsible news organizations. Editors and broadcast producers in the national media need to make their own news decisions and forgo chasing after scandalous or titillating stories that appear in the tabloids. Television news as well as *Time* and *Newsweek* seem to be seriously corrupted by this scramble for competitive advantage. Change will not be easy because much of the public seems conditioned to equate news with diversion and entertainment.

Second, the news business must find ways to improve the stature of journalists, whose public image has become so badly tranished. To do this, the news media must improve their performance. Political journalists must work to be again viewed as reliable, objective, and dispassionate news gatherers, rather then highly visible and opinionated performers.   The task of winning back the public's respect and admiration for journalists will be a difficult one.

The public must understand that there is a real difference between a journalist carefully reporting and explaining an important and complex story and a well-paid television celebrity interviewing a rock star or entertainment personality on a TV news magazine show. One is a public servant and the other is a quasi-entertainer.

Journalism has some, but not much, claim to being a profession such as law, medicine, or the clergy. The principal virtue that good journalism does have is that like recognized professions, journalism does provide an essential public service: the reporting and presentation of important news or public knowledge in a disinterested and objective manner. When journalism is practiced in that manner—and eschews the temptations to pontificate, mislead, sensationalize, or just be clever—the press merits the unusual protection it enjoys under the First Amendment that "Congress shall make no law . . . abridging freedom of speech or of the press."

Another perquisite of an emerging profession that journalism can some day become is the practice of monitoring and criticizing its own errant colleagues. In an open system of free expression, no journalist can be or should be coerced or restrained by government or by any private source, but no journalist or news medium is immune from incisive, scalding criticism or censure from their peers or the public.

As mentioned, a real strength of U.S. journalism is the longtime and still common practice of criticism of press performance from within the ranks of journalism. Such exchanges are healthy and evidence indicates that some egregious conduct has been modified. Prominent journalists are avoiding conflicts of interest by steering clear of the lecture circuits and the irresponsbile television shows.

Media criticism may be inhibited, of course, by the complications and practices of multimedia corporate giants. Will *Time* magazine critically report on Time Warner's control of cable channels? Will NBC News report fully General Electric's dealings with the U.S. government? Not likely. Despite such trends, more diversity still exists among U.S. news media than in any other democracy.

In the final analysis, diversity—the dissemination of news from as many different sources and different facets as possible—may be the most important value to cherish. The media, as well as the public and the courts, must ensure that the public will continue to have a variety of sources of information and opinions to choose from. When diversity disappears, in its place came orthodoxy and conformity.

Third, the news media must broaden and expand their audiences, particularly among younger readers and viewers. Newspapers and news itself is often viewed as obsolete or irrelevant among the 50 million who make up the 15–30 age group in America. Each new generation reads more news as it gets older but still reads less than the previous generation. News organizations are well-aware of the problem but are not having much success in dealing with it. In general, most agree that news content must be more relevant to the needs and interests of young people so that they will become dependent on those publications. Partly, of course, this is an education problem; many in the current generation do not read much and lack the general knowledge of modern history required to absorb and make sense of significant news. Schools must do a better job.

The growth of interactive newspapers on the Internet offers the potential of creating more news consumers among computer users who are mostly younger people.

Fourth, the Internet and other communication innovations will greatly impact on tomorrow's journalism and may prove crucial in redefining the future directions and format of news. One editor, Rem Rieder, believes the Internet needs the traditional values of journalism—news judgment, accuracy, fairness, and context—to make sense out of the tremendous volumes of information, most of it inaccurate, tendentious, and misleading that is available to computer users.

As the Internet matures, journalistic skills should play a key role. The onrush of raw data, including much garbage and misinformation, will require validators, that is, trusted editors and other experts, to separate the wheat from the chaff. The Internet will require interpretation and context, hence a need for individual, online judges to tell the surfers what it all means. Nonetheless, no one knows just how important a role journalism will play in cyberspace or how in time, journalism itself will be transformed.

Fifth, another priority for journalism is to restore and expand the importance of world news on the news agenda. It is ironic that at a time when the big players, Murdoch, Time Warner, Disney, and NBC, are all expanding their international operations and seeking foreign markets, the news media they own, as well as the public, are paying much less attention to the world outside our borders.

Two of America's best newspapers, *The Washington Post* and *The Los Angeles Times,* rose to prominence in the 1970s, in part, by expanding their corps of foreign correspondents and carrying much more authoritative news from overseas. Attention to world affairs seems a litmus test of quality journalism but too few other publications have emulated those two dailies.

America's pivotal role in the world would require greater attention to world affairs. Yet TV network news and many daily newspapers have been moving away from public affairs news and instead, featuring more self-help and personalized news on health, self-improvement, medical news, and personal needs. Similar to what is found in women's magazines, this soft news has the effect of pushing aside other more pressing news.

Despite the shortcomings of today's journalism and the low esteem in which many journalists are held today, there are reasons for hope and encouragement. The U.S. press still is the freest and most unfettered press in the world and is enjoying the most constitutional protection. Most news organizations are sound financially and make money.

Americans like to criticize journalists, just as they do politicians and football coaches, but all of us are dependent on the press to know what is happening in our communities and our world. We need the news to know what there is to criticize about the news.

Good journalism has a way of being there when we need it most. During times of national crisis in this century—the Great Depression, World War II, Korean and Vietnam wars, the civil rights struggle, the Cold War, the information revolution—Americans struggled to apprehend and understand these momentous events and were largely able to do so because they had access to independent and reliable information from their newspapers, radio, and television stations.

The importance and need of good journalism has not decreased in our society; if anything, we need it more than ever. Take a careful look at any of several leading publications—*The Washington Post, The Wall Street Journal, The Los Angeles Times,* or the *The New York Times*—and glance at the headlines or tune in NPR's "All Things Considered," and you will be reminded of how important a free flow of reliable public knowledge is to our personal well being and to the welfare of the Republic.

Good journalism does matter.

References

Adelson, A. (1994, May 9). More radio stations drop coverage of local news. *The New York Times*, p. C8.

Associated Press v. United States, 326 U.S. 1 (1945).

Auletta, K. (1995a, March 6). The race for a global network. *The New Yorker*, 53–54, 79–83.

Auletta, K. (1995b, November 27). The wages of synergy. *The New Yorker*, 8–9.

Auletta, K. (1996, July 29). No honeymoon, no marriage. *The New Yorker*, p. 29.

Bagdikian, B. (1992). *The media monopoly* (4th ed.). Boston: Beacon Press.

Bartlett, J., & Kaplan, J. (1992). *Bartlett's familiar quotations* (16th ed.). Boston; Little, Brown.

Blankenburg, W. B. (1995). Hard times and the news hole. *Journalism Quarterly, 72*, 634–641.

Blasi, V. (1977). The checking value in first amendment theory. *American Bar Foundation Research Journal 3*, 521–649.

Brandenburg v. Ohio, 395 U.S. 444 (1969).

Browne, M. (1991, March 3). The military vs. the press. *The New York Times*, p. 45.

Carmody, D. (1995, June 12). On the annual scoreboard of new magazines, it's sports, 67, sex, 44. *The New York Times*, p. C5.

Carter, B. (1997, February 6). After verdicts, will case still sell? *The New York Times*, p. A15.

Challenge: Responding to the challenge of change. (1996). *Journalism & Mass Communication Educator, 50*, 101–119.

Color of mendacity. (1996, July 19). *The New York Times*, p. A14.

Coulson, D. C., & Hansen, A. (1995, Spring). *The Louisville Courier-Journal's* news content after purchase by Gannett. *Journalism Quarterly, 72*, 205–215.

Dennis, E. (1992). Comment on the survey. *Intermedia, 20*, 31, 33, 36.

DeParle, J. (1991, July 3). 17 news executives criticize U.S. for "censorship" of gulf coverage. *The New York Times*, p. A4.

Diamond, E. (1993). *Behind the times: Inside the New York Times*. New York: Villard Books.

Drew, E. (1990, December 31). Letter from Washington. *The New Yorker*, 90–98.

Durocher, D. (1995). Times and Post cos. bow to mighty Singapore. *American Journalism Review*, 17,11.

El Zein, H., & Cooper, A. (1992). New York Times coverage of Africa, 1976–1990. In B. Hawk (Ed.), *Africa's media image* (pp. 133–146). New York: Praeger.

Emerson, T. (1985). Foreword. In P.Lahav (Ed.), *Press law in modern democracies* (pp. xi –xiii). New York: Longman.

Emerson, T. (1966). *Toward a general theory of the first amendment*. New York: Vintage Books.

Emery, M., Emery, E., & Roberts, N. (1996). *The press and America* (8th ed.). Boston: Allyn & Bacon.

Evans, H. (1990). Norman conquests: freedom of the press in Britain and America. In S. Serfaty (Ed.), *The media and foreign policy* (pp. 189–201). NewYork: St. Martins Press.

Fabricant, G. (1996a, July 20). Murdoch's world from a to z. *The New York Times*, p. C7.

Fabricant, G. (1996b, July 29). Murdoch bets heavily on a global vision. *The New York Times*, p. C1.

Fallows, J. (1996). *Breaking the news*. New York: Pantheon.

Fibich, L. (1995). Under siege. *American Journalism Review, 17*, 16–23.

Fibison, M. (1996). Washington Post's Broder aims at media dishonesty, "punditocracy." *Murphy Reporter, 43*, 1–2.

Forester, L. (1993, December 23). Protect the information underclass. *The New York Times*, p. A15.

Frankel, M. (1994, November 27). The shroud. *The New York Times Magazine*, 42–43.

Frankel, M. (1995, December 17). The murder broadcasting system. *The New York Times Magazine*, 46–47.

Frankel, M. (1996, September 22). An olympian injustice. *The New York Times Magazine*, 60–61.

French, H. (1995, November 17). On the Internet, Africa is far behind. *The New York Times*, p. A8.

French, H. (1994, November 20). An ignorance of Africa as vast as the continent. *The New York Times*, p. 3, Sec. E.

Gabler, N. (1994). *Winchell: Gossip, power, and the cult of celebrity.* New York: Knopf.

Getler, M. (1991, March 25–31). The gulf war "good news" policy is a dangerous precedent. *The Washington Post National Weekly Edition*, p. 24.

Geyer, G. A. (1996). *Who killed the foreign correspondent?* Red Smith Lecture in Journalism, University of Notre Dame, South Bend, Indiana, April 1996, 3-16.

Glaberson, W. (1994, October 9). The new press criticism: News as the enemy of hope. *The New York Times*, p. 1, sec. 4.

Glaberson, W. (1995a, July 30). The press: Bought and sold and gray all over. *The New York Times*, p. 1, sec. 4.

Glaberson, W. (1995b, November 17). "60 minutes" case illustrates a trend born of corporate pressure. *The New York Times*, p. A3.

Glass, Andrew. (1992, August 18). The last of an era. *Wisconsin State Journal*, p. 1C.

Goodman, W. (1995, June 16). In Jackson romp, echoes of two mergers. *The New York Times*, p. B1.

Gunther, G. (1994). *Learned Hand: The man and the judge.* New York: Knopf.

Gunther, M. (1995, October). All in the family. *American Journalism Review, 17*, 36–41.

Hachten, W. (1993). *The growth of media in the third world.* Ames: Iowa State University Press.

Hachten, W. (1996). *The world news prism* (4th ed.). Ames: Iowa State University Press.

Hachten, W. (1992). African censorship and American correspondents. In B. Hawk (Ed.), *Africa's media image* (pp. 38–48). New York: Praeger.

Hackworth, D. (1992, December 21). Learning how to cover a war. *Newsweek*, 33.

Harwood, R. (1995, June). Are journalists elitists? *American Journalism Review, 17*, 27–29.

Hawk, B. (1992). *Africa's media image.* New York: Praeger.

Hess, S. (1994, April). The cheaper solution. *American Journalism Review, 16*, 28–29.

Hess, S. (1996). *International news and foreign correspondents.* Washington, DC: Brookings Institution.

Hickey, N. (1996, November/December). Over there. *Columbia Journalism Review*, 53–54.

Hickey, N. (1995, September-October). The mega media are the message. *Columbia Journalism Review*, 20.

Hoge, J.F. (1994, July/August). Media pervasiveness. *Foreign Affairs 73*, 136–144.

Hultman, T. (1992). Dateline Africa: journalists assess Africa coverage. In B. Hawk (Ed.) *Africa's Media Image* (pp. 223–236). New York: Praeger.

Hume, E. (1996, March/April). Something's rotten.*Columbia Journalism Review*, 53–54.

Jacobson, G. (1996, May 20). For journalism graduates opportunities in new media. *The New York Times*, p. C7.

Johnston, D. H. (1979). *Journalism and the media.* New York: Barnes & Noble.

Kaplan, R. (1994, February). The coming anarchy. *Atlantic, 273*, 44–76.

Kees, Beverly. (1996, July). Some universities begin to rewrite the story of journalism education. *Freedom Forum*, 4–8.

Kimball, P. (1994). *Downsizing the news: Network cutbacks in the nation's capital.* Washington, DC: Woodrow Wilson Center/Johns Hopkins.

Knightley, P. (1975). *The first casualty.* New York: Harcourt Brace Jovanovich.

Knightley, P. (1982). The Falklands: How Britannia ruled the news. *Columbia Journalism Review*, 53–54.

Kolbert, E. (1995, October 15). Robert MacNeil gives a thoughtful goodbye. *The New York Times*, p. H39.

Kosicki, G., & Becker, L. (1996). Annual survey of enrollment and degrees awarded. *Journalism & Mass Communication Educator, 51,* 4–14.

Kovach, B. (1996, August 3). Big deals, with journalism thrown in. *The New York Times*, p. A17.

Kurtz, H. (1996). *Hot air: All talk, all the time.* New York: Times Books.

Kurtz, H. (1993). *Media circus.* New York: Times Books.

Lasswell, H. (1971).The structure and function of communication in society. In W. Schramm & D. Roberts, (Eds.), *The process and effects of mass communication* (pp. 84–99). Urbana: University of Illinois Press.

Lewis, P. (1996, January 2). On freedom of speech for the virtual press. *The New York Times*, p. B8.

Margolick, D. (1994, October 24). The Enquirer required reading in the Simpson case. *The New York Times*, p. 6.

Masses Publishing Co. v. Patten, 224 Fed. 535 (S.D.N.Y. 1917).

Miami Herald v. Tornillo, 418 U.S. 241 (1974).

Mifflin, L. (1996a, March l). For Rather, technology has drawbacks, too. *The New York Times*, p. C5.

Mifflin. L. (1996b, May 13). Media. *The New York Times*, p. C5.

Military censorship lives. (1994, September 21). *The New York Times*, p. A18.

Morton, J. (1995, October). Farewell to more family dynasties. *American Journalism Review, 17,* 67–69.

Mott, F. L. (1947). *American journalism.* New York: Macmillan.

Near v. Minnesota, 283 U.S. 697 (1931).

New York Times v. Sullivan, 376 U.S. 270 (1964).

New York Times v. United States, 403 U.S. 713 (1971).

Nieman poll finds decline in media quality (1995, Fall). *Nieman Reports,*38–39.

O'Reilly, B. (1994, February 26). We pay for news. We have to. *The New York Times*, p. 15.

Parker, R. (1995). *Mixed signals: The prospects for global television news.* New York: Twentieth Century Fund Press.

Pember, D. R. (1992). *Mass media in America* (6th ed.). New York: Macmillan.

Peterson, I. (1996a, January 12). Media. *The New York Times*, p. C7.

Peterson, I. (l996b, March 15). More journalists jailed, but fewer are killed. *The New York Times*, p. A5.

Peterson, I. (1996c, August 19). USA Today, the fast food of dailies, is expanding menu. *The New York Times*, pp. C1, C8.

Peterson, I. (1996d, September 9). Media. *The New York Times*, p. C5.

Peterson, I. (1997, May 19). Rethinking the news. *The New York Times* p. C1.

Pew Research Center for the People and the Press (1996, May). *TV news viewership declines* (news release). Washington, DC.

Pew Research Center for the People and the Press (1997, April). *The Times-Mirror news interest index 1989-1995.* (news release) Washington, DC.

Pfaff, W. (1995, January / February). A new colonialism? *Foreign Affairs, 7⁴*. 2–6.

Phillips, K. (l996, January 28). Bad news. *The New York Times Book Review*, p. 8.

Pogrebin, R. (1996, September 23). Foreign coverage less prominent in news magazines. *The New York Times*, p. C2.

Prato, L. (1996, September). Still tuning to radio news. *American Journalism Review, 18,* 52.

Rafferty, K. (1975). *That's what they said about the press.* New York: Vantage Press.

Red Lion Broadcasting Co. v. FCC, 395 U.S. 367 (1969).

Remnick, D. (1995, September 18). Last of the red hots. The New Yorker, 76–83.

Rich, F. (1994, October 24). He got the poop on America. *The New York Times Book Review, 1,* 31–33.

Rich, F. (1996, May 18). Media amok. *The New York Times,* p. 15.

Rieder, R. (1996, September). Primary values. *American Journalism Review, 18,* 6.

Rogers, E., & Chaffee, S. (1994, December). Communication and journalism from "Daddy" Bleyer to Wilbur Schramm: A palimpsest. *Journalism Monographs, 148,* 1–49.

Rosenstiel, T. (1994, August 22 & 29). The myth of CNN. *The New Republic* (Vol. 211), 27–33.

Rothstein, E. (1996, August 26). Anxiety in the land of gargoyles and giants. *The New York Times,* p. B1.

Rottenberg, D. (1994, May). "And that's the way it is."*American Journalism Review, 16,* 34–37.

Schell, J. (1996, August). The uncertain leviathan. *Atlantic, 278,* 70–78.

Schudson, M. (1995). *The power of news.* Cambridge: Harvard University Press.

Self-censorship at CBS. (1995, November 12). *The New York Times,* p. 14E.

Shaw, D. (1994, Spring). Surrender of the gatekeepers. *Nieman Reports,* 3–5.

Soifer, A. (1985). Freedom of the press in the United States. In P. Lahav (Ed.), *Press law in modern democracies* (pp. 79–133). New York: Longman.

Stepp, C. S. (1995, October). The thrill is gone. *American Journalism Review, 18,* 15–19.

Strentz, H., & Keel, V. (1995). North America. In J. Merrill (Ed.), *Global journalism* (pp. 355–394). White Plains: Longman.

Supperstone, M. (1985). Press law in the United Kingdom. In P. Lahav (Ed.), *Press law in modern democracies* (pp. 9–78). New York: Longman.

Wald, M. (1996, November 10). Cyber-mice that roar, implausibly. *The New York Times,* p. 5.

Walsh, K. L. (1996). *Feeding the beast.* New York: Random House.

Wicker, T. (1991, March 20). An unknown casualty. *The New York Times,* p. A15.

Zane, J. P. (1996, September 29) Liz's love life! Oprah's diet! Dole's foreign policy! *The New York Times,* p. 2, sec. 4.

Zuckerman, L. (1997, January 6). Don't stop the presses. *The New York Times,* pp. C1, C7.

Author Index

Subject Index